Octavius Glover, Heinrich Ewald

The Life of Jesus Christ

Octavius Glover, Heinrich Ewald

The Life of Jesus Christ

ISBN/EAN: 9783743382701

Manufactured in Europe, USA, Canada, Australia, Japa

Cover: Foto ©Lupo / pixelio.de

Manufactured and distributed by brebook publishing software (www.brebook.com)

Octavius Glover, Heinrich Ewald

The Life of Jesus Christ

THE LIFE

OF

JESUS CHRIST.

BY

H. EWALD.

TRANSLATED AND EDITED BY
OCTAVIUS GLOVER, B.D.
FELLOW OF EMMANUEL COLLEGE, CAMBRIDGE.

Cambridge:
DEIGHTON, BELL, AND CO.
LONDON: BELL AND DALDY.
1865.

CONTENTS.

CHAP.		Page.
	PREFACE	v
I.	The Sources of this History	1—9
II.	The Chronology of this History	10—18
III.	The Stages of this History	19—22

FIRST ADVANCE OF CHRISTIANITY.
THE ADVANCE TO MESSIAS.

IV.	John the Baptist	23—31
V.	The Carrying Out of the Idea of John the Baptist	32—38
VI.	The Baptist and Jesus of Nazareth	39—46
VII.	The History of Jesus before His Baptism	47—60
VIII.	Jesus' Baptism	61—67
IX.	The Baptist's End	68—71

SECOND ADVANCE OF CHRISTIANITY.
JESUS AS CHRIST.

X.	His Actions previous to the Baptist's Arrest—The Messianic Beginnings	72—74
XI.	The First Stirrings of the Messianic Power in Knowledge and Speech	75—81

CONTENTS.

Chap.		Page
XII.	Messianic Activity in Working and Helping	82—85
XIII.	The First more Public Appearance and Working, and the Beginning of the Recognition of Christ in Wider Circles	86—102
XIV.	The Happy Return to Galilee, and the New Position of the Messiah	103—106
XV.	The History of the Temptation	107—109
XVI.	The Founding of the Messianic Kingdom	110—118
XVII.	The Daily Occupation	119—122
XVIII.	The Journey of this year to the Feast	123—127
XIX.	The Opposition and Enmity of the World	128—139
XX.	The New Attitude of the Messiah towards the World	140—144
XXI.	The Founding of the Christian Church	145—155
XXII.	The Higher Teaching in the Kingdom of God and His Earthly Community	156—162
XXIII.	The Relation between the Lord of the New Church and Men and Spirits	163—167
XXIV.	The Practical Education of the Twelve through Travel with their Master	168—178
XXV.	The Practical Training through their own Mission	179—182
XXVI.	The Doubt of the Baptist, and his End	183—191
XXVII.	The Return of the Twelve, and their new Practice	192—204
XXVIII.	Increased Frequency and Extent of the Journeys with the Twelve	205—210
XXIX.	The distant Journeys in the North	211—224
XXX.	The Feast of Tabernacles in Jerusalem	225—237
XXXI.	The Stay on the East and on the West of the Jordan.—Decision of the Sanhedrim about Christ	238—248

CONTENTS.

THIRD ADVANCE OF CHRISTIANITY.

Chap.		Page
XXXII.	Christ's Temporal Fall and Eternal Victory.—His Resolution to meet the Crisis	249—254
XXXIII.	The Last Festal Journey	255—265
XXXIV.	The Entry into Jerusalem	266—270
XXXV.	The Last Public Working in Jerusalem	271—282
XXXVI.	The Betrayal.—The Bodily Death and the Eternal Hope.—The Bodily Separation and the Eternal Presence	283—302
XXXVII.	The Arrest and its Consequences	303—312
XXXVIII.	The Condemnation	313—323
XXXIX.	The Crucifixion and Burial	324—336
XL.	The Eternal Exaltation	337—348
	Notes	351

The Reader is requested to note the following Errata.

ERRATA.

Page 88, line 26, for "found" read "forced."
" 95, " 5, for "mere" read "more."
" 186, " 6, for "part" read "past."
" 194, " 5, for "gems" read "germs."
" 234, " 15, for "as no" read on.
" 248, " 8, *dele* "yet."
" 112, " 2 from bottom, *dele* "were."
" 123, " 1, for "effect" read "effort."

PREFACE.

THE following work is a translation of part of the Fifth Volume of Ewald's "Geschichte des Volk's Israel." It is, as far as the Editor is aware, the first attempt to introduce this great scholar and thinker to those who are unacquainted with the German language. It might seem at first surprising that the works of one, who has unquestionably had so great an influence on Biblical study, should never have been brought before English readers. Not to dwell on other reasons to explain this, it is sufficient to mention the daring boldness of his views. One who should only judge of the tendency of the book from a general statement of the author's principles of enquiry, and the results at which he arrives, would probably imagine it wanting in reverence, and tending to undermine the foundation of our religion. When we are told that the subjective turn of mind of the author leads him to look on the early history of the Jews as in large part mythical;—that in his view the history of the Patriarchs and of God's chosen people, in passing by tradition through the course of centuries, has not been miraculously preserved from the same fate which has befallen that of other ancient nations;—that he regards even the inspired Prophets as not so raised above human infirmities and the perverted or erroneous notions of their time, but that human passion may be traced in their writings;—when further we are taught to look on the Prophets rather as inspired preachers, than as foretellers of the future: on thus hearing of the author's views in bare outline, we are naturally led to look on the work as destructive to faith and to reverence for the Bible. But when we come to study the work, we find our first impressions in great part groundless. If we look on faith as the conviction, that what we have been led to believe can only have happened in the same literal objective sense in which we have been wont to regard it, in so far the history is dangerous to faith. But if we look on faith as a conviction that God has been and is guiding and governing His people; that national ungodliness will surely lead to the punishment of a nation, whilst even amid the sufferings of the nation God is leading on his faithful servants to higher and more spiritual views of Him and His governance of men: then this book is undoubtedly animated by the strongest faith and religious feeling. No work that I am acquainted with shews more clearly how God was teaching His people by their whole history to look to the Messiah as the only hope of their race.

I have spoken thus far of the author's history as a whole; partly not to lose the opportunity of expressing my humble admiration for the work. In spite of all blemishes, few who have read it can look on it as other than—to use the Dean of Westminster's words—'a noble work.' But partly, again, I have wished to diminish in some measure the prejudice which the name of Ewald might arouse against the following history.

I turn now to this particular work. It will be found nearly free from those bold speculations which offend in the earlier portion of the history. The supernatural is here never rejected *as* supernatural: the feeding of the multitude, and the raising of Lazarus, perhaps the two most stupendous miracles, are related with full faith in their supernatural character. The author, it is true, dwells much more on the moral purpose and spiritual meaning than on the outward miraculous features; but in so doing he is but following, he may plead, the example set by our Lord Himself. Excepting the narrative of the miraculous occurrences at the Crucifixion, which he looks on as poetic imagery, akin to that of the Prophet's language,—with this one exception, there are only two or three instances, in which He seems inclined to detract from the strangeness of the event as generally understood: but in all these cases he admits the truth of the observed facts, while inclined to doubt some of the causes imagined by the Evangelists, or, it may be, the sequel which men commonly supply from their own imaginations. Thus, while admitting the accuracy of the narrative of the healing the demoniac, and of the fate of the swine, he doubts whether the two events were connected in the way the Evangelist supposed. While admitting the truth of the narrative of the raising the widow's son at Nain, he is inclined to think that the supposed dead man may really have been suffering only from suspended animation: he is led to this view, it seems, simply from its having been passed over by the earlier Evangelists. That Peter at the Lord's command actually caught the fish with the stater in its mouth is, he says, a conclusion which the narrative does not warrant: that the command was merely a strong expression of the truth, that God by miraculous means, if necessary, will provide for the worldly wants of his own. I am not concerned with the probability or otherwise of these views, but simply with the fact that they do not in the least affect the credibility of the recorded *facts*. It will however be objected, and with some reason, that the author cares too little to maintain the credit of the Evangelists as true reporters of the outward facts of our Lord's life. This is especially noticeable in his remarks on the anointing of the Lord's feet, and on the two feedings of the multitude. He even regards variety of detail in narratives of an event as important for a testimony to the early currency of the narrative, and a token of its truth in the essential elements.

With regard to the discourses of our Lord, it will generally be allowed that the greater portion of them are given nearly verbatim, being given in essentially the same words by different Evangelists: other of His discourses again, though essentially the same in the different reports, are very different in expression (compare *e. g.* the discourses in Matt. xvi. 4—12, and Mark viii. 13—21). The author's conclusion is, that the more accurate report is a copy from notes taken by the disciples at the time. This is the work constantly referred to as the "Spruchsammlung." The other discourses, which have been more loosely reported, the author believes to have been drawn up by the Evangelists at a time when every saying and action of the Lord was reverentially recalled; then were many things recalled to mind "which the disciples understood not at the first, but after He had risen they remembered that He had told them of them." The principal real objection which, as I conceive, may be made to this work is, that the author is too fond of building on theory. A theory is very valuable as a guide to the observation of facts; but when recorded facts are explained away as inconsistent with the theory, it then becomes dangerous. Herein lies one both of the merits and defects of the book. It traces more clearly than any work I know the plan of our Lord's life conceived and carried out by Him, and thus invests Him with an increased human interest: but at the same time the author is led to dispute recorded facts as inconsistent with his idea of Christ's work, (see *e. g.* his remarks on the second temple cleansing).

I need not here specify all the points in which I am obliged to differ from the author: some of the principal of these have been noticed in the Notes at the end of the volume. These Notes, I may state here, make no pretension to offer a complete discussion of the matter they touch on: my object was the twofold one—first, where it seemed advisable, to signify my dissent from the views in the text; secondly, to elucidate the author's views from the Notes in the original work or from other works of his, especially " Die drei ersten Evangelien."

I will now only add a few words on my motives in publishing this translation. In the first place, I must admit the somewhat personal motive of the desire to make better known to the English public an author for whom I have so sincere an admiration, and to whose works I have been so much indebted. But in the second and principal place, it seemed that to minds whose faith may have been shaken by sceptics like Strauss or Rénan, a thinker so bold as Ewald, so unfettered by dogmatic prejudice, might speak with a persuasiveness and power, for which a less independent thinker could never hope. The author's disbelief in the Old Testament miracles serves as a dark background, which makes us more admire the firm faith in the works of Christ which shines forth from this volume. On one fundamental point this author's protest may, I hope, be useful—his protest I mean in favour of the genuineness of St. John's Gospel: modern scepticism is using every effort to throw discredit on this Gospel as a record of the works and sayings of our Lord. It feels that this is the grand bulwark of the Christian's faith in the divinity of Christ. The narrative of the supernatural birth of Christ and of the Resurrection it may explain as myths; but our Lord's language about Himself, as given in this Gospel, can only be set aside by denying the truth of the Gospel. I will notice one other objection which will probably be made to this work. The natural human element, it will be said, is dwelt on to the exclusion of the præternatural.

I should be sorry to make myself responsible for the writer's orthodoxy: yet if we, in accordance with the author's intention, bear in mind that it is the man Christ Jesus only whose history it is here intended to trace, not that of the Divine Word mysteriously and inseparably connected with Him; with such an understanding there is nothing, I think, which may not be reconciled with the orthodox view of the Person of Christ. Practically, I think, whilst we allow that our Lord in taking our nature took on Him the weaknesses and limitations of our body, we shrink from attributing to Him those of our minds and spirits. While we allow that the Divine omnipotence only broke forth at intervals from under the veil of Christ's humanity; we shrink from allowing that He was generally subject to the same limitations of thought and spirit as ourselves, the Divine omniscience only occasionally raising Him from human to divine knowledge.

I conclude with the expression of the hope, that the tender loving spirit which breathes through this biography may find a response in many hearts, that the vivid portrait herein contained may make Him to many more of a real living presence. In the prayer that all blemishes in it may be pardoned by Him it would set forth, the work is commended to the English public.

THE EDITOR.

LIFE OF JESUS CHRIST.

CHAPTER I.

INTRODUCTION.

THE SOURCES OF THIS HISTORY.

THE more important this history is to us in itself, the more carefully shall we enquire into the extent, the age, and the true nature of its sources. And here we must first without doubt lament, that we possess on the Non-Christian side no early and trustworthy information, worth speaking of, on the life, works, and fate of Christ. This cannot, it is true, be very surprising. No history, as will appear plainly further on, can be more quiet in presence of the turmoil of the world, and more inconspicuous, than that of the short public working of Christ, who never, as the Baptist, interfered with the public popular life of the time,—who, remote from all the world of that day, lived only for God as His Father, and for the establishment of the perfect kingdom of God; and whose Spirit, uncomprehended by that world, appeared immediately suffocated and crushed for ever directly it began to reveal itself completely in the world.

Even in the period next after this violent stifling, this mysterious stillness of the new Spirit in the world lasts on until it irresistibly penetrates it ever more strongly, and then soon both Jews and heathens say enough of it, when they had already lost the opportunity of being able to know most accurately about Christ. Thus Flavius Josephus is the only Non-Christian historian of the first century we possess who speaks of Christ. In the first indeed of his two great works—the history of the Jewish War—he did not speak of Him, he had no need in respect of the principal subject of it. But we cannot see how he, in the Antiquities, should have neglected to speak, however briefly, of Christ and His followers; as there he mentions much far less important, and that work professes to give a general history of the people, according to all its aims, various divisions, and manifold crises. Had he also in this work said *nothing* of Christianity, that could only be explained from a want of clear views on the subjects which had so completely fettered him, that he preferred to be silent on a matter so imperfectly known to him. He had certainly, when he wrote his work for the Roman-Greek world, a secret horror of every thing Messianic, and Christianity must have appeared to him, as to all the Jews of his views, something incomprehensible; and besides, as it was felt how much this last division had injured the Jews, it must have been a subject disagreeable and repugnant. But these grounds seem insufficient for his entirely overlooking it.

Now there are actually found in all manuscripts of

the Antiquities, two apparently corresponding passages where he speaks of Christ and His followers, but the first and more express of the two gives token of an unmistakeable Christian hand. We have too here every cause to readily believe in a change by Christian hands. For Josephus' works, written at first not for Jews so much as for heathen, soon, in consequence of the after destinies of the people, came into heathen and still more into Christian hands exclusively, and early became for the Christians a principal source of all their historical knowledge. It is no wonder then that an eminent Christian early so changed a passage on Christ therein contained, that the work became readable for Christians, and this change then passed into all Christian MSS. while all others have been lost. That the passage, without any occasion from the context, was first thrust in by a Christian, and thus is, in short, completely and in every word spurious, has been in later times without ground asserted by many: for if Josephus had not spoken of Christ at all, that would have been readily borne, as it did not occur to any Christian of the first or second century that he must first see the historical truth of Christ confirmed by Josephus. But it is equally false to imagine that the Christian hand found some unprejudiced statement in Josephus, for then it would have simply let stand an honest statement in any way readable, without caring to make it, by a couple of sentences added, a little more Christian. Rather we have every reason to suppose, first, that Josephus, as he could not quite pass over Him, described Christ, according to the view then spread among Jews and heathen, as a mere wizard (Goeten), who through such arts, as well as by a feigned holiness, had led astray the people and appeared dangerous to the rulers; and, secondly, that he, with most other intelligent Jews of his time, although disapproving of Christianity as a superstition, yet lamented the persecuting Christ to the death, and wished it undone: for now at length many of the most intelligent Jews were come to the milder view; besides the old opposition between the Pharisees and Sadducees might have contributed to this as Josephus was a Pharisee; whilst Annas the high priest, by whose instigation, with that of his son-in-law Caiaphas, Christ was crucified, was with his whole family an adherent of the Sadducees. The Christian hand altered then in the narrative almost the whole, and allowed to stand only two of the last sentences, in which Josephus' regret shews itself still tolerably plain. And this entire change in the passage by a Christian hand occurred certainly pretty early in the second century, at which time another Christian hand must have been similarly busy with the work on the Jewish War.

What the Jews later, after the entire separation of the two religions, in ever narrowed and more hostile feeling, thought and wrote on the history of Christ and of early Christianity, has no longer historical importance. It led at length in natural sequence to the incredibly low and tasteless fictions of the work written in the German Middle Ages (Sefer toledoth Jeshua ha Nozri): it has therein for ever condemned itself.

But on the Christian side the four Evangelists now give us the oldest, richest, and weightiest matter for this history. What in addition the rest of the New Testament, only however in allusion and slight touch, contains, is derived from just the same narrative matter, and agrees entirely with the four Gospels, but deals very little with particulars. Richer than the Apocryphal Gospels which have yet survived, are, it is true, the oldest surviving Christian writings, yet in the whole of them there are only a few additions in any way important which can be drawn from them. Thus we must have recourse principally to the right knowledge and appreciation of the historical contents of our four Gospels, if we in this whole subject would arrive at a higher certainty, and in the deep interest of the matter will look on the smallest matter as greater than any which we shall here ever again know.

As now in more recent and the most recent times, so many perverse and injurious views have been put forward, nay, have been zealously defended, on the origin and the nature, and hence also on the historical importance, of these four Gospels, and it seemed high time to arrive in this question on a course of safer principles, I have, since 1848, already put forward more at length my views thereon. What is there brought forward, and will be in part still further brought forward, forms here also the groundwork of all knowledge of this history. We shall too, in the course of this history of the last events of the earthly Israel and of the simultaneous rise of the immortal spiritual Israel, have repeatedly to recur to much of this subject.

The result of our enquiries is, that with all the richness and variety of Gospel narrative there are only two principal sources and classes of narrative which we must constantly distinguish. When the oldest narrative had been already spread very widely in manuscript, there first appeared in St. John's Gospel its true completion, whether we look at the deep importance and brilliance of this entire history, or whether we look at the number of particulars which, in themselves apparently unimportant, may yet become of great importance. Truly the wonderful history of Christ has found also at once its just as wonderful narrative: for what can in many respects be more wonderful than this very formation and structure of the Gospels? Men, who without themselves having been enlightened with the light of the Gospel would never have thought of any writing of their own or even the art of writing, became founders of a quite new kind of literature such as the world had never seen, so admirably simple, so brief and yet so satisfying, so unadorned and yet so attractive, telling of the highest which can be told of, actually without an effort surpassing the childlike as well as the heroic and sublime in the Old Testament narrative. But after this literature has thus been, with the greatest industry and incessant labour, already in the most manifold and varied manner formed in a long course of distinct writing, and its zeal now seems wearied out, its matter already exhausted; then at length it receives its proper completion and most brilliant illustration, by a writing which by itself alone is just as important as all the earlier together,—nay, not only outshines all earlier ones, but even for the first time shines on them and illuminates them, and which does it all as though without wishing it, simply through its own goodness and joy and satisfaction in its great object. That the fourth Gospel has the Apostle for its author, has indeed in Germany, in more recent and from less pure motives in the most recent times, been much denied, and yet is quite certain, as I have persistently publicly asserted since, and recently have shown more particularly. Only *one* circumstance could shake our belief in this: and I admit that I myself, when I saw it quite clearly, was for a moment struck by it. It is observed, in fact, that the writer not seldom lays as it were for the foundation of his own exposition a simpler expression which is found in one of the older Evangelists, especially too in the sayings of Christ: this might lead to the notion of the work of one however spiritually rich, still a second hand, as though the composer had been not the independent Apostle and confidant of the Lord, but one who leaning on the hand of the other Evangelists lost himself in this sublimity. But in fact this is mere appearance. That the composer before he went to his own work had some Gospels lying before him, and indeed the very oldest and best, is quite plain: but we also cannot see why the Apostle should *not* have done that in his great age. It could never occur to him at so late a period to compose a Gospel with special non-reference to all earlier ones; and it well beseemed him to compare the writings of a Matthew and Mark-Peter.

Nay, this all the more, if he, as is from many proofs plain, did not till quite old age make up his mind to compose a Gospel of his own to complete the earlier ones: the reading of the Gospels written much earlier, and by the men who were generally most trustworthy, revived then the full memory of bygone events, so that even many of their words became naturally to him the occasion of his peculiar living representation. And thus all doubt which one might first stumble on in reading this Gospel, as to its coming from the Apostle John, quite vanishes on further investigation. Now no unprejudiced man will mistake the simple truthfulness and the honest spirit, in which not merely our four, but also all the Gospels which preceded them were written. For the literature of the Gospels was, as I have there shewn, at first most various, and different according to the individual composers: because the great and difficult subject himself did not suffer himself to be so easily exhausted; but while in the spring time of this literature one writing might complete, in part also improve on another in this or that respect, in the strict love of truth and the avoidance of the intermixture of any foreign aim the earlier and also the four now preserved are alike. And if even the historical writings of the best times of the Old Covenant in harmony with the old true religion, in spite of all their other varieties, shew everywhere the deepest feeling for historical truth, how much more these Gospels, written but a short time after the might of the purest Truth had actually appeared on earth, and that too in the Truth's own history!

But true as all this is, we must yet never overlook that these Gospels, like the whole Christian period in which they came into existence, yet stand under the first impress of the entire manifestation, completely singular as it was, nay, infinitely sublime. This was the single grand subject of their narrative; and this, observe, is their greatest merit, that they give us this impression so truly and reflect it so continually. So far however as all portions of this entire great history, and above all the history of Christ Himself, has its meaning not only for those earliest times but also for our and all future time, it is our duty here to look above these first impressions, even into the primary and hence eternal meaning which this whole manifestation has. All the many peculiarities which the Gospels, and in some sort also other writings, afford to us, are only helps and contributions for this end: and if the mark corresponding to this aim stands so far from us that we can only gradually approach to it though ever more surely, yet may we never lose it in itself out of our sight.

All this being first premised, it will be found, on a careful use of the sources of this history, that although many of its several portions remain somewhat obscure to us, yet in respect to their chief objects and unmixed truths they quite satisfy us. And as though for the singular importance of this history the necessity had always made itself felt of having together as many trustworthy sources as possible, we have for this period of very few years a fulness of various accounts in the Bible itself such as exists nowhere else.

CHAPTER II.

THE CHRONOLOGY OF THIS HISTORY.

As the earliest Gospels proceeded in general from an inward sincerity and the quiet cheerfulness which is the true reflection of that inward happiness whose power is satisfied in itself, they were satisfied to note down even the most remarkable sayings and deeds of Jesus after some simple fashion of their own, without thinking about the accurate determination of their chronology, nay even without much thinking on the history external to this circle, and of fitting it in to the great History of the World: besides too it came into being and ran its course quite apart from its loud turmoil, and not till quite its termination connected itself with the name of a Roman viceroy. Further, at the time when these histories were written, the story did not go back so far, nor into so different a crisis of the world's history, for men to think in time of fixing its limits more accurately: it was known that these events were pretty recent, and had occurred in the yet peaceful period of the Roman Empire. Not until the period of the fall of the house of Augustus and the destruction of Jerusalem was a change produced, which even in respect to Christianity could not remain without results. Yet even John wrote his Gospel with the same complete indifference and unconcern about the connection of this history with the outer world. In truth, with his mode of handling Christianity this might seem to him a matter less important than to the composers of the other Gospels; but evidently their example influenced him also, so that he with less concern omitted what to him, as compared with the infinite importance of the matters in themselves, seemed unimportant. It then seemed through the mention of Pontius Pilate, omitted in none of our Gospels, that for simple readers the period in which the history lies was sufficiently indicated. But when once from the course of this history he has to recall to his mind more accurately, he gives out of its proper subject-matter many most valuable contributions to the more accurate knowledge of the several periods of the events. Nay, we might despair of arriving at a more accurate separation in time of many of the principal events of the history had we not the help of *this* history: St. John in fact looks on it as not worth while to define the years either in general or particular, nor to aim at chronology: but the occasional glimpses at profane matters, which he intermingles merely for the sake of the particular objects of the narrative, are so definite, so little inconsistent, and on more accurate enquiry fit in so well with everything else that is known to us, that they must be placed at the foundation, as for many points, quite the most trustworthy and instructive we have.

St. Luke quite otherwise, although he, like St. John, did not write till after the destruction of Jerusalem. He has (even St. John's Gospel was not before him) absolutely no more exact marks of time in the course of the history itself, or at least none such as could in any way help us to know the story chronologically more exactly in detail: but he tries by means of some certain dates to fit the story into its proper place in the world's history. Nay, this was plainly with him one principal object of his new history, and what he adds in this view to its chronological sources is quite peculiar to him. We cannot also fail to notice that he, just because it was a new principal object with him, made the most careful enquiries, and have only to regret that he yet gave fewer exact dates than we should now wish for. We must hence start from him, but when he leaves us, take the intimations of the other Evangelists, and especially of St. John, to help us. Now, strictly speaking, there are only two available dates of importance which St. Luke gives us. The one, that the Baptist appeared in the fifteenth year of the reign of Tiberius Cæsar; the other, that Jesus when he began to appear as Christ was about thirty years old (Luke iii. 1, 23). The last information is however in itself left somewhat indefinite, and is the less available for exact chronological determination, as it does not give more accurately the year in which the Baptist or Jesus was born. If the statement on the appearance of the Baptist is exact (of which we have no reason to doubt), that event falls in the year 781 U.C. or 28 A.D., according to our usual reckoning. That, however, Jesus appeared openly as Christ in the same year as the Baptist appeared, is not said by St. Luke. We must thus, in making a first approximation, leave *this* gap also unfilled; yet this is in itself probable, as St. Luke would probably otherwise have added a fresh date. But further, we assume here as certain what will appear afterwards as the result of our particular enquiry, that Jesus' public working lasted at least from three and a-half to four years, as may be concluded from St. John's statements. If several Church Fathers said Jesus' public working lasted three or four years, this was at least more likely than the opinion that it had only lasted one year: for the latter opinion was supported only by the apparent proof which the present Gospel according to St. Matthew, as well as that of St. Luke, might well spread, but how groundlessly will appear below.

Had St. Luke thought it worth while to state accurately the year also of the death of Jesus, we might thus easily lead to a safe conclusion what St. John lets us suppose on the duration of His public life. But for the end of his work there reappears that total unconcern about such observations, which, as above stated, affects from the first all the Evangelical literature: this may the less surprise us, as St. Luke yet later even in the "Acts" shews the same carelessness about a closer connection between the secular and religious sides of the whole history of the time.

But first in the history of Jesus' death, by all the Evangelists without distinction it is uniformly stated that the day of his death was a Friday: now this Friday, according to the more exact remembrance to be enquired into below, was the day of that year on the evening of which the Paschal week began, or the 14th of the month Nisan in that year. If then we can in that period find a year in which the 14th of this month, according to the rule then in existence for determining it, was a Friday, we should thus have a safe limit for the conclusion of this history. But now all authorities state with tolerable agreement, and according to all appearance from good remembrance, that Jesus' death happened 33 A.D., and on the 14th of the month, at the time of the Paschal offering towards evening; and it has been attempted to shew in later times, that according to astronomical accuracy that day was actually a Friday. If now we combine that beginning of the Baptist's work 28 A.D. with this year 33 A.D., we have a period of about five years, in which interval we may suppose comprised all that we know of the Baptist's as well as of Jesus' public life. This period is further, looked at generally, not too short for the unfolding of the extraordinary activity of the Baptist, and still more of Jesus: but however remarkable, on the other hand, this activity may have been, we can hardly imagine that it can have lasted a considerably shorter time. Further, with this agree all the dates and traces of the universal history of that time, as well as the history of the profane side of the story (as has been earlier shewn in the author's history), and in some particulars is still further to be touched on. Finally, entirely without design the intimations in St. John's Gospel agree admirably therewith, which the more incidentally they have been recorded are so much the more welcome, as they serve from quite another source to corroborate the principal proof. The Gospel of St. John actually gives us a further proof, quite distinct, for the accuracy of the beginning of the time named. In quoting a speech of the chief priest's on the temple, immediately after Jesus' first appearance, he makes them say that the temple (that is, as it then was) had been built in not fewer than forty-six years, (John ii. 29). This refers to the building of the temple by Herod, which was long continued after Herod's death (Bd. iv. s. 191), and begun in the year 20 B.C. This year 20 being an incomplete year, and the 28th year A.D. being likewise an incomplete year, and therefore not included, we arrive at the interval here given—46 years. Supposing even it was St. John himself who gave these words with so accurate a mark of time, one sees in any case that he could have fixed the time of Jesus' first appearance quite as well as St. Luke, and that he (had he set any importance on it) would have been quite capable of fitting the Gospel history in all its parts into its place in universal history. Only the interval between the Baptist's and Jesus' appearance seems with him to have been less taken account of. But this interval was after all not very great, and it seems in remembrance to have grown ever less. In what then concerns the period of the public activity of the Baptist and of Jesus, and a number of important events besides this, we have information enough. Many particulars of it will probably never again be clear to us in their perfectly accurate sequence; but much can, by continued closer investigation, grow ever more certainly again clear to us, and much, on the certainty of which in more recent times doubts were felt, will become instead continually plainer. Still we must never forget that very many of the several events of this entire history are not of the kind for which their exact chronological place is of much importance, as they have for their first object only the fuller knowledge of the whole life and working of Jesus.

The enquiry reserved, however, on the duration of the public working of both men, and especially of Jesus, is far harder to determine with the same certainty. It is too in fact, for this history, itself of little importance to know exactly how old Jesus was when he began to work, and the older Gospels pass over this entirely. St. Luke indeed thought to define this by the sentence "he was about thirty years of age," but this expression is itself far from definite, and has hence given rise to many misconceptions. If we take this "about thirty years," in spite of the uncertainty in which St. Luke has left it, in the strictest sense as thirty, and compare therewith the date given by St. Luke as the year of the Baptist's appearance, and as is natural to suppose that also of Jesus, namely the 15th year of the reign of Tiberius, or 781-782 U.C., we must arrive at 751-752 as the year of His birth, or if He were supposed to appear not until two years after the Baptist, the year 754 U.C.

This reckoning, through the ignorance, as is allowed, of the early middle ages, became in Europe the foundation of our present reckoning of time before and after Christ. But if Jesus was born in the reign of Herod the Great, as we are informed by the last composer of St. Matthew's Gospel, and quite independently by St. Luke, this period for our Lord's life is too short, as Herod died 750 U.C. Nay, we might probably put His birth a year earlier, as He, according to the meaning of the passages about his birth, could hardly have been born in the very last year of the reign of Herod. It is true, the account in St. Luke about the Roman census during which Jesus was born, seems to lead to a more exact conclusion about this year. But the year for which Augustus ordered such a census over all the world is neither defined in this account, nor is it from other accounts clear to us. In truth this account, as St. Luke gives it, according to plain tokens, is merely repeated by him from an earlier writer, and St. Luke in a short parenthesis is contented with merely remarking on his own part, that this census is not to be confounded with the one under Quirinus. Now as this account here taken up by St. Luke describes only very generally everything of the outward universal history which concerns it, it is manifestly only a more distant tradition of such a census "of the whole world" under Augustus in Herod's lifetime, which in this part is its authority. The registration which Augustus ordered could have reference evidently only to Romans and Roman subjects, and so could not properly have reference to Palestine, as not at that time a member of the Roman confederacy; the census too is here described as accomplished not as after Roman but as after old Hebrew fashion, by families. But Augustus had, as was known, designed to carry out accurate enumerations of the number of inhabitants of the Roman empire, including those of the confederated countries, and had appointed a Roman census for 746 U.C.: the aged Herod, become continually more dependent on him, had certainly met his views in this wish for an exact account of the number of inhabitants of his country; and we know further that he, in one of the last years before his death, had made the whole people take a solemn oath of fidelity in his own and Augustus' name, which probably was done with the men assembled for the census. From this might be formed that more definite idea, which in so far was not without historical reminiscence. If we cannot then determine quite accurately the birth year of our Lord, it is yet plain from all tokens that the expression of St. Luke "about thirty years" is rather *thus* to be taken, that He at the time of His entrance on His ministry was already some years over thirty years old. And this is the most probable conclusion which we could maintain in respect to diverse opinions which it was sought to establish in ancient times.

CHAPTER III.

The Stages of this History.

When however we look from the external temporal limitations of this history of a few years to the progress and gradations of its inner development, we cannot be enough surprised at the way in which all its grandeur is compressed into so small a space, and yet at the same time passes through three such various gradations until it completes itself and arrives at a preliminary rest. But thus also the whole power and the whole long labour of the germinating, flowering, and fructifying of a noble tree is compressed in short time into the marvel of the small thick growing fruit, that this successively germinating, forming, and ripening may render yet far richer produce. And here too we have an entirely peculiar tree of noblest sort, and a fruit at length ripening after 2000 years.

The perfected Man of God was to come as founder of the perfected Kingdom of God and healer of all the sins of the world: to this unfathomable thought and to this ardent longing had the people now, in the course of its long life and painful striving after true religion, raised itself: but He *must* come even now, if this whole life and struggling, with all its hard labours and sufferings was not to be, after all, fruitless at last. There is something gigantic and eternal which lay in this thought: even the clear thinking on, hoping for, longing for such a consummator, embracing and collecting in Himself what was most salutary in all true religion, must wonderfully quicken and exalt the spirit, the never-wearying faithful waiting for Him give to the spirit a decided tendency to all perfection and an ever lively tension. But just as this people, as Jehovah's people, (see Bd. II. s. 188 ff.) appeared in the world's history with a gigantic idea and enterprise, out of which sprang all of noblest and most heroic which in the course of many centuries was active in it, after that this enterprise become historical, historically could no further advance, this people appears with a yet more gigantic view of the future, which however quite corresponds to the first, and was evoked by it. If it has become apparent in the history of 1500 years that there is yet no perfect people of God, nay, that this, just when it must be at its greatest perfection, to sustain itself at all on the earth, sank to the lowest depths and is continually sinking, then must there first come a perfect Man of God: and that He may come will now be the object of all deepest longing and striving: that the people, notwithstanding its increasing disruption and weakness, hopes for Him so firmly, is its greatest merit.

His actual coming is now the great advance which was here yet possible, the fulfilment of the gigantic higher consciousness and aspirations, so far as these could then be immediately fulfilled. And secondly, the true advance, if it is really to be the advance to the perfect true religion, must itself be the coming Messiah's own working. But that it might be also actually even possible, and that the true Messias might be able to appear, it needed—first because He must spring forth from this people—a last meeting and striving by the whole people to this end. Were however, lastly, the true culmination of all advance here possible, by means of the people's own striving and complete working once arrived at, this advance must of itself lead to the advance which at once extends itself beyond the individual Messiah into the great whole, and which first brings about the true conclusion of the whole of this great advance; because it is after all not the perfection of the individual Messias, but of the very Kingdom of God in the world; it is this to which all converges, and which can begin so soon as the perfect Messias is there. The great advance then which forms the fairest part of the whole history of this people divides itself immediately into three particular advances, of which the first is ever the condition of the others and pushes them on; but of these however each one is of quite peculiar kind; these develope themselves in their periods with wonderful rapidity and encroach on each other, and yet each of them will have its own peculiar time. In Christ they are all combined, and He alone forms the second of the three as the purest and highest of all these advances. He extends into the first, but so that He is only moved and impelled by it; and He goes on further spontaneously into the third, but in such sort that He rather suffers than works, and His suffering is itself the transition to the third advance so varied in its manifestations—that advance with which the germ of the Perfect advances indestructible into the great world, and Christianity, or the immortal part of Israel, has already become a never-ending blessing to humanity.

CHAPTER IV.

FIRST ADVANCE.

THE ADVANCE TO MESSIAS (CHRIST).

JOHN THE BAPTIST.

It may in many respects be regretted that we possess so little old and express information on John the Baptist. For of the late writings of those who only, in opposition to Christianity when it had become mighty, thought good to announce themselves adherents of the Baptist, we need make the less mention, as they are entirely unproductive of historical knowledge. We thus now possess on him and his earliest followers, besides the New Testament account, only the short one of Flavius Josephus (Antiq. 18 v. 2), which is superficial and unsatisfactory in proportion to the inability of this writer to understand anything which breathes a Christian spirit. The higher glory and the entire perfection of Christ outshone soon the brilliancy and fame as well as the whole undertaking and effort of the Baptist: but looked at from the past, he was assuredly one of the greatest heroes of Israel, his work the deepest and the truest which in all these last times could be attempted, and the entire elevation of spirit and definiteness of the effort to which he called the people, was doubtless the first and most necessary step to the only possible and true salvation of the period, nay, the surprising fulfilment of the first of those three conditions of its fulfilment above described. And therefore it is that the information about him in the New Testament is, with all its shortness and fragmentary character, not only the oldest but also the most express and instructive, exactly because it could the best bring forward the earliest and noblest of his views, and what he in fact set forward destined to find its completion only in Christianity. The actually perfect may well and safely look back on its own real beginnings; ripe and decided manhood look back on its youth: thus the New Testament looks back on the Baptist. But the more necessary then is it that we also know truly this first breaking of the new day, and estimate that hero after his noble nature, who ventured on the first mighty step to raise himself and the people above all hitherto realised, in order to bring it in effect nearer to the perfect of men's aspirations. In the oldest sources our John is never distinguished more particularly in his descent and race: the name "Baptist" affixed suffices with them, as well as in Flavius Josephus, to distinguish him from the numerous other Johns (for particularly since Hyrcanus I. this was a very favourite man's name); so memorable a feature must at first have been the baptism in his case. Still, in the somewhat later and more artificial account of his appearance in the public world which St. Luke has adopted in his history, Zacharias and Elizabeth are spoken of as his parents, the city of Judah (by which doubtless is meant the old capital and city of the priests—Hebron) is named his father's city (Luke i. 23, 39): his father according to this account belonged to one of the 24 priestly families, which after ancient custom had to provide for the temple service in proper succession, and thus when it came to their turn betake themselves from their home to the temple. And we have every reason to accept as historical these reminiscences from the history of the parentage of the Baptist. Our John might have as a priest's son, nay, as according to St. Luke's narrative, a particularly late born child, grown up accordingly and lived on in all honour and the abundance of common life: but we see repeated once more in him all the stricter view of life and willing devotion, which, as on many occasions we saw above, is with no priesthood of antiquity so peculiar as with that which the true religion subsequent to Moses had established among this people. Nay, it is remarkable enough, that now towards the conclusion of the course of this whole history, when the deepest, the strongest and most enduring which lay in the people was incited once more to reveal itself most strongly and aim at everything possible to it; it is again a born priest, who out of the purest impulses of true religion prepared a new spiritual movement and advance, which must go beyond everything which in former times an Aaron, a Samuel, or an Ezra had attempted and effected. If, in fact, we will rightly appreciate his life-work, we must well observe the entire foundation on which it rested, and which we yet may know well enough from his own words and deeds. And here we must first of all notice, that *he* it was first who among the people reflected more deeply on the hope of the Messiah, and consequently made it for the first time a true life-question for the whole people. He knew assuredly, with all clearness of conception, that this hope might not be left unproductive and barren in books, in mere thought and reminiscence, but that it was high time to take up with all honesty, as well of spirit as of action, what it involves as a moral call immediately practicable for the whole people: and he was resolved boldly and skilfully enough not merely to rightly know all this, but also to carry it out for himself and the whole people. In this double power of true knowledge of what was necessary for the time, and of the decided and persistent action corresponding thereto, herein lies his peculiar importance and his lasting service: but that his work was in itself so successful and so lofty, and through the success of the revival kindled by him produced such a wonderful after effect even beyond its own limits, the cause of this lay not in him but in the pure truth and infinite loftiness of the conception of the hope itself: the miraculous power of the Truth raised any spirit which had the simple courage to trust to its leading, so far as it was capable of being led by it. It is not right, and least of all at this time is it right, to wait doing nothing for the Messiah and His coming: His coming is truly to be expected, and never more than now: but if He is to come for the salvation of Israel, Israel must prepare itself rightly to receive Him when He comes. He will, as almost every king, come as a strict ruler to set up His Kingdom with the proper sharers in it; but at the same time as quite a different king from any that had been on earth, as the king of the kingdom of the perfect true religion. Let the people then raise itself to the perfect true religion, that the Messiah, when He comes, may use it as the right instrument of His Kingdom; let it go resolutely out from the inrooted errors, perversities, and corruptions of the whole life of the day, and leave behind it all the deficiencies of its whole bygone history, in order to raise itself to that new pure life which the Messiah when He comes can approve, and to which He can attach the strongest threads of His blessing-bringing rule.

Israel is indeed His first people to whom He will come and whom He will rule: but not Israel as a people and the ancient Church is properly that which He will seek and which He will bless with His salvation: the perfecting of the true religion and its kingdom is that which He will seek and which He will bring; but *Israel* He will exalt to His salvation only in so far as it is worthy of this kingdom. (vgl. s. 101.) Therefore, in sum, it concerns Israel not as a whole people, but individuals in it: each individual then must prepare himself for this true kingdom, and as a completely regenerate man seek to be more receptive of all that is pure, perfect, and best; nay, as a man not drawing back even before the highest when it comes, wait for the mysterious and yet certain coming of the Lord. This is indisputably the close connection of all the first thoughts and intuitions of the Baptist, from which he started and which so powerfully filled his soul beforehand, that they quite early determined the whole direction of his life, and made him the singular man of his time, which he actually was. What he thus strove for was something completely new in its firmly resolved faithful direction towards the certain and speedy coming of Christ, and in its severe moral preparation for it, which indeed already in effect was made into a new law of life. And yet the requiring strict penitence and an entire return to the first declared divine will, with the giving up also of all national pride, was nothing strictly new in Israel.

The old prophets had already demanded all this; but with more eloquence and with greater depth had the "Great Unnamed One" at the end of the banishment exhorted to such a complete national regeneration, and to the bold conception of the perfect true religion (Bd. IV. s. 54 ff), and, in fact, many of his inspired words were plainly what now distinctly reechoed, and helped to urge on the Baptist to his enterprise. But if that "Great Unnamed," in the beginning of this whole last great revolution in the history of Israel, had at the same time to exhort to a new gathering of the dispersed people, it had now likewise long become plain that even with the revived ancient people, completely reformed into a new people, the Perfect was not yet come: and while that mighty call, which sounded at the beginning of this new phase of history, reechoed yet more mightily towards its end, it at the same time took quite another direction and proceeded from a penetrating truth, which at that time could not properly be sounded aloud. In fact, John undertook what at his time could most rightly be undertaken by the purest and deepest spirits of the people, and what had never been undertaken before. That the Messiah could not come so easily, since Isaiah's times were past and his prophecies had sounded apparently without result, was a dim feeling which became ever more overmastering, and after short intervals of excited hope ever returned: hence there arose along with this hope, as has been shown more at length (s. 93 ff.), the other consciousness, that a great prophet must first return to prepare the way of the Lord by the preparation of His people for Him—a consciousness which could not be more true and exact, and by which the whole circle of the Messianic hopes would at length be so closed, that these could now rest and wait for their own fulfilment. But was now the coming of such a prophetic forerunner of Christ in this prophetless time not likewise very difficult? That this prophet, in order to lead the people and transform it from the lowest depths to worthily meet the Messiah, must be of the mightiest power, was likewise doubtless felt; and hence there had (Nach. s. 94 f.) formed itself the hope, that none less than Elias would return to execute the indispensable work preparatory for the Messiah. But could not men wait in the same inaction for the coming of Elias as for that of Christ Himself? Could not some timid, self-fancying, acute interpretation of Malachi's prophecy find in it actually a duty to do absolutely nothing for the furtherance of the great cause, till Elias, from heaven or from some other place of His concealment, should return in His own body and prove Himself the true Elias? Yet all this did not frighten back our John before he became the Baptist; he recognised the divine call to his age as directed most specially to him, and followed it as though he had thus simply to fulfil his duty. And as towards the end of the long course of the history of Israel, all the greatest, the purest, and mightiest which ever stirred in it is compressed into the smallest and compactest form, and long-perished power returned wonderfully renewed; so does this John, in the time now become quite prophetless, yet become a prophet, but a prophet of quite different sort from those whose time was long gone by.

He promises with all prophetic certainty the near advent of the Messiah, and requires with all true prophetic strictness a life conformable thereto: but as though by his own deepest striving to hasten the coming of Messiah's time, he exchanges the whole previous life of the community for a new life alone worthy of the coming Messiah, will lead the united people without exception to Him, and live with his disciples as though the hourly Expected were already come. Thus was he urged on to fulfil the first of the three above described previous conditions of the coming of Perfection. The agonizing grief that the Expected still comes not, this served to goad on his thoughts and actions; while his clear view on the divine call to his time, and on the extent and limits of his own higher duty, made him collected and calm in his bold enterprise.

CHAPTER V.

The Carrying out of the Idea of John; The Baptism.

Urgent and unspeakably seductive as was the idea of the Baptist, equally great was the difficulty of its execution: here stood one against the whole people, and would with it prepare himself for a perfect state of things waiting to appear, which *he* only inwardly divined and hoped for, but did not see further into and comprehend, so that he would never have thought himself capable of introducing it.

For this reason there is repeated once again in the course of this history, and now most strongly, that spasmodic and violent beginning, which we often saw appear at the commencement of great developments, only now softened and glorified because the Perfect, to which men not in vain wished gradually to approach, threw forth already its rays from the darkness, and would spread its soft light even before it actually burst forth.

As he had to entirely reject for its tendency all the civilisation of the day, noble and brilliant as it was in many respects, and, yet more, all the ruling powers of the day, he retired out of this luxurious world to the solitudes and wilderness on the Jordan, and took Elias for his model in his mode of life. Like him he clothed himself in a rough garment of camel's hair kept together by a girdle of skin, and lived on nothing but what the wilderness spontaneously offered him, locusts and wild honey, which he might collect in the season and the places where they could be gathered in greater abundance, and keep them in his hut which was as simple as his life. No one then could begin with greater earnestness and resolution, and more entire renunciation of the old world, that new life soaring towards the Messiah, whose speedy coming was constantly expected, than did John: but this life struggling towards the Messiah was assuredly one also of deep mourning and sighing, which, as well through all the other deepest efforts of the soul, as in particular by frequent praying, weeping, and fasting, would excite as it were God's mercy to send the Messiah, and would strike sparks out of the hard stone of the present. Thus teaching and thus living he gathered around him a circle of closer friends and followers, to whom he opened all his inner life, whom he consecrated to be his closest fellow-soldiers in his mighty undertaking, and who with him would not fear even all the hardest efforts of mourning and fasting. He also taught his disciples new prayers, which were long used amongst them. They doubtless shewed forth in the most pointed expressions the elevation to which he would raise his followers. In this retirement from out of the luxurious world, and in his dwelling in the wilderness on the

Jordan, he seemed only an old Nazarite or modern Essene, in frequent praying and fasting to be only perhaps a stricter Pharisee: and yet how different was he in the depth of his aims from all such older sects! Accordingly, for a right initiation, and for the putting a stamp on this his real effort, all former modes of life and symbols did not suffice: an entirely new symbol must be formed for him, in order to be both the actual beginning and the plain expression of what he would found in Israel; potent enough to serve for the commencement, and yet simple enough to be applied indifferently by all members of the people, as they in view of the effort needed were all alike. This instrument and this sign was found by him in Baptism after sincere confession of sins: every member of the people who would look on himself as meet for the speedy coming of the Messiah and his salvation, must with all sincerity confess his sins before him who called him to repentance, and promise a new and better life; then, at the hand of him, whose it was to make this sacred promise in God's stead, immersed in the depths of the water, rise purified from the stain of his deeply repented sins to the new life which had already been explained to him in its meaning and its duties; and then, at the conclusion of that which was the very instrument and token of his cleansing, receive the divine promise of forgiveness of sins and fresh grace. The immersion in the depths of the flowing water under the Baptist's hand became thus the strongest visible and sensible token of the life-cleansing and spiritual regeneration of this race, and served, as it were, for a pledge that every one thus born again was worthy of the coming salvation of the Messiah, so long as he remains as pure as he had then vowed to remain. It need hardly be said that this baptism, regarded even outwardly, was of a far mightier and more downright kind than that which in the following period, gradually enfeebled, proceeded from it. It is true, this instrument of cleansing seemed at first far less sensibly impressive and less sensibly enduring than the original circumcision, the place of which it now almost occupied, for the purpose was now to found a new, purer, and worthier Israel: but it was evidently intended originally to cause a momentarily violent shock and trembling through the whole man after the confession of sins which had just been made. Nor is it demonstrable, or even probable, that the baptism, as John applied it, was to be extended also to children or women; or that, from its intention, it could be repeated: it would thus only have suffered in its true meaning. It further hardly needs remarking that it was with John something entirely new, and just as creative as the thought itself, of which it became the answering expression and visible token. For though bathing in the Jordan had been earlier looked on as purifying and healing, and highly also as bathing in certain holy places of the Ganges and other "Tirthas" was esteemed by the Western Indians at that time, who have become gradually better known; still this deep immersion under the hand of a confessor, with this strict acknowledgment of sins, this vow, and this forgiveness of sins which it was to symbolize, as well as this whole preparation for the Messiah,—this was something which as yet had not been, and the most striking mark of the mighty change of thought, totally new, which was to be brought about in Israel. But in fact, too, the magnificent ideas and images of certain prophetic passages might hover before him, and lead him to the choice of this very symbol of his purpose. And certainly he could choose no simpler and yet more impressive token of his successful effort.

For that John for a time produced a remarkably great effect, and made a most salutary impression on the whole people in all its orders, sects, and aims, appears in all the traces of the history; and we should certainly know it more clearly if we knew more particulars concerning the beginning of his active working. The people streamed to him in continually increasing numbers, most of them from Judea as well as Peræa and the neighbouring provinces, but evidently also from the more distant Galilee: many even from the learned schools of that time did not hold back. The bold speaking and unwonted actions of the man attracted both luxurious and irreclaimable men of the day to follow the new strong attraction of hearts to him, in order, through a lightly spoken confession of sins and the shock of immersion, to receive the promised new life with its attractive fruits: but the severe man demanded more than an outward confession, desired a complete renunciation of all even the most widely spread and cherished errors, and of all even the national perverted pride; and declared to every single order, nay, to every individual man, to whose spirit he approached more closely, what was to be done by him in particular and what left undone. The more sharply he thus dealt, and the more severely he chastised the prejudices and destructive tendencies of the time, the sooner must he have frightened away the proud schoolmen of his time, Pharisees as well as Sadducees, who thought themselves so clever, and driven them most generally from his simple, rough work-place: very few comprehended him and approved of his initiation for long, still less submitted to his call and his baptism. That the Sanhedrim also at Jerusalem did not overlook his undertaking, which was so striking and so successful, and sent to him, as to a distinguished priest's son, priests and Levites, but these selected at the same time from the school of the crafty and learned Pharisees, to try him with captious questions, as the fourth Evangelist briefly tells us, is quite credible. Accordingly they put to him the questions, whether he took himself for Christ or for Elias, or, even more indefinitely, for the prophet promised in the Pentateuch, like unto Moses, (s. 83): but he was able dexterously to evade the questions, as he in fact was undertaking something which had never been even imagined of this kind and manner, and he never thought of being or seeming a prophet of the old sort, not to say a great prophet, no more than he even gave signs after the old sort, did miracles, or wished to do them. He knew that he was simply doing his duty as God required from that time: and that he would thus prepare for the Messiah, *that* he had never denied, for it was the ground and impulse of his whole life, nor even now did he deny it before his spiritual authorities: but the Sanhedrim also could not utterly deny the Messiah, nor have any handle against a simple preacher of repentance who pointed to Him. From this quarter they must likewise give him free play, and, so far as we know, in spite of the Sanhedrim and the doctors, the result of his activity went on ever increasing. The extended field for his labours became soon too large for his own exertions: he already allowed his more intimate followers to baptize. And how deeply he had worked on the spirit, of some in particular, of these his nearer friends and adherents, appeared quite clearly at his death and in the time following, as is further to be enquired into below.

CHAPTER VI.

THE BAPTIST AND JESUS OF NAZARETH.

YET the greatest result of his activity was that result humanly least expected: it actually called forth not without his cooperation the Messiah, but this Messiah was quite different from him whom he had expected, and yet the only proper Messiah. In the following this thread, lies the whole of the further history which has here to be told, as it developes itself from the already explained commencement; quite consistently, yet, humanly speaking, out of the most unexpected and sharpest contrasts. For first it is indubitable that the Baptist, his whole position and mighty effect being really such as above described, could not hesitate on any external ground to accept as the Messiah one who came before him bearing the right tokens. For as surely as he had not expected to see the old Elias, in the vulgar sense, again come forth from his concealment, but, following the divine call to that period, himself did what he recognised as his duty: so must he also conceive as possible a Messiah who should not, in the vulgar sense, descend from heaven in the clouds in a moment;

the one thought in fact leads to the other. Nay, that he the first in this, so far as we can know, could have such clear insight into the heavenly kingdom, *this* was in truth one of the first and richest fruits of his own effort. And if he, according to his whole doctrine as well as his own strict conduct, held fast to this above all, that the overmastering strength of sin alone has to answer for the ruin of the people and the delay of the divine salvation promised to it, he could not be strange to the thought and hope, that One in whom he could find no trace of the power of sin might be He whom the divine purpose had appointed to be the Messiah, and on whom, at the right time, all the divine power might descend for the accomplishment of His infinitely exalted work. What is great and extraordinary in the Baptist is, that he was not only a man for the most difficult enterprise and the hardest labour, as well as of the purest honesty and the boldest speech, but, at the same time, of the most cheerful hope and most intense expectation: and nothing but the greatness and nobleness of these could render endurable to him the burden of his hard labour. No one hitherto had stood like him between two worlds, in action, in views, in hopes, and in faithful waiting, and raised his eye so boldly and so deliberately into the boundless regions of the obscure future: nay, his whole effort, according to his deeper view and its best consequences, was directed to this—the drawing forth from under the repulsion of the old perversity and confusion, the purest and highest possible in Israel, which could only be accomplished through the

Messiah. And can it be conceived that, in this his agonised seeking and most ardent hoping, he should have failed to discern such an one as came to him bearing the tokens of the possible Messiah, and from Him expect the fulfilment of His own difficult work? Assuredly his spirit must cheer him on when it met him. He could, it is true, only think to see the divine marks of the future Messiah, and then meet Him with His elevating, hopeful address, leaving to the future the way in which the Messiah would carry out under God's government the whole work of the Messiah shewn beforehand by Holy Scripture: just as he, on a smaller scale, had had striking experience of in his own case: but to cheerfully recognise these marks, and when they should shew themselves, joyfully to greet them, this was, through his whole calling, held by God before him as his aim, and as the second, the higher and fairer half of his whole work, whenever his prophetic eye met unmistakeably such tokens in any one who came across him, as he learnt to know him more accurately. He could not certainly proceed in his own person to look for and anxiously weary himself to find these marks; but when they unmistakeably came across his spirit, cheerfully hopeful and an experienced enquirer, skilled in men and spirits as he was, *then* not to fail to discern them was his duty, and thereto his innermost spirit impelled him. The vital point, in fine, was that he should not deceive himself when his eye perhaps lighted on one unworthy, not hold back when it lighted on the true Messiah: and, as a good intimation of the correctness of his eye and the honesty of his faithful finding, this is remarkable, that we never find a trace of his having wavered between two or more future Messiahs, and having lightly cast his eye from one to another.

Nay, it is not to be gainsaid (and this is the second preliminary important point) that he, until he had half run through the course of his noble activity, knew nothing of Him in whom he then thought to find the tokens, and was not at all previously acquainted with Him. The older Gospels presuppose this as self-evident; but our present fourth Evangelist, who had an especial reason for telling more exactly and completely, both in this and everything else, all which concerns the relationship between the Baptist and Jesus, expresses this sufficiently plainly by the words in which he makes the Baptist exclaim immediately after the baptism of Jesus: "I knew him not," nor have begun, as one might think, all my labour in Israel because I knew Him before, or in order that He might after my wish come to me; *but* I am a Baptist, and stir up Israel *in order that He*, although unknown to me, through my human activity indeed, but without my aiming at it, and thus through divine arrangement *alone*, should be revealed to Israel as the true future Messiah. And how important this is, and how certainly he had indeed (according to our previous expression) borne in mind the marks of the Messiah, but had not known Jesus up to the moment of His baptism, the Apostle points out again by a new saying of the Baptist, expressing the same, only yet clearer and more definitely. (John i. 32 f.)

We must hence hold fast this circumstance as one of the highest importance for the whole connection of the previous history, and consequently not be led astray by the narrative at the beginning of St. Luke's Gospel, as to a relationship and particular friendship of the two mothers, and the visit of Mary in her pregnancy to Elizabeth. For, however the whole of this account, which is quite peculiar to St. Luke, may have appeared, it must not do away with the great important truth of the history which we see here. The most decisive account of the feelings, the hopes, and the certainties of the Baptist's mind previous to this moment, is that which the fourth Gospel likewise expresses in short and pointed but clear words, wherein it makes the Baptist exclaim, at the beginning of his ministry, "There standeth one among you whom ye know not," the true Messiah, of whom you do not even know the right tokens, much less His real being, so that you may easily quite fail to know Him when He appears; *He* who comes after me," (briefly to describe His real being as I have known it) although He, as already said, is in the midst of you, though He is not indeed visible among you, but will not come till after me, yet assuredly will come, as already in spirit present among you, and is only waiting for the right moment of His visible manifestation; whose shoe latchets, when He appears, I am not worthy to loose— the true Messiah (John i. 26 f.); or, in a yet shorter, more pointed, more mysterious expression, "He that cometh after me has been before me, for He was before me:" with yet, that is, more decided reference to the doctrine of the Logos, according to which the true Messiah was already existing in His heavenly concealment from the beginning of creation; nay, before it—how much more before all then living! With such a view of the Messiah, a view especially of such clearness and certainty, incomprehensible to the world in its heartiness and confidence, the Baptist, in fact, could not but, from the beginning of his work, hope for the speedy coming of the true Messiah, nay, with his eye of faith look on Him as already present; and in the eternal truths which the view of the true Messiah embraces in one in their remotest issues and apparent contradictions, is wrapped the meaning—mysterious to the common mind—of this short, decided, but yet clear expression. Allowing that the Baptist may not perhaps in quite these very words and short pointed sentences have expressed his meaning, there is yet not the least doubt that the same pious hope in its essential and necessary elements filled him from the first, and so determined with the warmest glow as well as bright clearness all his actions, to an extent found in no other single member of his people.

This all being so, it follows that we have a quite unexpected meeting of the two men, and a real prophetic event before us, which is for us now as infinitely great and momentous, and then likewise was as significant for the moment, as the meeting of such spirits in such time and such circumstances must be; and the same results from all the recorded reminiscences, as well the oldest and briefest, as those somewhat later and gradually more definite expressions.

Every divine truth and power, which appearing in the history of mankind becomes an eternal possession and an inextinguishable spark to kindle humanity, can only, through the deeper emotion of a moment and a shock of the soul at the right time, spring forth from the world's mysterious bosom, and go forth into the world a sturdy form from its birth. For if every deeper truth of mere science can only by an emotion of the spirit, seizing in their deepest meaning and conglomerating the several materials and threads which make it up, or, so to speak, by violent rubbing and kindling strike a spark; much more *such* a truth which is for man no truth at all, unless it be at the same time a corresponding power which strengthens and drives him to action, and such is a truth of religion: so that in short it is really rather a power than merely a truth to be grasped by the intellect. The several components and primary materials of such a truth may long be present, nay, for many centuries be stirring themselves on their proper ground, and, ever more living and energetic, strive more and more to meet each other: but only the most violent emotion and shock of a moment so drives them to and into each other, that the whole new truth and power, which will form itself out of them, shoots forth in effect like sudden fire, and quite fills and glows through that spirit or those spirits which are meet for it. And if this happens generally, most of all here at this moment, which will be the true beginning of the highest perfection of all this long history. Hence, this is precisely also the true prophetic or the creative in religion, which now in this history, after so long subsidence, again appears mighty, as though it would at one blow and at one mighty advance seize on all the ultimate results which in the whole course of this great history are yet possible to it, and all that is past as well. In the Baptist we have the climax of the previous prophetic spirit, rising at once to the highest prophecy which, after that of the old prophets, was yet possible through the collision of the most real searchings for and evocations of the Messiah. But as what is in itself prophetic-creative seeks also always for its corresponding expression and finds it, even so does this shew itself here in a new most important case, as well as in all similar cases, in the history which is now quickly rising to its zenith. We saw above the several efforts now at work. We saw, too, the mighty beginning and the life and doings of the Baptist, calling forth all that survived in Israel most deep and mysterious, nay, as with irresistible supremacy driving it forth.

CHAPTER VII.

THE HISTORY OF JESUS BEFORE HIS BAPTISM.

JESUS of Nazareth now first came into this sphere; and not only the older Gospels, the form of which is still preserved to us in the Gospel of St. Mark, but also the Apostle John himself, in much later time, does not deem it worth while to tell anything of his earthly being and life before this moment; because all the historical importance of it, singularly high as it stands, not only begins with this moment, but at this moment becomes at once so clear and radiant, that all that goes further back vanishes, as it were, before this brilliant appearance, and in fact is hardly worth mentioning, so soon as one is bent only on firmly grasping the simple principal fact on which all at last depends. Yet can it not be forbidden to glance back over these limits into the earliest life and being of the Christ of history: curiosity is here excited from the most varied impulses: and as many Gospels so early met this craving, we have now—in order that we may rightly understand the infinitely important moment before us—the great crisis in the history of the coming completion; we have yet stronger motives to look back so far as we may into this previous history, unrivalled as it is in its kind. Jesus the Son of Joseph was of Nazareth in Galilee, where His father's house had plainly been long settled and seemed naturalized. Joseph was a master workman, and Jesus was supposed to have intended following His father in this employment; His mother Mary had besides Him four younger sons and several younger daughters; among his brethren, James, Jose (as was now very often said for Joseph), Judah, and Simon, were later, particularly the eldest and next to him the third, to become more celebrated. The father of the house died some years before Jesus came to the Baptist; and the mother was now generally looked on as the head of the house, so that Jesus was distinguished among the people from others of the name shortly as her son: for the name Jesus was not uncommon, and Joseph was quite one of the commonest names of that time. Although the family were now looked on as naturalized in the little town of Nazareth, which is not once mentioned in the Old Testament, and here lived the sisters of Jesus, doubtless married, they appear however, from reasons of which we have now no more particular knowledge (probably because after the father's death they found here no further livelihood), to have changed their abode, a short time before Jesus' baptism, to the somewhat more northernly Kana, and not long after that to have moved to the greater commercial city of Kafar-nahúm on the western shore of the lake of Galilee, and here remained living during the largest period of the public ministry of Jesus.

They moved to Kafar-nahúm, from all appearances, because they found here the best friends and relations: a like motive probably prevailed for their migration to Kana.

If we enquire more particularly into the kindred of the family, something at least more precise can be discovered about it. On one hand, the mother of the two sons of Zebedee, James and John, named Salome, was, according to all the evidences we can discover, a sister of the mother of Jesus: the early acquaintance of these two (later so famous) Apostles with Jesus, and the special advantages in the kingdom which their mother seems to have thought she might ask and expect for her two sons from Christ, are thus most simply explained. This relationship might be looked on as probable from the earlier Gospels: but if they rather presuppose as known the relationship between the two sisters, St. John remarks it more distinctly, though, quite in keeping with his well-known delicate feeling on such matters, rather with brief allusion than with any boast of such relationship. The father Zebedee was a well-to-do fisherman (Mark i. 20) living in Bethsaida on the lake of Galilee, but appears to have died during Christ's public ministry, so that in later time it would be more natural for the mother to accompany her sons. On the other hand, the mother of Jesus was, according to undoubted recollections, related to the Baptist's mother, (for further remarks on which see below). The father Joseph had, on the contrary, so far as we can see, no relations in Galilee as the mother had; so that it is the more easily explained how his family, as above remarked, had no fixed abode in Galilee. As the family then, though it may have resided in Nazareth about thirty years, was at any rate not so rooted here through old inherited landed property, but that it could easily move elsewhere, it is in itself not improbable that in earlier times it probably lived in other places outside of Galilee. The Apostle John indeed, who does not elsewhere in his Gospel shew himself very well informed and communicative on such information about home and family matters, mentions nothing of another birthplace of Jesus. With him Jesus is simply a Nazarene and a Galilæan, and so He was everywhere generally regarded. Yet no importance must be attached to this, as this Evangelist in general, as above remarked, passes over as unessential all which concerns the birth and childhood of Jesus, and begins the earthly history of Jesus with His baptism. But the two Evangelists who embrace in their view the previous history of Jesus, in spite of the great divergencies in other respects in their independent narrative agree in this, that the parents about the time of His birth were on a journey: according to both He was born in Bethlehem of Judæa while Herod the Great was still reigning: according to St. Matthew, this was followed by a journey to Egypt, and the parents did not till after Herod's death, from fear of the cruelty of his successor in Judæa, Archelaus, settle designedly far from Judæa, in Nazareth: according to St. Luke they resided here before, and went merely to Bethlehem on a visit on an external ground; and when they were here Jesus was born. And in truth these recollections cannot be quite without grounds. For, allowing that all accounts about the early history, as they are given us in these two Gospels, were certainly composed comparatively late, when Mary, and most of the others who had more exact knowledge of these distant events, were already dead, and only scattered reminiscences could be collected about them; allowing also that it is actually the higher Christian view which does not collect these records in their dispersion with mere curiosity, but fills them with its spiritual knowledge, and through a creative power puts new life into them, and this again very differently in St. Matthew and St. Luke, so that we can see very plainly from St. Luke, as compared with St. Matthew, the nature of the progress of the whole of this more definite formation of the narratives of the early history; also that the accounts found in St. Luke must have arisen quite irrespective of those in St. Matthew, and hence cannot be objectively harmonized with them; yet on this very account whatever is common to them must all the more be reckoned as their proper earlier foundations. But to this category belong especially these recollections of the birth of Jesus in Bethlehem, as they appear in the existing St. Matthew's Gospel, shorter indeed and more abrupt, but evidently much simpler, more original, and in their actual matter more complete than in St. Luke. Very intimately dependent on this recollection of the birth of Jesus in Bethlehem, David's city, is that of his descent from David; and we must assuredly pronounce a like verdict on this. For though one might readily suppose that the idea of deducing Christ's lineage from David—and hence, too, the idea of his birth in Bethlehem sprang originally from the wish to see in this too the fulfilment of the prophecies of Isaiah and Micah in his person; yet this supposition is in itself a quite arbitrary, nay, quite groundless one, because the Christian spirit in the Apostolic age, supposing it were known that Jesus was not descended from David, would very readily have thought of another mode of reconciling with each other the known history and the Old Testament prophecies. But now we find in the actual narrative, that Jesus, after He was well known and recognised, was greeted, by those who perhaps wished to flatter Him, as David's Son: that He, while not entirely rejecting this title, lays no weight at all on such a name and reputation, would rather discern something else and infinitely higher recognised in the Messiah, before which all such human descent and human glory vanishes utterly. From these considerations, then, we have all the less reason (even had not the recollection of his descent from David in very manifold ways been interwoven in the narrative of the early history) for looking on it as simply unhistorical. Rather, here too the very variety of the structure of these recollections, as we now find them in the two mentioned Gospels, refers us to a true ancient historical basis. Then too it admits of no doubt, that even in this late century many of the race of David, in spite of having lost all outward respect, and in fact also having now become defenceless and unsettled, might very well be known and pointed out. We know how much importance was laid, and necessarily laid, on exact genealogies: but, least of all could the descendants of David's house be readily forgotten: and how little they were forgotten in these centuries, and how a residue of faint hope ever clung to them in the minds of many, we know also well enough. It may however be readily imagined, that it was often difficult, without long investigation, to trace out the descent in the case of any one who lived 600 years after Zerubbabel: and thus in St. Luke a quite different stem-tree has been preserved from that in St. Matthew; for that given by the latter appears more like a mere first attempt, that adopted by St. Luke, on the other hand, as the result of more exact investigation. Besides, the descent from David (putting aside these Gospels) appears early enough, not only in the Apocalyptic John, but also in St. Paul. But in truth the Apostle John, in direct contrast to the Apocalyptic John, expressly mentions that Jesus' assumed mere Galilæan descent, excluding his descent in Bethlehem from David, was to many a stumbling-block. And at least on his mother's side, He seems to have been of not quite unmixed descent from David, as (for example) the high priest who could take a wife only out of the tribe of Levi. That Mary was of the race of David, the accounts in St. Luke do not tell us: according to those in St. Luke she was, as related to the priestly house of the Baptist, rather of the tribe of Levi; and although this relationship itself, as before shewn, can have little historical meaning, its mention in St. Luke shews that he had no fear of putting her down as of the tribe of Levi. In many Apocryphal Gospels yet in existence she appears indeed of the race of David, but in other older ones her descent was either left undetermined, or traced back to Levi: and how widely spread this view was at the beginning of the second century after Christ, is seen from another book written at that time.

But we can pursue all this much more definitely in detail. When St. John mentions that Jesus' coat was, as at the crucifixion may generally have been seen, a seamless coat, and so woven all in one piece, he can only have brought forward this as important, in order to shew his descent from a mother of the priestly tribe; as their sons appear to have had the privilege of wearing such a coat. And St. John, being (see above) the son of the sister of our Lord's mother, we find also in his case tokens of a relationship with the priestly race. Had, then, in the earliest Christian period, any one wished rightly to exalt Christ in human fashion, he might have been able to allege how in Him the best blood of ancient Israel, that of David and that of Levi, flowed together, as it were to form a higher whole. But the New Testament nowhere lays weight on such matters, as Christ's own dignity far outshines all such outward advantages.

That Jesus was born in the lifetime of Herod the Great, on this, too, the narratives from the two sources agree in a remarkable manner, as has already been more particularly investigated (Chap. II.): thus this, too, belongs to the basis of older reminiscence and tradition.

But in respect of the early fate of the child born in Bethlehem, the two traditions diverge so widely from each other, that it would be vain to try to unite them by violence. To bring forward here only one principal aspect of these divergencies, the pictures in St. Luke, generally esteemed as of more depth and brilliance, point to a circle of a so thoroughly peaceful, heaven-blessed life of the families of Jesus and of the Baptist and their neighbourhood, that we should not in the least dream of severe persecutions and misfortunes with which they were visited. But it is quite otherwise in St. Matthew: the narrative brings us into the storm-troubled beginning of this life, beside which the penetrating sunshine of delivering grace, together with the backward glance on the already risen star out of Judah, promises a so much brighter day; and, plainly, much more of original tradition has been preserved in these shorter but many-sided reminiscences in St. Matthew.

Certain however as it is that these narratives, not formed till the second half of the Apostolic time, express only weak and very scattered reminiscences, we may not, in an historical point of view, overvalue them, nor deduce from them anything not otherwise supported. Much less close is the view into the misty period in the background which the story in St. Luke, of Jesus when twelve years old, offers to us.

The 12th year of the boy was the time at which, according to old custom in Israel, he ceased to be looked on as a child, and for the first time could share in the higher religious ceremonies of the people. We must then imagine to ourselves, that Jesus also then, for the first time, was taken by his parents up with them on their yearly journey from Galilee to Jerusalem for the passover, and for the first time was taken into the temple and into the halls built around for renowned teachers of the law. How He now here for the first occasion, and to Him the most memorable, forgot his parents and everything human, discussed with the wisest doctors as one who was a match for them, nay, to the supreme astonishment of all present, all day long, and replied to the parents seeking Him sorrowing, and at length finding Him, " Wist they not that He must be about his Father's business," and yet immediately, with childlike obedience, again submitted to the parental will; this gives us a distant view indeed, but yet a very clear one, into a boundless and sublime fulness of expectation, quite in harmony with that which we afterwards see realized in his great public history. But it is only a single glance which we can cast from this into the threshold of the history, for on the whole of this life, before the baptism in the Jordan, the New Testament has nothing further to tell us. What the after-shoots of the Gospel literature, which we now name Apocryphal Gospels, tell us about the parents of Jesus and Mary, as well as about the history of his birth, childhood, and youth, is too unhistorical for us to pause at. We cannot, to sum up, say anything more definite than that the New Testament narratives allow us to cast a glance on the two stages in life before the riper manhood of Jesus and his baptism, synchronous with this—into the time of childhood and that of youth at the very beginning of each; a glance just sufficient to stir our curiosity to know more closely the great public history which follows, as the unfolding of those first mysterious tender germs; and enough to enable us to know this much at least for certain, that He, before the outwardly great and decisive moment now to follow, was in spirit always the same; nay, that He, from the first conceivable beginning, was by the Divine will already destined for that, which now in Him is visibly to shew itself to the whole world. And in the attempt, which some of these narratives adventure on, to open an expectant glance on all the infinite loftiness and uniqueness of the life to follow, if the human side of the history draws back somewhat to make way for the purely Divine, the story is yet, because, breathed on closely enough and quickened by the first Christian spirit, too healthy to be able to quite overlook the human side and leave it unmentioned. We see this particularly in the natural, briefly-told, events where such narratives betray an inner impulse to drop again from their height to the more earthly and human. We only know one thing more of those early times, and this is in many respects important. In Jerusalem there still existed (vgl. oben) a high School for the Doctors of the Law, which was much looked up to, and education at which was esteemed as a particular distinction. Now we know by a definite testimony that Jesus never visited it, and received there no sort of foundation for his education. Not till we know this does the story of the boy Jesus, when twelve years old, become quite plain, when He, who later also never needed instruction in this high School, could maintain so young with its masters the most learned disputes. But, in truth, all education of old turned almost exclusively on the true religion, and the high School had little power of restricting this privilege, open to the least member of the community, of enquiry and instruction. So well had a happy freedom in this respect been maintained as well for scholars as teachers. But that Jesus had no inward need of the high School of that time, only shews us all the plainer what spirit from the beginning had dwelt in Him. In fact, Jesus would not have become what, as seen in the light of his great public history, He subsequently became, had not his spirit from his earthly beginning received the Divine appointment and full powers for it. All that is purely spiritual is above history, being itself the first spring and life of all history; and in contemplating it, we are led to a mysterious height which we can but acknowledge for what it is, and bow before it: we have here the most remarkable example and proof of this. When the spiritual, nay the very highest spiritual substance, or from its origin and source the Divine substance itself, entered the human body, it became indeed subjected to all the necessary limitations and weaknesses of this; and the knowledge of the individual, that is of the mundane, is for the individual spirit just as much subject to the limitations of space and time as action is, so far as it has reference to and acts on the individual: but amid these limitations and these weaknesses, the individual spirit can in knowledge and action not only completely recover the purely Divine, but even completely hold it fast and give itself up wholly to its working; so that its knowledge and its actions, though more or less limited by time and space, yet in its clear subject-matter, as well as in its goodness and happiness, becomes the Divine itself; and the weak, the mortal, and the changeable is transfigured to the mightiest, immortal, and eternal, where the world sees these glorified in human body. And either this higher ideal is never realized in the world's history, or it is first realized in one made wholly fit for it: but where it has actually been wholly realized in one, then the perfect true religion has come forth into history as a pattern shining bright and conspicuous, never to be lost out of it, because its appearance and rule is the goal of all human history. The perfect true religion, or the Fulfilment, was at that time most markedly in Israel, as in the ground alone prepared for it, sought for above everything, and, as become the most indispensable, summoned forth from this country with the mightiest spiritual struggles. If, then, on this proper ground the spirit made capable for it were actually there, then must his bearing in face of the task before Him, his approach to it and entering on it, all his doing, striving, and suffering for it, themselves be the evolution of this completion, and the highest life-work could here be accomplished which had ever been appointed to any single spirit in the frail human body.

There is a wonderful charm in the nature of a task which germinates by Divine appointment and necessity, and places itself face to face with the spirit: when the right man comes face to face with it, it shews him all its real difficulty, but also the majesty of its recompense which beckons him on, and leaves him no rest till the task is done; and the more gigantic the task, the greater struggle does it impose on him, but adds therewith all the higher eternal recompense. Here was the highest task set which could be set to any, even the ablest spirit. It had long been imagined, and was waiting for him who should satisfy it; it floated however singularly near since the Baptist had brought it forth from the mists of the time and placed it radiant in heavenly splendour. Who as the true Messiah is to bring the completion, as the old Prophets in prescient glance had beheld it, as all the pious faithful of centuries had waited for it, as now the Baptist with most living energy was longing for and hastening it? Who, after that the first condition of the three above-mentioned had been accomplished by the Baptist himself, is sufficient for the two other far harder ones, which, even though they did not float before the Baptist's eye so clearly as they have been above deduced, yet lay in the task itself? Who first has even the courage to enter with thought and action into the meaning and the requirements of this task? Him indeed who had the human courage and the divine capacity to enter thoroughly into them; on him must they themselves react with their giant power in wonderfully exalting and bearing him on. But who could rightly think to see and keep before him the never-sought, the immeasurable, which its accomplishment requires, or from whom could one in faith hope for this?

CHAPTER VIII.

Jesus' Baptism.

One thing however could the Baptist, from his nature as above described, know; and that he knew this one thing rightly and in faith held it fast, nay, allowed himself to be guided aright in divine faith by what he knew aright, this forms the keystone to the whole of the further development. He knew for certain, as has already been said, that he only who is quite free from the power of sin can be the true Messiah: and if this divine token should come across him on any one coming to baptism, he was resolved for certain to announce to him this divine destination, and wait for the further consequences from it. Nay, this consideration and this resolution must spring from him quite spontaneously out of his calling as confessor and forgiver of sins. For no one had learnt to know the infinite consequences and fearfulness of sin as it then so visibly and unveiled appeared in Israel, as he had; he who before all others had indisputably struggled much with its power in himself, and only by putting on himself the severest discipline could become such a preacher of repentance: but he had certainly found no one yet, in whom he had not discerned the power of sin, and whom he could not consequently have forgiven his sins. But now, how if at last he found such an one? Should he treat him too, from first to last, just like the others? or must not his heart, if he were really a pious and faithful man in Israel, exult in having at length found the desired One, and in faith submit himself to him, in place of merely forgiving him his sins as his spiritual lord? That he should not deceive himself in doing this was ensured by the probable circumstantiality which the conversation and address before and after baptism allowed; for, as above observed, we have every reason to think that he was very particular, and was in no hurry with any one who desired baptism from him. When Jesus came for baptism, He was following the better feature of that time as described above; nor was He the first Galilæan who came for baptism and tarried some time with him: and certainly the Baptist had at that time long been known, for the Galilæans, after an express historical reminiscence (Mark i. 5, Matt. iii 5), were the last who visited him in great crowds. The Baptist, of course, first conversed at some length with Him on his desiring baptism from him; then must he soon discern that he conversed with one like none other who had come before him, and his heart must tell him with joy, that here at length appears *He* whom he had been continually seeking; and according to the fourth Evangelist he said, with an Old Testament expression (Isa. liii. 7, quoted freely), "Behold the Lamb of God who takes on Himself the sins of the world!" He said in this only what he, practically at least, must have actually experienced and known as true; for He who, free Himself from the power of sin, comes into the world for man's redemption from it (as the Baptist, engaged as he was with sin and its burden, expected from the Messiah), *He* must now take the burden of them on Himself, as in a less degree every one who will keep himself freer from sin, and yet will help the world, must first resolve to suffer *with them* from their sins. Supposing at least, among the other Messianic characteristics which the Baptist directly thought to see in Him, were marked mildness and gentleness in no small degree, he might naturally be led to this expression, as he could not at least at first expect in Him only the severe judge: whether indeed he expressed his first feelings exactly in these words or in others, is for the history itself of less importance. According to the present St. Matthew's Gospel the Baptist speaks more simply, merely objecting to Him, "I must be baptized of Thee, and Thou comest to me?" Yet Jesus persisted in his request to be baptized, expressly assuring us, according to St. Matthew, "thus it becometh us to fulfil all righteousness," to shrink from nothing which God demands from Israel as His duty, on the same principle which later also ever guides Him, as will appear below. This whole divine commencement of the Baptist was the necessary portal for the coming of the Messiah Himself: no living member of the community might keep from Him, at least according to the higher obligation, not even he who might become the Messiah, but was not yet. So He came and was baptized: and as this shock of baptism, following deep self-searching, was adapted to work strongly on every catechumen, so that his countenance, as it came forth from under the Baptist's hand, furnished to his sharp practised glance various tokens as to the effect of the whole on him and the true condition of his inward purification and renewal; so must He, whose characteristics the Baptist had discerned beforehand, have come forth, another indeed than he had been, but in his own purity and majesty only more markedly resplendent. The Baptist must at this moment have clearly discerned in Him that heavenly token which he was ever expecting; and not less must the moment for the Saviour Himself, if the baptism were to be not without effect and result for Him, and not rather most strongly seize on Him just as on others under the Baptist's hand, thrill through and cleanse, it must become likewise to him a complete purification and regeneration; but the cleansing was for Him only that He, at the Baptist's call and consecration, suddenly, as Messiah felt himself become another man, free from the duties of the past life now seeming to him as quite cut off, became simply conscious to himself of the highest divine appointment as the new obligation and duty of his life, and in all sincerity consecrated himself to it alone. This glorious moment thus became the true birth-hour of Christianity: the highest in all previous antiquity was compressed in Him to form a New which must be the very perfect, and this New developes itself from this moment, unchangeable and irresistible, according to its proper spirit, so that all futurity rests in him. And in face of this great fact, it is indeed of slight importance in what outward signs the eternal truth, greatness, and exaltation of the moment may have immediately expressed themselves. Yet, as the most spiritual and highest ever seeks, and finds also, its fitting tokens and most striking expressions; so, very early the infinite and purely divine facts which are here before us were compressed into two most lively pictures and striking words, and a whole short Gospel narrative has formed itself which is quite sufficient to let shine through it clearly and strikingly what was here actually disclosed. The Holy Ghost in His whole fulness and power descended on Him as He emerged from the water; and descended not merely fluttering and hovering doubtfully, but abode on Him, and was seen as certainly as a dove descending from heaven can be seen: this is, in the most touching picture, the truest conception of this moment, since the eye too would see the Divine where it reveals itself, and can see it in innocence: the Holy Ghost in all His living fulness must rest on the Messiah, if He is what the Messiah must be; this was indeed the Old Testament thought (Isa. xi. 2, xlii. 1, and other places). But if the Old Testament in its early times could conceive the descent of God Himself upon the portentous Cherub, it is something quite new that the Holy Ghost also is looked on as so coming down, yet, as beseems his delicate tender nature, only as a small white dove; and thus was given the first speaking picture in which Christianity with creative power revealed a bright picture of one of the most forcible ideas of its peculiar truth. And at the same time (as the plain word may still less be wanting) a heavenly voice proclaims Him aloud the Messiah, again in Old Testament words (Ps. ii. 7, Isa. xlii. 1), and thus *He* was here divinely appointed, whose coming had been long expected, and for whom such Old Testament words had long waited their fulfilment. What is there in all this which was not ratified by the event, and is thus only expressing itself in the shorter and most striking manner? Further, nothing can be by this intended, which according to the purport of the narrative could not have been literally seen and heard by every one—for it is a matter of course that this as well as every other baptism was quite public; and at least the two principal actors in it must, according to the purport of the narrative, have at the same time experienced all this. It is true that the oldest and simplest narrative, as it has essentially survived in all the first Gospels, confines the seeing and hearing to the Saviour, but plainly only on account of the shortness and artlessness of the story. If the fourth Evangelist, on the contrary, lays particular stress on the Baptist so seeing and hearing and maintaining aloud that he had both seen and heard, he is in this only in so far completing what, strictly speaking, was a matter of course: for to him, who is here ever the principal actor, the prophetic man, in the simplest sense the heaven opened to let him see and hear from out of it what no one else saw and heard; just as, according to the Old Testament, heaven can open to every true prophet, and to him immediately.

This is all which we now know for certain of the meeting of Jesus with the Baptist. It might probably be supposed that the mere particular day and moment of the Saviour's baptism was of little importance, and that it is the present narratives in the New Testament which first thus condensed all that was most important into this one moment: for that Jesus would not have become Christ without the powerful impulse which the Baptist gave to the whole period, and without the meeting with the Baptist, this is certain. We may conclude with truth out of the fourth Gospel, that Jesus' meeting with him lasted several days. Of a stay however of any length with him, as a scholar with his teacher, no trace is anywhere visible: and as baptism in these first times in general had something extremely violent and overmastering in it, the power of the moment could at most quickly call to light all which already lay concealed deeper in the spirit. The Baptist's lightning struck nowhere on such a subject as it did on Jesus. And thus we have no ground for imagining differently to ourselves the essential truth in those narratives.

CHAPTER IX.

The Baptist's End.

Once, eleven centuries ago, when the first human kingdom was established in Israel, a rightful longing for it had long prevailed; and when at that time, in Samuel, the true prophet came to stablish it rightly, a prophetic glance had also quickly decided on the right man for it: so piercing like a lightning flash is the prophetic eye, and with such necessity is that, which had long in the secret sway and commotion of all virtuous energies been prepared, at length decided by a single piercing glance and the higher emotion of *one* divine moment. At that time also the tokens of divine salvation shone round him who had thus been chosen, and all the future tokens of high success before the first steps of him who thus became king, ushered him in. Then also through the new kingdom the true theocracy purposed to receive new youth and strength. All this is now repeated after long waiting and yet deeper longing. Here at length stands forth a recognised great Prophet, and there comes a King summoned by him as it were from far, and then in the happy moment acknowledged and consecrated as

King, who, like the former, has first to collect his followers and found his kingdom. But this King, emerging from the water of the Jordan, holy of old, was to found quite a different kingdom with quite different means from what Samuel had once expected from Saul and afterwards from David: this, too, the Baptist knew, only he could not know and recognise it so particularly as *He* who then himself took it in hand. And just because the kingdom of perfection, if it were the true, must become, and soon did become, actually a quite different one from what the most penetrating prophetic glance had been able to foresee and the warmest desire to wish for; accordingly the ways, and hence also the views and hopes, of the two heroes of the Regeneration must again diverge ever more widely. It was not that the men wished to separate, still less become hostile; but the very change of position and effort which each, and the Saviour especially, must now follow, led them, the longer they went on, the further from each other, as is to be shewn below. As the perfect religion could never have come into being without all the foundations of the true religion as laid in the Old Testament, still less could the religion of Christ without that of the Baptist. The whole deeply earnest, inflexible tendency of the grand ancient truth towards the Perfect, with that strict requirement of most sincere repentance and complete renewal and purification of life which belongs to the essence of the Baptist's religion, nay, is its very purest and original essence, passed over from him into Christianity, and for ever forms its deepest foundation and most necessary condition. In fact, Christianity in youth lives and moves in the thoughts, efforts, words, and ideas of the Baptist's religion; and rises from this basis gradually, ever loftier, more independent and imperative: even the great instrument and token of this mighty purification and regeneration, Baptism, has passed from it to Christianity, and although gradually changing its form, yet points plainly enough to its origin in time, as well as to its indispensable eternal antitype. We can certainly not rate the Baptist and his work too highly; and yet Christianity, summoned forth by him as it were by force (so far as this lies in man), such as it actually formed and perpetuated itself, is something quite different and higher.

He laboured and lived after that moment above described, which we may well name the highest moment of his life, long enough to rejoice in the first progress of Christianity called forth by him, and himself advance it; but long enough also to go astray, on its further development (see below). But his days were numbered: the rulers feared his word and his work, for he was much respected by the people; and though the Sanhedrim could find nothing against him, soon enough another yet more powerful imagined he had all sorts of danger to fear from him for himself.

He did not stay at any fixed place on the Jordan, but on both banks of the river, as he thought best to advance his mission; mostly indeed on the southern Jordan, but also further north. He could not allow his energy to be limited by the provinces of the various rulers of the time; and he could not be anxiously careful to spare with the severe word of his mouth these rulers themselves, when it seemed necessary. So he had—(either on this or the other side Jordan in Peræa, which had been put into the hands of the Tetrarch Herod Antipas), we know not on what occasion, but certainly in no unjust censure—spoken out about the immoral, sinful second marriage of this Tetrarch; and such free speech had come to the ears of this prince. This led him to take prisoner the strict preacher of repentance, who was so gladly listened to by the people, and thus might easily become dangerous: this probably happened once, when he was without suspicion following his mission somewhere beyond Jordan: yet fearful in every quarter as this prince was, he could not have him executed, spite of the repeated urgent prayers of his wife, who rightly felt herself the most injured; but put him instead in the fort Macharus as prisoner, visited him indeed here also, wondered at the force of his address, and often became serious when he heard him. This state of things must have lasted some time, as will further appear below: his disciples were meanwhile allowed freely to converse with him. But at length Herodias drew from the prince the order for his execution, through (as St. Mark tells us) a surprise of the prince. Among the people, many found in the unfortunate war of the Tetrarch soon following, a divine punishment for this murder of so righteous a man: while his disciples not only continued his labours even after his death, but buried with all honour his body dishonoured by the execution.

CHAPTER X.

SECOND ADVANCE OF CHRISTIANITY.

JESUS AS CHRIST.

HIS ACTIONS PREVIOUS TO THE BAPTIST'S ARREST; THE MESSIANIC BEGINNINGS.

ON this earlier period of the public activity of Christ, the earliest sources are almost entirely silent: in such remote background did it lie for the general remembrance, and so certainly did this activity become, after the Baptist's removal from the scene of this great drama, far greater and more public. We must hence acknowledge all the more thankfully, in every respect, that St. John in his particular Gospel has made it one of his aims to complete this very deficiency: a considerable portion of his Gospel is given up merely to this; and although the Gospel as usual holds it superfluous to indicate this its view of filling up the deficiency by any express statement, it is yet from the work itself unmistakeable. There are given the words and doings of Christ till He returned the second time out of Jerusalem and Judæa to Galilee, each time distinguishing his first entrance into it by one of his most memorable miracles: and though he found the first time very little belief in Galilee, his country in the more restricted sense, (according to the well-known experience of the little honour of a prophet in his own country), he found the second time, on returning out of Jerusalem and Judæa, immediately on his entrance into Galilee, all the more general recognition and willing belief, for that he had in Jerusalem done much in public. This is the simple summary into which the Apostle groups the reminiscences of that earliest period. And soon after it the Baptist must also have been taken prisoner, as this Gospel does not indeed particularly inform us, but intelligibly enough intimates.

But also these accounts, from their contents, undesignedly shew themselves true reminiscences of the real first times of commencement. Every one who knows them more intimately and comprehends them with more lively interest, readily feels how surely the Saviour, when He began to work and be recognised as Christ, must come forward in public much in the way which is here described: it seems as if the Apostle had with all the more affectionate care recalled to recollection this very portion neglected by the earlier narrators. In truth there lies, on this account, a peculiar charm in these narratives: we are sensible here of, as it were, the fresh delicate scent of the early manhood of the future Christ, and see Him rising before our own eyes to his full greatness and power. If the highest manifestation historically possible, even at the time when its flower is pushing forth with all its power, only shoots forth when stirred by the world itself, with a so to speak cool fanning; we see clearly in this history the way the world itself animates the future Christ; first in true presentiment and speech, as well as in mighty works, to shew Himself *Him* whom He must become. But hardly has He so done, not forcing himself forward, nor drawing back from proper calls upon Him, and already discovers his royal power in full activity when this power in return forces Him, unasked even by the world, to shew Himself, as well in working as in teaching, the true Lord and King in his own province: and He is recognised even by dwellers at a distance, if at first only by individuals, yet by people of the most various kind; till He at last gives free play to the power of His Spirit's ever more mighty working. We have here the course of the inner development of the spiritual powers once set in motion in the mutual contact of spirits: and this progress is so direct from its first timid beginning, that nothing can be conceived more direct and more majestic as well as more simple in its advance. The duration of this beginning time cannot be defined quite accurately; it probably was not more than a year. A tradition tells us the Saviour's active working began in spring; but this is connected with the erroneous view (Chap. II.) that his whole ministry only lasted one year.

CHAPTER XI.

The first Stirrings of the Messianic Power in Knowledge and Speech.

True power never thrusts itself forward uncalled for, at least in the commencement and before it has quite learned to know itself: it is rather timid and reserved, free from all presumption, and, as it were, mistrusting itself, till it unexpectedly is led from without by an irresistibly favourable call for working. And this in every kind of working, and first in the mere knowing presentiment and speaking. For assuredly the power of the true Christ must express itself in the glance which penetrates into man's deepest soul, and most truly knows his thoughts as well as in the quickly striking appropriate saying, or indeed in this first of all.

An occasion was found soon enough after the baptism of the Saviour. He staid for some time in the Baptist's neighbourhood; and when the Baptist used to see Him appear even at a distance walking about, the sight constantly called forth in him the very feeling already described, and he broke forth constantly in the same words of higher wonder and expectation. Now once, when he was thus speaking of Him as He went by, while two of his disciples who were just out of Galilee stood round, they, all the more that they were Galilæans, conceived a strong desire to go up to the Man thus pointed out: they went after Him; but when He in a friendly way turned to them asking what they wished; somewhat put out at the first moment, they had no reply but that they wished to know where the teacher (Rabbi) had his dwelling. With the simple reply "Come and you shall see it" he invited them to follow Him to it: they followed Him thither were at once taken by His discourse, His doctrine, and His whole nature; and without noticing how the time passed, spent the night with Him, although it was forenoon when they met with Him. Nay, they were at once within these hours so entirely convinced that He was Messiah, that one of them even the next morning would not again leave Him; while the other, named Andrew, went to look for his brother Simon, communicated to him his new-found joy in having found the Messiah, and at once brought him likewise to Jesus. Jesus had hardly cast on him a more serious look, when He discerned in him the unwonted blunt firmness, tenacious power of soul, and quiet decision, which remained with him through life even to the death, and the future King and Lord had found in him His most rock-like servant and confessor; the man who, even under the most violent change of inward revolution in his own spirit, and the most violent storms of the world rising ever higher, never again became in heart untrue to Him. It is not surprising that the

Saviour immediately named him a rock, and that since then this name, gladly repeated by him, and by others not less gladly used, became his surname Kêfa, which, afterwards rendered also into Greek Peter, almost threw into the shade his original name, and became one of the highest names of honour in the new community. Where an entirely new spiritual tendency, or rather a new community, will form itself, there also arise naturally new names, accidental as at first the origin of any particular one may be: we see this recurring here, but in the most eminent example. Who one of the two who first sought for Jesus was, the Apostle John does not inform us, but certainly only from the same modesty and loveable reserve which leads this tenderly-fashioned spirit throughout his Gospel to at most gently intimate his singular personal relation to Him, never to boast of and speak loud of it. Doubtless it was he himself, who first with Andrew sought out Jesus from the Baptist and his school, but directly on his first meeting with Him was so taken captive by His royal spirit, that he was happier with no one than with Him, in sweet fancy, as it were, forgot himself when close to Him, and never again went from his side for long. In what advances from this first moment his faith grew, and his love to the Saviour passed into that nameless charm which raised it above all mere belief, and thus made him through a long life even to his late death most specially the Lord's disciple,—this we are not further told by him: but we cannot take it amiss that he allows to be clearly conspicuous in his own history that first moment in which he who wrote and lived also latest; before all others, came into Christ's presence the first time. Not until quite the close of this highest earthly history does he suffer some like traits to appear: the event can but most strongly carry on and confirm in the highest degree the connection which so charms at its first commencement.

In the other older historical sources, John and James, (the latter, because always put first, certainly the older), belonging to a well-to-do family (as we can conclude from the tokens of it, Mark i. 20), with the other two brothers, Simon and Andrew, are constantly spoken of as the earliest disciples of Christ. We see how firmly this fundamental element of all recollections of the earlier times was rooted. But if in their common narrative Peter with his brother is always named first, this is to be explained by his higher dignity, just as simply as the reason why John, in his particular narrative, neither here nor elsewhere speaks of James; for his sensitiveness and the reserve of his language doubtless extended thus far. These four firstlings of grace had this too in common, that they were alike descended from two families of fishermen comfortably off on the lake of Galilee, nay, were strictly from the same town of Bethsaida, (John i. 44, xii. 21). But if in the earlier narrative the call of this double pair of brothers is transferred in the Gospels to Galilee by the lake of Genesareth, this is quite consistent with the whole tenor of this earlier narrative, according to which the public working of Jesus falls in that somewhat later period. And, in fact, the more constant living together of these four first Apostles and Christ cannot have resulted at once; we shall see later the time and the causes of its commencement. When He took later these four into his closest confidence to live constantly and inseparably with Him, and marked them out thereby before all others who had hitherto been somewhat more closely bound to Him, then may He also, in natural allusion to their previous employment of fishermen, which they were now to abandon, have used that beautiful image, that from henceforth He would make them fishers of men: that image, with the deeper thoughts which lay at its root, belongs quite to that time. At present however the relation between the Master (Rabbi) and the disciples who became his more intimate friends was a somewhat loose one. It is however a matter of course, though following from the "*we* have found" in the mouth of Philip (John i. 45), that these three or (probably with James) four accompanied Him on the return to Galilee which soon followed: and when He, on the day of His journey home, met with Philip, who was of the same town with Him, it needed only one word on the Saviour's side to make him also a companion. Thus was the fourth (or the fifth) about Him of those who later made up the number of the twelve.

The journey home was (as remarked earlier) to Kana in Galilee. But on the journey this Philip had recognised so completely the truth of Christ, that directly on arriving at Kana he looked for his friend Nathaniel, declared to him with high elevation of spirit, " he had found Him of whom Moses in the law and the prophets had written," and silenced his unbelief, which had broken forth in the question "Can there any good thing come out of Nazareth?" with calling him to come and see for himself. Jesus now, when He saw him coming to Him, only, as was his wont for others, dropped the remark "There comes a true Israelite in whom is no guile;" for He had seen before in him at the first glance, when passing by unobserved, a guilelessness and simplicity of spirit, such as every member of God's true community must have. But struck with the inner truth of this exclamation, which was well heard by him, he replies quickly "Whence knowest thou me?" And on Jesus replying to him "Before that Philip called thee, when thou wast under the fig-tree, I saw thee;" he quickly remembers himself likewise the deep and difficult thoughts to which his mind had been drawn on, when sitting under the fig-tree of his house and concealed by its branches, thinking himself alone: he sees, guileless, as he had been described, the deepest thoughts of his soul suddenly in a mysteriously surprising manner spread clearly before Jesus' spiritual eye, and sinks at the Master's feet with the most sincere confession of belief in Him as the Son of God and the King of Israel. The first remark had at once deeply struck him: the memory of the moment just passed, when he, thinking himself quite alone, full of deep desire, was thinking probably on the misery of Israel, and unawares was seen and rightly judged by the Master, quickly completed his belief. Yet this first overflow of belief is not enough for Him: He, as with admiration, points him and all standing round on to the time when, if he now believes because he had seen himself known when unnoticed under the fig-tree, they all shall soon find quite other causes for belief in Him; should see heaven open, and the angels of God ascending and descending upon the Son of Man. For so soon as the Messiah with all his heavenly powers is in full activity, this far higher spectacle opens for every one to recognise who will not mistake it, and is most clearly to be seen, looking at it from the end after its accomplishment, as did the Apostle, who dashes in these slight sketches of reminiscence of the earliest beginning of the public activity of Jesus: and has learnt from the conclusion constantly to look back with infinite ecstacy on all this which he too had once experienced. So unsought and yet so inevitably shews itself the activity of the true Messianic knowledge of the depths of man's heart, and its grasping them also by the correct glance and the true word; and already this power is in full operation. Who this Nathaniel was, appears to us at first somewhat obscure, as the name is only found in this Gospel: yet he must certainly have been a man of great importance in the circle of the first confessors of Christ, as he once more appears in this Gospel in such a way that he must be accounted one of the twelve (John xxi. 2). Now as in the ancient catalogue of the Apostles Bartholemas constantly follows close on Philip, we have full right to look on these as the same: St. John might then have kept his proper name; the Apostolic catalogue on the other hand, the name by which he was popularly known, Bar Tolmai.

CHAPTER XII.

Messianic Activity in Working and Helping.

The Messianic activity shews itself soon enough, quite spontaneously, nay, almost against its will, and for this very reason from a higher necessity. On the third day after the return to Kana, the story goes on, there was a marriage, to which Jesus' mother as well as He Himself and His disciples were invited. Now His mother had observed the change which had lately come over Him more plainly than all others; she looks accordingly to Him as Messiah, more full of expectation than His as yet few disciples: and when at the wedding, visited by so many, the wine ran out, she says to Him "they have no wine," as though she would say, how well it would be if He would give help in the unexpected difficulty, especially as He Himself, with an unexpected number of His disciples, had been invited. He is surprised by the presumption of His mother, and refuses her request, because "His hour was not yet come," and therefore He does not yet feel in Himself the full Messianic power: but she keeps her favourable belief in it, and bids the servants do what Jesus says to them.

Thus is it then, this motherly belief, which suddenly for the first time drives forth the whole slumbering power in Him. He just now felt a timidity keeping him back from acting and helping; just now He felt his hour not yet come, but suddenly it is come; and the water, which at his command was poured into six large water-pots standing by, serving at other times for washing the hands before or after meals, changes at his will into such excellent wine, that the master of the feast himself, unprompted, pronounces it better than the first. Thus this first of the miracles of Christ appears in every respect a true beginning work, and in this very respect is most instructive. It appeared in the midst of a cheerful time which might easily become disorderly, as it were in the sport of life, yet was it great and solemn enough: even in the midst of the joy of life, in which He and his disciples are guilelessly sharing, He is collected and earnest. The action was suitable as well to the unusually cheerful season of this family feast, as to the commencing Messianic activity. To change water into wine is otherwise not one of the usual miracles of the first Christian times, yet here it is as it were a cheerful gift for the commencement of the whole royal life-work now coming on; somewhat as other kings, on the happy days of their coronation, cheer the people's hearts with distribution of wine. But here is quite another King just entering on his kingdom with full power; here is no outer preparation, no worldly riches and worldly substance of his own which this future King could or would distribute: He has no wine, and yet he has—the water itself becomes under his Spirit the best wine: He does not think about preparing it for this day to celebrate this occasion with it, and receives it unsought, nay, almost against his will, at the right time for its celebration, (δόξα, John ii. 11). We should ourselves dilute the wine which since that time may yet ever flow for us, if we ask here in the material sense how from mere water wine could be made in a moment; for must not the water in the best sense everywhere even now become wine, where his Spirit is in full activity? Without question, this side also of the Apostolic reminiscence and Christian intuition might have been touched on at length and for spiritual improvement: our Apostle in other places does not miss doing this. But here, in this first work, which he relates as an example more expressly, he is more concerned to bring into prominence the right beginning itself; and in this respect the narrative, in spite of its brevity, is plain and instructive enough. No good, blessed, beneficent work follows the independent human willing, urging it on, least of all a commencement work: reserve and delicate modesty, a quiet and patient endurance, till, unobserved at the right time, the Spirit itself comes with power and impulse, this is here a first and higher command; but with what wonderful greatness and power can this Spirit itself work, when it thus comes in the right manner and in the right time! then it works infinitely more than the man himself shortly before thought, and then bestows powers and blessings which surpass all which the modest mind shortly before expected: but pious belief, meeting from without the inner power and encouraging it to its benevolent work, is thus the beginning of the miraculous itself. If this is so everywhere, so in the highest and plainest manner in the case of the Messiah: and if the first great work of beneficence be everywhere the hardest and at first seem almost impossible, so that in it especially true divine modesty and reserve must combine with right belief coming from all sides, this was also the case with the first Messianic miracle. The mother's faith at the right time met Him for the right work, unexpected as it was, exalting and encouraging: thus the whole hidden power of the Messianic Spirit slumbering in Him came forth in Him suddenly, when it had been once awakened in the right way and at the right time for a beneficent work; never to fail again in activity and helping power, but carry forward the Messianic life-work thus begun, without interruption and without fainting, to its proper highest end. This is the special lesson of this first story of its sort in St. John's Gospel: and, as was to be expected from that Evangelist, this narrative of the first Messianic miracle has something much more instructive, and penetrates deeper into the boundless depths of this whole history, than the narratives corresponding to it in the other Gospels.

CHAPTER XIII.

THE FIRST MORE PUBLIC APPEARANCE AND WORKING, AND THE BEGINNING OF THE RECOGNITION OF CHRIST IN WIDER CIRCLES.

CHRIST did not however remain long dwelling with his mother, his brethren and disciples in Kana; the family moved to Kaphar-Nahûm on the western shore of the lake of Galilee, where we see them afterwards permanently settled, and where too Peter and Andrew lived, both of them in the house of Peter's mother-in-law (Mark i. 29—31). Thus in Kaphar-Nahûm (Capernaum) several families of friends seem to have met. Not far from it, probably somewhat to the south, lay the Bethsaida already spoken of, which is mentioned rather as a small place, and, probably in another direction, Chorazin; two places of which as yet no certain traces have been recovered. Within the limits of these three towns, as far as we can now be certain, the earliest Messianic activity of the Saviour appeared. It was a somewhat small circle in which it first moved, but the surer was the ground on which it gradually rose, and that higher experience which might here be gathered. In truth this experience which these three towns offered was little encouraging, although Jesus dedicated to them the first flower of all his now so powerfully blossoming activity: even in later times this better remembrance forms a deep enough undertone, little softened as it were by the remembrance of the following period. But all the more urgent on Him was it, outside also of this more contracted circle, even at the very highest place of the time, to let Himself publicly be known as He whom He would be and was. Only Jerusalem and the temple, with its halls of learning and all its other advantages, was the proper place for this: and if He would be known to any effect as the Messiah, He must from this high centre shew publicly as soon as possible that He was the Messiah, and what sort of Messiah He wished to be. Not that corner, nay, not even the whole of Galilee, was sufficiently suited for his end: and though this little country had many advantages (as will appear below) which even Jerusalem did not offer, yet, in all which concerned the temporal and spiritual rule, it looked always only too humbly and expectant to Jerusalem. Now the Saviour would doubtless, in any case, have taken at this time the usual journey to the feast in Jerusalem; but the fact that He, in spite of his Messianic sayings and doings, found little true recognition in the first smaller circle, contributed to determine Him, so soon as possible, namely at the next passover, to make a pilgrimage to Jerusalem. (John ii. 13, iv. 43—54).

There is just one action of this his first stay as Messiah in Jerusalem, which the Apostle brings forward as important, and relates more at length. He certainly did not go there to make an outward cleansing of the temple; but when He saw the dishonouring abuse of the holy places, which was carried on from mere covetousness and love of comfort, the Messianic zeal which had already been stirred within Him overmastered Him, and with irrestrainable power, with the help of a scourge hastily made from small cords, He drove forth the sellers of sacrificial animals, with the animals themselves, out of the fore court of the temple; overthrew the tables of the money-changers, who had stationed themselves here, (because indeed by old custom all the dues of the temple must be paid only with coin of the country, not with foreign coin), and did not suffer that such vessels as did not belong to the temple service should be carried in or out. Such profanation of the holy places is in truth everywhere possible enough, and has often even in Christian times been repeated, and is not seldom even called forth through the priest's laziness or even covetousness: but never was it more insufferable than in that sanctuary, which would be looked on as unique and could alone minister to the true religion.

And every good man may easily be zealous thereat; so that it is hard to say how one should properly punish the individual, who feels himself more powerfully impelled to put an end to the disorder which has found itself in. But before all others can, nay must, the occasion being given, the Messiah feel Himself destined thereto. He has, it is true, what is much greater to purify and amend; yet even the less must He not disdain to purify, when the occasion for it calls Him so closely and irresistibly as it did then: and besides, when He is at the commencement of his higher activity, He may not despise even the smaller, as this may serve of itself for the token and beginning of yet greater purifications. Thus was this surprising action not designed after any far-fetched plan, nor out of place, but proper in its place and full of meaning for its time; not one to be hastily begun by any one, still less to be hastily carried out, but conceived by his heroic zeal, to be carried out also with his irresistible, heroic strength. He Himself appealed in it to nothing but some passages of the Bible here appropriate; and his followers, although at first sight astonished at the strangeness of it, could readily compose their minds by thinking on similar passages of the Bible. The priests and temple warders could only put it as a question to Him, how He dared do such things? and what particular right for it can He shew? And so, according to St. John, they did in fact ask Him what sign (from God), that is, what particular divine credentials and authority, He has to shew for doing such things. But this question in truth made Him think not only of his own right as Messiah, but at the same time, or rather yet more in the final view, of the right of the whole existing state of things: and those who asked such a question should have first asked themselves, whence comes their weakness in face of such profanation of the sanctuary; and whether some one else besides the Messiah might not completely cleanse this sanctuary, not merely partially and for a time, but for ever and completely.

Thus He meets them with an answer, which if possible might surprise them yet more than did the deed itself, "Destroy this temple, and in three days I will build it again;" not going beyond the temple in his reply, as was necessary, but leading them on at once to something infinitely higher, as likewise He must do in order to silence them. "Your whole religion, as it rests on this temple, is corrupt and perverted; but *He* also is present, who, when it passes away, as it must pass away, will easily restore it again in far higher majesty, and thus is able to accomplish, not merely a common miracle as you ask, but the very highest miracle." That was precisely his meaning in that riddle; here, as is elsewhere his wont, at once rising above the vulgar thoughts and purposes, to the highest which are directly in question, and raising the more vulgar strife from the dust of this earth into its heavenly height and eternal purport. "Will you indeed have a token from Me in reference to my divine authority over the temple? be it so; you shall have the highest which you can expect and ask of any one: Destroy this temple, which so long as it stands I wish to see purified and worthy, but which will yet certainly one day fall; destroy it yourselves if you will, and throw away with it all your perverted religion: I tell you that in a short time I will rebuild it, the eternal and indestructible Temple, which will be, of course, infinitely nobler than this visible defaced one." How little they were in truth able to reply, and how they preferred understanding the noblest spiritual words in a material sense, nay, tried thus to laugh at it, is at once apparent: but then they had to leave Him in peace, whose offer they could not take, and whose riddle they could not solve.

If now the action was surprising, still more the answer and declaration. In it lies already the whole boundless presentiment of all futurity: He has already in his mind the true indestructible Temple just as much as at the close of his whole earthly activity. And if every fire and every zeal, when first it can break out quite freely and spread itself, is likely also to be the most violent, so is this action and this saying. Nay, this saying is so extremely abrupt and sharp and so mysteriously sublime, that we cannot be surprised at the many misconceptions to which it gave occasion. How it stuck to his enemies' ears in variously perverted forms, and at length, at the final capital arraignment of the bold speaker, how it was made use of, will appear below. The issue of the whole history is so closely connected with its beginning, as happens in all great developments, that with the very first step the last is given. That splendid temple of incomparable sanctity was destroyed soon enough, chiefly through the guilt of those who would most carefully maintain it with all its abuses; and, not after its outward destruction, but in a wonderful way, almost before it fell, in the stillness of the period, another had been built in its place of simply imperishable nature: yet *He*, who at the beginning of his course in mysterious presentiment announced it, and before anyone desired it was building this incomparably firm new temple, fell a victim to the truth of this riddle when it was intentionally perverted; and thus was the truth which might lie in His prophetic word, fulfilled in another far more immediate and visible manner.

The yet far more wonderful and nobler Temple of his own body had been destroyed by his enemies, and was yet raised again by Him in three days. It is no wonder that John, with other disciples, applied the remark to this, nay to this in preference. Against the enemy it had almost as much meaning, nay, for those early Apostolic times more immediate meaning: for this interpretation of our Lord's saying certainly originated at the time when the temple was yet standing; and from that time it must have been so retained in St. John's mind, that he actually repeats it at the time when the temple was already overthrown, and when the more natural and higher explanation of the saying would have been much easier. We however, who this long time have been able to look at it with less prepossession, must turn to the strict meaning of the whole story and the full sublimity of the saying and deed of Christ, but thank the Apostle for having preserved it to us in its first abrupt sublimity. But if now the Saviour, through many such words and actions, whose wonderful power and effect may be discerned in the examples above given, thus aroused the general observation in the metropolis in Jerusalem, it is readily intelligible that here too many began to believe on Him. But it might seem surprising that He took into his closer circle none from all the multitude in Jerusalem, and especially from the great scribes and eminent men here assembled: and that, although many trusted (believed)

Him, yet He trusted Himself to none of them, not in the way in which He took the well-known Galilæans, some at least, into his closer confidence. But what we see here occurs again later. It must then have a general cause, and this is not very obscure. The Galilæans stood in every respect closer to Him; and if He wished closer confidence He found it sufficiently among them, at least among some, for a large number is here out of the question. The people of Jerusalem were, on the contrary, (as frequently in all capitals) compared with the more simple agriculturists, on the whole, rather a curious and novelty-loving people than deeply earnest: and the old scholasticism here flourishing was little adapted to understand Him more intimately, and join Him more closely, as the result will on the whole shew. The penetrating glance of Jesus saw this truly from the beginning; and, besides, He had no need of human support and help, with trouble sought for and retained.

There were many among those of high renown and influence in Jerusalem, who felt vaguely the deficiencies of the dominant scholasticism and priest-rule; and neither enjoyed the rule of Herod nor of the Romans, and who consequently would have been well inclined to adhere to a true King of Israel, nay, who silently marvelled at Christ, and were ready to acknowledge Him, if it had appeared sufficiently safe for them so to do. But the Apostle (who though in his Gospel he relates so much of Jerusalem, yet felt himself before all a Galilæan, and knew that Jesus had only Galilæans for His closest friends) observes on this occasion that He had determined not to trust Himself to those of Jerusalem, " because He knew all men, and needed not that any should testify of the man," that is of Himself as man, (though He did not despise witness to Him as to God's Son when it came to him freely); for He well knew what was in man, whether men wished, merely in consequence of His surprising works and miracles, to honour Him as a human King, and did or did not expect a Messianic kingdom from Him. He who in the usual manner will rule among men, must look around for influential men, who humanly, *i. e.* from temporal grounds, because they seek thereby their own human profit, as is acknowledged by the general feeling of men, praise and recommend him, who would fain become his closest counsellors and ministers, to spread and support his kingdom, which is not grounded on eternal truth. *Such* He neither sought nor needed.

Yet a Pharisee named Nicodemus, a man of position and wealth, and a member of the Sanhedrim, seemed to wish to make an exception to the general holding back of the great men of Jerusalem: he was struck by the great deeds of Jesus, and felt some wish to confide more closely in Him as the true Messiah, in order to get for a time behind this secret of the age, seeming to him so remarkable, or indeed to offer himself to Him as his first friend and counsellor, but at first only secretly. So he came to Him by night, and joined Him in confidential conversation; he had a real longing " to see the kingdom of God," and himself to share it, and thus wished likewise to know its conditions, and how Jesus will introduce it. We cannot doubt the historic truth of this partly earnest inclination of such a man to the Saviour and his undertaking. He became in fact, through the mere confidential conversations with Him, confirmed in his growing belief, and subsequently shewed publicly, so far as he thought safe, his earnest interest in Him: still he, in his position as a distinguished man and privy-councillor in Jerusalem, could not become such a disciple as the twelve, and like to them; the Saviour therefore, while disclosing to him the full truth, makes no further effort to draw him to Himself. He thus remained honouring Him in silence; not reflecting that in face of clear truths and duties, silent honouring is only fit for women and children, while all the great evils of the time are advancing in spite of them. But the extended discourse, in which the Saviour places before him the true conditions of participation in God's kingdom, has in its peculiar structure (as all such in this Evangelist) received its definite form from the narrator. That this Apostle repeats single sayings of the Saviour in their most exact and original form, we have lately seen in the history of the temple cleansing: but of course this cannot be the case with all longer artificially elaborated discourses. So with this discourse, it is a model of Christian truth and perspicuity, and certainly, in its deepest foundation grown out of thoughts which Christ Himself constantly announced: little more than the putting together of the words in this whole is the Apostle's own.

The fundamental condition of sharing in the kingdom

of God and His salvation is regeneration (as the Baptist had already required); but this must result not merely (as in baptism for example) through water, but at the same time through the Spirit, so that man becomes a wholly willing instrument of the Divine Spirit, and lets himself be driven by Him as by a favourable breeze. But if this is obscure to any one, so that he does not comprehend how he can suffer himself to be taken hold of by God's Spirit and led to eternal salvation, let him believe on *Him* in whom this has all been most completely fulfilled, and who is destined by God, through the deepest suffering and the highest glory, to bring in eternal life, and at the same time the judgment of the world; let him *thus* look rightly into these heavenly secrets, in which to believe is difficult indeed, and which yet must be believed by everyone whom the Spirit has not led as powerfully and as certainly as Christ Himself. In these three propositions lies, in fact, the deepest and most exhaustive declaration of the course which each one must tread, who will really share in God's kingdom and salvation. But the peculiar intuitions and phraseology of St. John in the colouring of the sayings, appear more freely the longer and more freely the discourse pours forth; and the two questions which St. John makes Nicodemus himself throw in, serve, in fact, only for the inner advance of the evolution of the long discourse, and for the clearer defence of the three great propositions about which it all turns.

Meanwhile the Saviour was tarrying with his disciples yet longer in the country of Judæa; and his closer followers, who had earlier (see above) been themselves disciples of the Baptist, and so could be used by the Baptist to help him in baptism, continued the baptism at the water proper for it; but now, of course, baptized in the name not of the Messiah undefined, but on the coming Messiah appointed in Jesus. That the baptism must be continued generally in Christianity, we saw above (Chapter IV.): but though baptism, so soon as Christianity was established, must in so far, as will be seen below, take a somewhat different shape, seeing that now the very giving of the Holy Ghost was the principal point, so that, even former disciples of John were rebaptized; it could at that time, when Christ had hardly appeared, and in the whole time of his earthly life, only differ from John's baptism in that the hope of the catechumen was no more to be directed to the undetermined Messiah, but quite definitely to the Messiah to be hoped for in Jesus, as shewn above (Chap. VI.). Besides, as Christ from the beginning defined the purity of spirit which baptism was to give quite differently in many respects from the Baptist, and changed the uncultured life which he called for into a life of divine joy and love; baptism at once within His circle received a new meaning, which might lead to great variances from the Baptist's views and principles.

Of course the Saviour must allow this new baptism, but could not Himself baptize, as otherwise He would have had to baptize into Himself, which on account of his dignity He could not do (no more than a Christian, that is a conscientious, king with us will offer the oath of fealty to himself), even had He not avoided it from modesty, as unbecoming. Some certainly of Jesus' disciples began first at that time their particular baptism, the baptism in the water of Jordan or in other places appropriated to it: the baptism in the consecrated waters of Jordan was still too new and attractive; this new baptism found quickly so many friends, that the disciples of John, who continued the old sort, soon fell into a dispute with a Jew who maintained that the purification which the new baptism furnished must be much more potent and spiritual than the old. When John's disciples now complained of this to the Baptist himself, and sought to irritate him against the rapid progress of the new baptism, he soothed them, and shewed them that a quick growth of the new movement was only a matter of joy. The way the Apostle makes the Baptist speak on this occasion is, in its phraseology, rather coloured in the Apostle's style, than an exact repetition of what the Baptist may have said of the Saviour: but that he then expressed himself in this sense, admits of no doubt. He was in this only true to that which he from the beginning (Chap. VIII.) had felt and wished about Jesus: but if he had not then expected that Jesus would so long delay the full Messianic appearing, nay would himself allow a new kind of baptism and preparation, yet anything which seemed to him an essential part of the evolution of the new movement, as did this baptism, must be to him an object of desire.

He might then, in fact, admirably, in the figure intimated by the Apostle, compare himself with the bosom friend of a bridegroom, who must rejoice at his bringing home the bride as soon as possible, and who waits attentively on all his steps and commands, if at length there may come the proud moment of boundless joy at the actual bringing home the bride. The bride which *he* meant, as did Christ, was the perfected Church of God and God's kingdom itself; only that he had other views of the way of winning and bringing home this bride. His touching figure often returns in those times of boundless expectation and joyful hope.

Meanwhile the year, at the commencement of whose passover Jesus had gone up to Jerusalem, was already far advanced: there were but four months to the coming harvest (John iv. 35). The new kind of baptism of his disciples, too, had not a little aroused the attention of the Pharisees and other clever men of the capital: but He held it better for the present to go out of the way of their rising suspicion, and resolved to return to Galilee through Samaria.

Making experiment, that is, of all for the first time, He had at present no reason for avoiding Samaria, as He certainly had later: still less had He any fear about bringing his truth, should it be enquired after, into a half heathen land. He thus arrived in the neighbourhood of the ancient and as yet very large town of Sichem, at a small town named Sykhar; and as it was already rather late, about six in the evening, He sat Himself, wearied as He was, on Jacob's well lying here on the way, which, famed of old, was peculiarly holy to the Samaritans as a monument to the ancient renown of their own country. Whilst now his disciples had gone into the town to buy food, He begged a drink of water from a Samaritan woman just come to draw water: when she wondered how a Jew, from the known enmity between the two people, could speak to her about anything, and was little inclined to give him anything, He spoke of the infinitely better return which He could give to her of inexhaustible water of life, and explained to her somewhat more closely, on her not at once comprehending, what this is. Still somewhat confused as to his exact meaning, yet become very eager, she begs now very urgently for the gift of this water of life: but as she was yet not at all prepared to understand, He suddenly turns the conversation to something apparently strange and unimportant, telling her to call her husband. She then is detected in her attempt to hide the true state of her immoral life from His penetrating eye, and cannot help at length clearly feeling that a remarkable prophet stands before her; and, further, the misgiving will force itself on her, that the advantage possessed by the Jewish religion which brings forth such prophets may be well founded (John iv. 20). Then is the time arrived for explaining to her the whole relation of true and false religion; to point her to the completion of all true religion, which must at length be expected, rather is already coming with power, and to tell her things which she had never before heard in this way. Already she divines, and then hears, that surely the Messiah Himself stands before her, and hurries into the town to impart her growing belief to others. The disciples before this were returning from the town, but find the two not engaged in strife and angry conversation (as they might have feared, from the hostility between the Jews and Samaritans), but in the most unexpected peace, and the woman now hurrying for joy into the town. Astonished themselves at this spectacle of a converted Samaritan, they at length, when she had gone away, invite Him to eat: but He is now so occupied Himself with the fresh truth of what He had just been teaching, and with the thought of the completion one day of the conversion even of non-Jews here begun, that He has forgotten bodily hunger and thirst, and prefers for Himself thinking on that eternal food which the carrying out and completion of his work offers to Him; and, although all this is only a first slight beginning, and as it were a first scattering of seed, already in spirit He sees the great harvest ripen, yet more for the disciples than for Himself. For if Samaritans indeed believe, what new ground for hope of the general completion of his work! just as *then*, at seed-time, the harvest at the end of autumn seemed yet very distant, but his Spirit could see the fields already white to harvest. And in fact, the story tells us, the Samaritans now came forward to Him so friendly, that He had to stay with them longer than He meant; nay, many believed in his claims, not on account of the mere saying of the woman, but led to it as well by their own growing conviction. Thus every, apparently even most trivial occasion may serve for the unfolding even of the highest truth; and as certainly there must at length vanish before this truth even the most hardened enmities of nationalities and of existing religions: these are at first sight some great truths which this story may give us in passing. We have the less ground here for doubting an historical basis of the story, as we are here brought so completely into the first commencements of the Messianic activity; although here also we must not fail to recognise that the Apostle, whilst he went in memory back to those commencement times, with their apparently trifling and yet so weighty occurrences, could not fill up the several points of the picture without the colouring of his own language and higher intuition.

CHAPTER XIV.

The Happy Return to Galilee, and the New Position of the Messiah.

When He returned this time to Galilee, as a man who had much approved Himself in the capital, He was received with much greater belief than before; and immediately on his entrance into the midst of this country a miracle took place, which, in consequence partly of its similarity of time and place, but also in itself, seemed to the Apostle worthy of being placed as the second, beside that at the marriage-feast, already mentioned as the first.

He returned to Capernahum by Kana, which had earlier been so dear to his spirit; it was, too, no great way round to pass by this. Immediately on his arrival, there spread quickly, even to Capernahum, the news of his slow return. There hurried then to meet Him from thence a man of note, who had for some time settled there, a captain in the service of the prince; who, though himself a heathen, had long taken great interest in the welfare of the Jews, and, in fact, had helped in the most practical manner in the building of the synagogue there.

His son was now very ill, and, accompanied by the thankful rulers of the synagogue, he came to Kana to meet the Saviour, to pray for the healing of his son, and for a quick return to Capernahum afterwards. Jesus, although actually begged by the principal Jews to help the son of the heathen, at first refuses his help; displeased with reason that they should want always signs and wonders in order to believe in his higher truth. But the simple firm belief of the man would not give way. According to one account, he was, like a true soldier, so staunch, but withal so simple, that he thought, just as he, as captain, obeyed a higher command, and himself, on the other hand, imposed on his soldiers unconditional obedience, so can the Messiah command, by a word, the great and less demons to leave the man tormented by them.

So the Saviour promised him help, and bade him journey back in hope. It was in the evening: he passed the night in Kana. But, the next morning early, servants from his house met him on his way with news that his son was better, and he learnt to his astonishment that the fever had left him at exactly seven oclock the evening before. He felt consequently wonderfully confirmed in his belief; and his whole household as well, embracing many members, believed, offering at once the first and a great example of its kind. But the whole was important for this as well, that it was a heathen household. The story of this event must have soon spread widely, and for this very reason taken many different forms. It appears essentially again in the older circle of traditions, and is there, according to their system of grouping, transferred to a somewhat later time; but it appears there, too, at the passing through an important crisis in Christ's public life.

At this time, in fact, or soon after, must the Baptist have been put into prison: we cannot indeed specify the date quite accurately; but we know for certain that the event falls somewhere at this period. This had also an important reaction on the Saviour's work now just commencing. His work was, in its temporal purpose, a carrying on and completion of that of the Baptist: the external ground was now as it were shaken, on which the bolder edifice of his own work was rising. And if the world with such malice threatened and busied itself to overthrow the essentially far less work of the Baptist, much more must He fear that it would likewise soon seek to violently crush and annihilate with all its power his own hardly commenced undertaking. Unless then content to immediately drop his work, now was his very time for continuing it more earnestly and powerfully, nay, one might say for beginning it again from the beginning. For hitherto the great work of giving new life to Israel, and the mighty effort for the perfecting of all its higher blessings, rested in almost equal proportions on the elder well-known man and on the younger, who was just beginning to be rightly known: hence, when the Baptist fell, and his disciples also evidently suffered a hard blow through the captivity of their master, the higher duty of not letting this whole work fall to pieces again fell at once on the Saviour alone; and the new obligation began for Him, of now first actually beginning his true life-work, as it were from the beginning, with a power and decision, but also with a foresight and higher wisdom, none of which had before been necessary. All his Messianic work till now had been only a prelude and trial of strength for that which now rose of itself facing Him; and must in later times all the more so appear, the greater the development of the work proved, which now began to reveal itself to the world. This was a principal cause of the memory of it in the usual Gospel story quite early fading away, while it could not be utterly lost.

CHAPTER XV.

The History of the Temptation.

It is thus readily apparent how the narrative of the earlier Evangelists might make the imprisonment of the Baptist the great beginning of the Messianic activity of Jesus: it was usually by them simply stated, that after the apprehension He went into Galilee, to begin the clear announcement of the Gospel. Yet the space between Jesus' baptism and this his first appearance in Galilee was left for that simpler narrative by no means unfilled, so enduring had been the thought that there had intervened here an interval of some length. The thought, too, lasted, that the interval must have been a time of first trial and of the right preparation of spirit: for only when the spirit first tries itself, can it prepare itself to win the final strength, clearness, and decision, which for the real beginning and the successful carrying through of a great work is indispensable. But when a mere attempt (versuch) is first in progress, there just as closely lurks always temptation (versuchung), for the wholly right is not yet in progress; so that errors also, of all sorts, injustice and wrong, stir themselves yet more strongly, at least in thought, and the power of error may try again to come at least into closer converse with the spirit as a power, and rule it. This is temptation as it may present itself even to the purest and strongest spirit, as it comes more inevitably the greater the work to be attempted: and, while it is in fact providentially necessary, in order to remove the possible error before great activity, it may, too, providentially become rich in blessings, if it serve merely in any particular work to separate these possible kinds of error, and to dismiss them beforehand. Nay, we may also, in so far, deem it a Divine mercy for the Messianic as the greatest life-work in the world's history, as it would commence and perfect itself too in Jesus, that, before it had after the Baptist's removal to immediately reveal itself in the purest and highest activity, at the right time a short interval was found for self-trial and the learning to know completely all the various forms and powers of error, and for ever reject them, which must have been to Him dangerous, nay, destructive, had they not in advance been put to the most decisive rout. Whilst now that interval in the Saviour's life from the baptism, where He received from God power to become Messiah to the moment after the Baptist's removal, survived in memory, only as a dark, but yet for the following time most important commencement; it was early learnt to take it as the time of the Messiah's temptation, and thus the way was prepared for a true representation, which only needed to be carried out by the higher contemplation of his whole history to illustrate an abundance of higher truths belonging to the very commencement time, truths themselves taught us by it; as is seen in the more detailed history of the temptation. But the immediate occasion of the particular account (that this temptation which, according to the well-known examples in the Old Testament, lasted forty days, and was carried by Satan into the wilderness, inhabited by wild beasts alone) was due, doubtless, to the remembrance of the above-described stay of Jesus in southern Judæa and in the Baptist's neighbourhood: this residence had also, from the evidences given above, lasted some time; so that forty days for it gave a particularly suitable estimate: from it, too, he had immediately gone to Galilee to make a complete beginning of the great work which we are about to witness. In so far, then, there is a good deal of true recollection in this narrative also. But further, of this first Messianic time, while we have to thank St. John for preserving more accurately to us some single features in the narrative, some single features have been preserved to us in the earlier Gospels: they have, however, in them been moved forward to other connections of time. We have noticed some above in their several places: probably some more belong here, only that it is difficult now to bring them back into their original order in time.

CHAPTER XVI.

The Founding of the Messianic Kingdom.

Looking now at the new position of the Messianic proclamation and the personal labour which the Saviour now took on Him, it only consisted, in its innermost nature, in a still more decided direction of every power to the one mark which had already been put up and become perfectly plain; and hence also in, if possible, yet greater laboriousness and consistency, as well as decision, publicity, and boldness, united with that greater foresight and wise reserve, which this greater decision as well as his previous experience demanded. Thus it must be from the necessity of the case, and thus the surviving traces of historical reminiscence shew that it was. It was not *He* that now changed in the depth of his spirit, in thought, will, and effort; but his position in the world had changed, as this world had changed. His task was now to shew Himself, in every respect and unremittingly already perfect, as the actual ruler in his kingdom: and it needed his peculiar elevation and nobility of character to approve themselves at once, at this stage of his calling, through all its duties and labours, as well as its joys and victories.

But when the whole activity reaches its greatest intensity and effort, then must it necessarily all the more limit its sphere of action, if it would not, through unnecessary fragmentary work, weaken and annihilate itself. And as in the whole Messianic activity the inner necessity of Jesus and the outward constraint meet so wonderfully and so perfectly, so is it also here. For if the widely extended, as yet quite unlimited, activity, which in that time of beginning and trial was perfectly right, must now be limited by its own higher intensity; this concurred with his previous experience, which constrained him and shewed him the right way.

For already it had been proved that the great majority of the wise and mighty in the proud capital had themselves no sense of the deep meaning of his enterprise: whilst it had likewise appeared, how ready the countrymen of his own Galilee were to enter into his meaning, after having witnessed his great deeds in Jerusalem, and the high respect to which, in the minds of some at least, He had attained. He resolved then to devote Himself in general wholly to the Galilæans, and in that smaller but so much the more intimate circle, to lay the most enduring foundation of his kingdom: and to this resolve the peculiar circumstances of the Galilæans might in themselves contribute. For the Galilæans stood, as remote country people, in no high esteem with the proud inhabitants of the capital; and people were offended with their less refined pronunciation, by which they could be easily known: but, in fact, none of the populations, then so various of the ancient Holy Land, were so capable and so available for receiving the Gospel into their hearts from its earliest, and consequently most difficult, beginning, as were these very Galilæans. No corner of the Holy Land, since the first days of the decline of the old power of the people, had suffered so much through the encroachment of the heathen as the northern and the eastern portions of the land, according to its ancient limits, as we find the great prophets bitterly complaining; but the communities, often quite scattered, which under these severest sufferings and longest trials had yet remained faithful to the true religion, only approved themselves the more in all new hours of danger. And if the eastern lands had been continually more occupied by heathen populations, the Galilæans, at least within extensive tracts, lived close together, and, since the erection of the modern Jerusalem, had adhered all the more decidedly and simply to the new Temple; and, in spite of all distresses of war and other various trials through all these five centuries, had remained true. (Bd. IV. s. 109, 359 f.)

The Samaritans, indeed, gradually formed, between them and the Jews proper, an intermediate population, evermore decidedly and harshly separating them, and on all sides, too, these Galilæan Jews were much straightened by heathen towns, and without fixed boundaries; but only the more tenaciously for that did they always cleave to the distant sanctuary. Compared with the inhabitants of the capital and their neighbours, the Galilæans were, in their fruitful plain in the south, their mountainous country in the north full of caves, and the rich and prosperous shores of the lake of Gennesareth, and the right bank of Jordan; had yet remained simpler, more vigorous, and more susceptible of enduring impressions.

We observed, coming into prominence, since the days of the Asmonæan dynasty, a more powerful influence of these simpler and sincerer Galilæans on the southern Jews; often the Jews persecuted in Judah fled into their castles, ravines, and caves, and readily found amongst them their most tenacious defenders. But now they were to range themselves round one out of their midst, as champions of an all-unknown kingdom; and strange as was the call, never has a call in the end been so completely answered, as this was by chosen spirits among these Galilæan peasants, fishermen, and publicans: but, in truth, neither had any corner of the earth before resounded with such a call, and been filled with such a new miraculous vital power, as were these not less checkered than confined and torn, thickly populated tracts of Galilee. And if it be an internal law of the higher retribution, that, like everything unreasonably despised, so also a much humbled and despised land, often misused for centuries, arrives at length at all the higher honour; here is the beginning of the most splendid ennobling of this hitherto all but ruined corner of the Holy Land: and *then* indeed, after that this ennobling, already patent enough, had been made a part of universal history, certain passages of the Old Testament must seem to have received a quite new, nay, their best fulfilment—the passages in which once the heart of the great prophet, overpowered by the sad spectacle of the sufferings of these countries, raised to a bolder flight by the hope of the Messiah, saw in spirit a just future ennobling also of these. But the same higher effort which induced Jesus now to confine his activity principally to Galilee, led Him also to take some of these Galilæans into his closer intimacy, that they might be constantly about Him and suffer his spirit to pass wholly into them. It was not *the Twelve*, whose appointment will be found later: a definite number in the case of these was as yet of no importance, nor was instruction and practising needed so definite, as we shall see below in the case of the Twelve. But assuredly the relation to Him of these now taken for his constant companions, was quite different to that of his first companions and disciples: if they had most of them joined Him uninvited, and He only did not send them back; these lived probably at home and in company with Him, and went with Him wherever He wished. Many might for this reason not find it suit them: and, according to a permanent reminiscence, this select circle only comprised the four, who (see above) had voluntarily and at first joined Him, and whom He had for some time known more intimately—the brothers Simon and Andrew, and the sons of Zebedee, James and John. He may at this time have called to Him these fishermen's sons with the saying, which seems long to have been well remembered, "Come, that I may make you (something much better) fishers of men," as He meant now to take them for ever into His closer life-companionship: we may well suppose that they at once followed Him all the more willingly; even the sons of Zebedee, although they came from a home of some wealth, and now left it almost for ever. The two pairs of brothers lived, we see from this, by the lake of Galilee, not far from each other.

In place of this simpler narrative, St. Luke has adopted from a somewhat later account, one more grandly conceived, in which only Christ and Peter are the two principal actors, and the two sons of Zebedee appear merely as Peter's companions in occupation, and subsequent companions in faith: here, too, the commencement of the higher faith is painted with more depth. Whilst the Saviour is engaged in the teaching at length of the people, He sees on the bank of the lake two boats lying unoccupied, whose sailors are now occupied with the mending of their nets: they have taken nothing in the past night. He enters Peter's boat, desires him to let it down somewhat further into the water, and thus from the high prow of the boat teaches the people, who were standing closely packed on the shore. Then He has the boat pushed further into the lake, and gives orders to cast out the net. Peter has at first, from the bad luck of the night before, doubts of a successful haul; but, on the other hand, He has been so penetrated by the higher faith through the teaching of Christ which he had just heard, that he now at His word throws out the net. He then takes more than could have been expected for both ships, even with the most successful haul; and the first impression of this undeserved blessing on him is so overpowering, that he sinks at the

Lord's feet, as of one too holy for him: for, however the neighbourhood of the Holy One may bring blessings, the man oppressed with the burden of sins feels himself more bowed down than exalted by it; because he must fear that the same power which he has had experience of in unexpected blessing, another time, when he perhaps unwittingly sins against it, may just as unexpectedly crush him. But, rejoiced at this sincerity also of Peter, Christ raises him, comforting him the more, driving away the troubled fear into entire closeness to Himself; and now, raised by Christ to be fishers of men instead, the three follow Him, who seem generally in the reminiscences of the Gospel closest to Him, now more entirely forsaking everything earthly.

Many of the higher features of this narrative doubtless owe their origin to a generally more spiritual class reminiscences. But, however the story may have received this its form, based on a thousand earlier spiritual intuitions and perceptions, its ultimate teaching is but, how the lower faith is transfigured into the higher, and, this that is the consequence of all true following of Christ. Even for earthly good and bodily blessing, the active nearness of the true Spirit, and Christ's own, may be a blessing, and in its joy be received with double measure of joy: this is one blessed truth of the Gospel experience and history which recurs in other times, and some actual experience must originally have lain at its root: but he who experiences merely this blessing, to him there yet cleaves from it a lower fear which must first be transfigured into the higher, in order to arrive at the right commencement for right serving the Lord in and with all. Of others, whom the Saviour during this period took into his closest confidence, Levi, the son of Alphæus, is now only mentioned. He was a well-to-do collector of customs, and as such was in no good repute: yet the Saviour invited him to Himself, and he gladly gave up, to follow the call, all his previous earthly advantages. We know however nothing of his later fate: he afterwards certainly did not belong to the twelve. But the house of Alphæus appears later also, as one joined in close friendship with Christ: and the James out of this house, who subsequently appears among the twelve, was probably a younger brother of this Levi. Such was, in a general view, the position of Jesus at this time. As the commencement period of his most perfect and uninterrupted Messianic activity, in which the very first lasting foundations of his kingdom were to be laid, it must have been, in many respects, most laborious and difficult, full of the most endless efforts and exhausting labours; and this time lasted, as will appear below, about a full year. But of the characteristics of this time of laying the deepest foundation of the whole Messianic structure, we still know less than we might perhaps wish. For firstly this time also, although in it everything is now pressing on towards perfection, yet lies behind the time of the highest perfection of the Messianic activity; so that even the Gospel of St. Mark, to which alone we are indebted for a somewhat fuller and more distinct picture of this period, relates comparatively but little of it.

Secondly, just at the period when the older Gospel narrative began to enter more fully into the distinctive features, the Gospel of St. John, with its more lively recollection of these earlier times, ceases, evidently not without design; for St. John for the subsequent time,—for what at least concerned the Galilæan activity of Jesus,—looked on the older narratives as so complete on the subjects, that he found nothing of much importance to add. Still, so soon as we only carefully put together all that the Gospel of St. John has preserved to us of the period, we may sketch a tolerably satisfactory picture of it; if not giving all particular points exactly in their proper order, yet accurate in respect to the principal sides of the Saviour's activity in the course of its most fundamental and laborious effort.

CHAPTER XVII.

THE DAILY OCCUPATION.

OF the nature of his daily occupation at this time St. Mark's Gospel gives a sketch, in the description at length of all his manifold activity on one day and the time next following. It is the picture of his active work on the first day of his entering Capernahum as the permanent seat of his future life: this day however serves but as an example for all similar ones during this whole period, whenever not much broken into by special accidents. It was a Sabbath, He went early into the synagogue to teach; and his mode of teaching was so different from that of the scribes, and the matter of the doctrine itself so mightily overpowering, that there was general and natural wondering how the divine power, out of which it flowed, was poured into Him. But in the synagogue was also present a man tormented with an unclean spirit: and it seemed as though this spirit, the more powerfully the discourse was inspired by the divine Spirit, and the more deeply all others present were affected by it, could the less keep himself quiet and hide his true nature. At length, unable to contain himself longer before the Holy One, he broke forth in loud talk; and as though he felt himself one with all his kind, he bade Jesus cease: "they knew well that He was the Holy One of God, and that He was come to destroy them." But, on the contrary, Jesus bade him be silent and come out; nay, He pressed him so strongly that he, rending and crying aloud, gave much pain to the man, but at length came out and let him go. Thus was shewn that the new doctrine and power of Christ's quiet word does not even leave the unclean spirits at rest, till at length, so soon as they are excited, a stronger word of His express command drives them utterly out: and if the flight of evil spirits before Him caused astonishment, the world must have been yet more astonished that the power merely of the new doctrine is so great, and that all ultimately results from this alone. Well are we told that this very thing spread his fame everywhere, even in the whole neighbourhood of Galilee. On coming out of the synagogue, accompanied by the sons of Zebedee, He visits Peter's dwelling: he was then already married, and his mother-in-law, in whose house he lived with his brother Andrew, lay now sick of the fever, which they did not conceal from Him. But going in and taking her by the hand, He raised her up; and the fever left her so suddenly that she was actually able on that very day to prepare a meal, and be present at it as hostess. Then the evening came on: He betook Himself to his own house. But now they were bringing in the cool of the day—the Sabbath too being over—all the sick with their various bodily or mental diseases, and it was as though the whole city had assembled before his door. He healed many sick of each kind: but He sought to quiet beforehand the spirits of the possessed, that they might not break out into so painful wild a cry about Him as the dreaded Messiah, as they had done in the synagogue.

After a short night's rest, He arose very early when it was yet dawn, to go into a solitary place before the city. He was here praying, alone with God: but Peter and his friends soon went after Him, discovered Him, and told Him that already many were seeking Him in the city. But He bade them to visit with Him the smaller adjacent places, to work there also as He had for that end now left the city. So He journeyed with His redoubled activity to the remaining places of Galilee.

Thus wide in its extent and laborious was the Saviour's day's work at that time, as shewn us by St. Mark, who sets it before us the most clearly. We know, from the same Gospel also, the occasion of the somewhat violent interruption of this peaceful life, so calm in its self-collectedness, with all its zeal and all its powerful activity.

While the Saviour was staying somewhere in Galilee, a leper pressed in on Him into the house, quite against the law, which expressly shut such an one out of society. But the Saviour, touched with deep compassion, laid on the unhappy man, who in faith trusted Him entirely, his healing hand; immediately however, after healing him, commanded Him in the strictest terms to go forth in all haste from the house and from the whole country, to tell no one about his healing, but before all, announce himself to the priests at Jerusalem, according to law, as a healed man, and then quietly to return to his occupation. But the man could not, for his great joy at his recovery, do without telling aloud everywhere the history of it; so that Jesus, known everywhere in consequence, and expected beforehand in every town, could hardly enter one of them quietly, and preferred remaining outside the towns in lonely places. But even so they came to Him from all sides continually seeking help. He returned of course in time to Capernahum as his fixed abode.

CHAPTER XVIII.

The Journey of this Year to the Feast.

If however the position and effect of the Saviour was in this whole period as above described, it was the natural consequence that He preferred staying in Galilee as permanently as possible, to making the customary journeys to the Feasts. To make every one of these journeys three times a year, was for the dweller at a distance not absolutely necessary; there were admissible excuses for him, and indeed he might also perform all connected with his offerings by representatives. And the Saviour had, in truth, now something more important to do. Just at this point St. John's narrative comes in again with its more exact discrimination of times and circumstances. According to it, Jesus journeyed in this year once at least to the feast: for, that the narrative of such a journey (John v.) should be placed just at the commencement of this time, admits of no doubt. St. John, it is true, does not define here more exactly which of the three yearly feasts it was. For the substance of the narrative here to be related, a more exact definition was not much needed, and for this reason he might be contented with the briefer expression. If however we must mention the most probable conjecture about it, it was the great Feast of Tabernacles, to which the Saviour now journeyed to Jerusalem: at the Passover, as appears above, He had not been long in Galilee; and yet He wished now, for a time at least, to confine Himself as much as possible to Galilee: for this reason then we naturally think of the Feast of Tabernacles. To these considerations may be added the parallel case in the following year (as will be explained below), when also He journeyed to Jerusalem for this feast. And if this be the feast intended, the explanation is most simple of St. John long afterwards calling it a feast of the Jews: it was very far then from having for Christians the importance of the Passover, and might, at the late period of the composition of this Gospel, and by a man like St. John, be thus denoted briefly. But the subject of the discourse, too, which Jesus, according to this Gospel, then delivered in Jerusalem, quite suits this year: and it is principally for the sake of the great truths of the discourse that St. John relates the journey itself, and the more immediate occasion of the speaking of these exact words.

At a north-eastern gate of Jerusalem, named (probably from the many sheep here entering to be sacrificed) the "Sheep Gate," was a pool—Bethesda; whose water being not far from the Temple, might all the more be looked on as health-restoring, as it seemed in a mysterious manner to sink and rise: according to the common notion an angel in the air moved it at times, and the first sick man who then went in, might according to the same notion be healed. In the five halls built about it by public charity, there lay constantly a multitude of blind, lame, withered, and other sick; also a man who had been a cripple for thirty-eight years, who, arrived at length probably from a distance, had yet found no sympathetic hand to help him at such a moment of the water's rising, and prevent others pressing in. Jesus wished, as was to be expected from his whole present position, to avoid at this time all notice in Jerusalem; yet seized with sympathy for the poor man, He healed him without using that half superstitious means, bade him take up his bed with his own hand and go forth, and immediately, apparently intentionally, was lost again in the press close by. But, as it was now the sabbath, the Jews reproached the man with a breach of the law, which forbad changing one's abode on the sabbath, and desired he should name Him who had commanded it: he could not however find again his benefactor. Some days later Jesus met him in the Temple, and gave him now further admonitions to keep his recovered strength by stricter morals: the man now first named Jesus to his earlier complainants as He whose advice he had then followed. When called to account by them, He answered as He was wont in the cases, not rare, of such a complaint about sabbath-breaking. But as Messiah, He could, in the rising ardour of his discourse, point out that in such help, administered even on the sabbath, He was only following the example of his heavenly Father, who since the Creation does not cease working for man's help, not even on the sabbath. Even this admirable and quite logical and decided thesis for the final laying of doubt, by which Jesus must have only the more irritated the sneaking enmity of the prejudiced Jews, was now, according to St. John, the occasion of a very diffuse and precise discussion of the relation of Jesus as Messiah to God, which forms the true principal subject of this whole account. In this freer outpouring of deepest truths, the conception and colouring of the speech is due to this Apostle's tone of thought, which appears more unconstrained the harder it is to exhaustively represent these truths. There are four such truths, which, brought together here according to their inner sequence, exhaust all which belongs to the subject. It is shewn here, first, how certain is the essential unity of will and similarity of working of God and Messiah, which now in its highest working subsists for the salvation of man; a salvation which extends from the moment of the immediate present to the last limits of all development of human history, and which the more miraculous and incredible it is, will only the more certainly arrive. But on account of this complete highest unity of will and of working of the Messiah and of God for man's eternal salvation, the last and only ultimately decisive testimony for the truth of the Messiah must be his own divine mission, appearance, and activity; although the Holy Scriptures of the Jews themselves, which are by them so infinitely honoured, when rightly searched out and known in their deepest sense and purpose, give testimony for Him. But though the nature of the exposition of these four fundamental truths here given is peculiarly St. John's, they certainly lay in the Saviour's mind, and were by Him, in words and actions, for the man of intelligence and faith everywhere literally taught. And at no time taught by Him more plainly and definitely than, as opportunity offered, at this very time, when He, after the Baptist's removal, had fully revealed Himself as the Messiah, and when He had to discuss with calm grasp even the highest relations, the solution of which now pressed.

CHAPTER XIX.

The Opposition and Enmity of the World.

We saw how strictly Jesus at this time, everywhere, as well in the city of his more permanent residence as in the towns where He made a shorter stay, and in Jerusalem not less than in Galilee, avoided attracting notice, and how firmly He adhered to the wise limitation which He had prescribed to Himself. He did not wish to check the circulation and publication of the truths which He proclaimed: neither would He reject the Messianic acknowledgment of his working, when it met Him freely without his cooperation from its own inspiration and the genuine beginnings of a faithful recognition. But when He worked his miraculous cures, He did all He could to avoid notice and calling forth the public excitement, which singular, unwonted, and at the same time so beneficial actions naturally occasion: and thus He worked cures only when his inmost compassion was too strongly stirred, and sought most to withdraw Himself and his mission from the world, when He might probably suppose that it would be forced into the world unnecessarily and injuriously.

For He had to fear above everything, any too early and too injurious disturbance of his great work, and He knew for certain how easily such an arbitrary disturbance of it might proceed from the rulers of the time. And in such a determination He persisted, as will appear below, even during the following first development of his work as a whole. But yet no wise foresight and self-constraint sufficed to prevent the tidings of his deeds being carried ever more widely, and the general notice of Him becoming ever more excited: his whole mode of acting too was so entirely different from the customary; and in his discourses and thoughts likewise, which He could least hold in, there was matter enough to wound the prejudices of the time, and call forth ever more decidedly the opposition of the world. The attention of the highest authorities in the country was not, it is true, at this time so turned on Him as to cause Him apprehension from them; but the dominant tendencies and schools of his time came into collision soon enough, in the most varied ways, with his working and his nature; and it was just these who, through his mere existence and public working, must feel most deeply threatened and most unexpectedly attacked. We saw above some cases, in which He sought in vain to check greater attention to his works and his words: but a very lifelike and historically remarkably instructive picture of a multitude of such cases, where his deeds and actions excited the embittered observation, and soon the censure and the envy, nay the evil suspicions, of the ruling tendencies, is sketched by St. Mark's Gospel in a continued series of the most speaking characteristics.

When He some time after returned from the tour above mentioned to his home at Capernahum, and the news had hardly spread, immediately such a crowd assembled, that the open space before his door did not suffice to hold them. While He was now fully occupied instructing the throng from the window of his house, there was brought a man so completely crippled, that he had to be carried by four men on a light bed; and as it was impossible to get at the door with the bed through the throng, they carried him up by a staircase lying at the back of the house to the flat roof, no doubt, according to their way of building, provided with an upper storey; they took off the tiles at a part behind, and so let down the sick man into the roomy chamber where Jesus was discoursing from the window to the people. This desire, in spite of all difficulties, to approach the healing Hand of the Saviour, certainly proceeded chiefly from the cripple himself: Jesus then was, at sight of the strong belief of the sick man as well as of his benevolent bearers, taken with compassion, and began the healing at once, by offering to the sick man the higher trust in divine help and the comfort of absolution, to impart which lay entirely in his prerogative. But in the same room were sitting not far off some scribes, curious, and full of inward suspicion, listening to all that He said: these did not express themselves aloud on the forgiveness of sins, which the Saviour here again was assuming to Himself, but He knew exactly what was passing within them. Like true scribes of the time, they doubtless thought (if we would enter somewhat more closely into their line of thought) the sick man should first bring the offerings prescribed in the Old Testament, if he felt himself oppressed by the consciousness of his earthly unworthiness or sin, in order then to receive in God's name from no one but the regular priest the forgiveness of sins; thus, forgiveness of sins by another appeared to them nothing less than an attack on the divine prerogative, and, since the name of God was brought in, blasphemy against God Himself. To leave them in this error as to his authority was not Christ's part, and, as usual, He at once overthrows the error most directly, by urging against it not only its opposite, but also the higher and final truth, and thus leads the question through a bold but true advance to its best end: so now asking them at once openly, which then is easier, to announce the forgiveness of sins to a sick man, or actually to help him as well? He at once heals the sick man, and bids him straightway take up his bed himself, and go forth with sound limbs. For all relieving and strengthening of the spirit, through the elevating assurance of new divine grace and forgiveness of sins, can and ought only to prepare the man to be not unworthy of healing, and not to fail of it, when it now is waiting to come, and is perhaps already near: but this itself is something higher, and only even to powerfully stimulate and further its coming, is something far higher than the mere expression of forgiveness of sins: this power of healing is, when it reveals and approves itself, a proof of the inward power of the spirit, which passes immediately into the divine itself and cooperates with it. Through the most practical proof possible were thus then refuted these doctors, dried up in their law-books; and all the people as well, standing round, were, as this reminiscence concludes, astonished at the sight of this Messianic power, and praised God "who had given such new power to men:" for it is quite a part of the first Christian feeling, as something almost of course, that the new higher powers of the Spirit brought by Christ into the world, and by Him first revealed, survive also in his people, and thus bring forth fruit a thousand fold.

If it was now the greatness of the action at which the Scribes were offended, and yet could do nothing, there were on other occasions customs of His which appeared to them too low and unworthy, on which they fastened their astonishment and censure.

When He, on escaping again to the shore of the lake, found sitting at the toll-house the Levi mentioned above, and he at the Saviour's call willingly followed Him, and, perhaps on the evening of the first day of his accompanying Him, prepared for Him in his house a feast, at which, besides his earlier disciples, many publicans and others accounted sinners took part, partly as invited by the host, and partly as lately having joined his company more closely; the Scribes and Pharisees could not contain their astonishment at his eating "with publicans and sinners," and censured this behaviour publicly in presence of their own disciples. But this was not the place for going into the question of the greater or less guilt of the publicans and of other men: He therefore replied to their reproach only by a general reference to the nature of his Messianic mission.

On the other hand, He was blamed another time for not keeping fasts, as was customary in the schools of John's disciples and of the Pharisees: it might then be the very time after the Feast of Purim and before the Passover, when fasting, on account of the time of year, might readily seem peculiarly appropriate, and thus have been introduced by the stricter schools. This censure might have been intended, as well as taken up, more earnestly, as it was known that He Himself had originally passed through the baptism, and so also in a certain sense through the discipline of the Baptist; and some also of his disciples had passed through the school of the Baptist. Add too, that the whole period tended towards this more gloomy strictness, and the very school of the Baptist was then (see above) in such tokens of earnestness, of yet more earnest and fresher zeal than the Pharisaic, so that the latter could at this time be moved to new zeal in it. But not only was it in general accordance with Christ's spirit to leave such exercises and tokens of earnest piety to the free impulse of the spirit, but He reminded them now with yet greater truth of the exceptional case of the time, in which his disciples, gathered round their Lord and Messiah, could with more reason turn, as if at a wedding-day, to the brighter side of life; the more surely that one day after his departure they must give way to gloomy mourning.

But as concerned in particular the views of John's disciples, He specified them in striking figures as half views and self-contradictory, as in consistency they must actually and wholly desire the New, and so the Messianic with its bright glory, cheerfulness, and joy, and yet would hold fast the Old with its more gloomy constraint, and thus join together elements incompatible and necessarily repugnant to each other.

With the disciples of John He came, on this almost solitary occasion, into a somewhat closer contact: otherwise He plainly took care to keep from strife these two shoots, still so weak, of the same noble stem, and suffered, even after the Baptist's imprisonment, the working of his disciples along with his own: only rarely did the followers of these two schools (see above) come into controversy. But the remaining schools of the time reproached Him, as well in his life as in his works, with downright offences of all sorts against the daily practice of the established laws. On one sabbath, perhaps fourteen days after Easter, when some of the first crops (barley especially) might be standing ripe, his disciples, in walking through them, plucked some ears for immediate eating. The Law allowed this to a hungry man (die Alterthümer, s. 213), but the Pharisees reproached Him for this as a breach against that most holy special law, which commanded to take nothing required for eating on the sabbath, but to have everything prepared for it beforehand. He refuted them then as well from examples out of history, as from the thing itself. The sabbath is for man, not man for the sabbath: man was not made merely to serve the sabbath as a supreme moral law, in no single case to be broken, as he must serve God; He told them too what want of charity it shewed to condemn innocent men; that Messiah as such is empowered to remove even the rigidity of the existing law when it would overthrow the highest divine duties of compassion and love. When one now examines all reproaches made against Him by the world, and which seem now to have taken such fixed and definite form that nothing strictly new was added in the time yet remaining of his public activity, there were essentially only two subjects at which the existing spiritual power could take offence, according to the laws of the true religion as then understood and applied. For that his aims were Messianic, and that He spoke of the fulfilment of the kingdom of God, nay, even (as was by degrees commonly known) did not wholly reject fealty to the Messiah when it freely met Him, all this could not seriously be objected against Him, for the hope of the Messiah belonged to the treasure of all Israel's consecrated hopes; and besides, every one saw He would set up no common kingdom. If the whole undertaking of his public work, as He carried it out, had been completely revolutionary in this community of the true religion which might not renounce the spiritual power, *then* assuredly it would not have been so long tolerated. It was then only firstly the forgiveness of sins at which (see above, in this chapter) legal offence could be taken. But where the Law expressly enjoined certain offerings for one to be cleansed (as for example for a leper), Jesus in the case of one healed by Him always urged the fulfilment of the legal duty. Again, spiritual assurance and consolation might be given to each other by all members of the true religion according to its fundamental laws: and the wholly new peculiar way in which Jesus offered it was consistent with his Messianic beginning, which no one could check. Here too then, in spite of all ill-will, no proper occasion could be found for legal punishment.

It was, in the second place, especially the laws on the sabbath, in their then minute development, against which the scribes learnt to watch for slips on his part. And we must allow that this was the point most open to attack. The sabbath had become, since the founding of the community of the true religion, their most peculiar and highest sacrament, afterwards in these late times, in accordance with their whole spirit, had been most painfully elaborated, and was regarded as the proper token of a true Jew, to be shewn forth in every part of the world. But just because in this law, as it was then treated, the whole perverted elaboration of the true religion culminated as it were in one point, Christ might here least of all follow the prejudices and dangerous traditions of the schoolmen: and thus on this very subject a number of disputes arose, which, springing doubtless from other much weightier causes, became ever more decided, and of which the whole history of His public working is full.

St. Mark relates a similar event, which had worse consequences, and for the first time shewed him quite plainly what fearful rage had already gathered against Him among his enemies in Galilee. Once, when He returned to Capernahum from one of his Galilæan tours and had gone into the synagogue on the sabbath, there appeared before Him, begging help, a man with a badly twisted and withered hand: but He remarked how the Pharisees, already watching Him, were noticing whether He, in spite of their repeated admonitions, would on that day again desecrate the sabbath by healing, that is, in their view, by a work. So He the more made the petitioner come quite openly before their eyes, asked them whether to do good and save, or the contrary, is forbidden on the sabbath, was strongly indignant against them, as they, in their embitterment and hardness of heart which had long grown in secret against Him, would never answer his natural questions, and threatened Him with public accusation before the council of the synagogue if He still persisted in healing; He then at once healed the man's hand, seized with compassion for him, with deep sorrow for them. But the Pharisees now departed at once with open hostility, and it was soon found that they, with their enemies the Herodians, were devising a plan to destroy Him. The Pharisees, proud of their moral purity and observance of the Law, from whose midst had proceeded the Zealots abhorring every human kingdom (oben Judas der Gaulonäer), who were always in danger of merging into them again, now united with those who before were their direct opponents, with the morally lax Herodians, who were well disposed to the king and flattered the house of Herod; and this merely because these were in Galilee then powerful enough to destroy Him, whose nature must seem to them every week more inexplicable and alarming.

This first outbreak of plain mortal enmity followed perhaps late in the summer of this year: probably this was now a principal purpose of his visit to Jerusalem to the Feast of Tabernacles (above spoken of), that during it the irritated fury of his Galilæan enemies might somewhat abate. But in Jerusalem, also, He was, in spite of all reserve, entangled in the very similar dispute on sabbath-breaking described in the last chapter: and this also concluded with the same embittering of the men of the Law, so that these, here too, formed plans for destroying Him. In both halves of the Jewish country, then, He was openly threatened with the danger of destruction in the world, in spite of all wise foresight and reserve: and as He might be charged, unlike John the Baptist, with blasphemy against the Highest, a violent end was easy to be foreseen by Himself. Probably at Jerusalem there followed thus early the suspension over Him of the lesser excommunication, or thrusting out of the synagogue, under the pretence that He by breaking the sabbath had made Himself unworthy to teach or appear in the synagogue. It was the mildest penalty which they thought in Jerusalem they could now apply against Him; and under this there was concealed for the present the deadly hatred which gathered against him in Jerusalem. That the Pharisees, in fact, somewhat about this time carried such a measure, and first indeed in Jerusalem, St. John's Gospel intimates very clearly; and the proceeding is quite in accordance with the further unravelling of the now tangled skein of this whole history.

The measure doubtless appeared to its originators tolerably mild. The lesser excommunication was only for a single synagogue, as we see that Jesus some time after this appeared in the Galilean synagogues: it could, besides, after some time be again removed. Still it was quite hard enough for Jesus, such as they deemed Him, because they knew how much He had hitherto discoursed and worked in the synagogues, and how much He liked this public activity. Add too, that the example once given by the synagogue of the capital might likely be imitated by the others.

CHAPTER XX.

THE NEW ATTITUDE OF THE MESSIAH TOWARDS THE WORLD.

It was however, in fact, not his own death which Christ feared or in any way tried to avoid; nor did his spirit now for the first time recognise and dread its necessity: for, from the first commencement of his Messianic working He must have made Himself familiar with this thought. The only thing which He had now every reason to fear, was the premature interruption and destruction of his work in the world: for this had now been begun right earnestly, but was yet far from completion, too far at least for Him to remove from it as yet his earthly hand. But one thing had been unmistakeably taught by the course of the last year: that the world, as it then was, would not suffer either Him or much more his work, nay, was resolved to crush it in the bud. Hence, if He would not suffer this his work to be overthrown by it, when it was yet hardly grounded, He must put it now in quite a different attitude towards the world, in order to ground it unshakeably in the world, in spite of his too probable violent death. And the right means thereto could not be doubted.

His work was the founding and active commencement of the perfect kingdom of God, by the forming a community to close in round Him as its founder and visible head.

This community had to be made from its commencement quite different from that of the existing true religion: for that this, as it then was, was past mending, and therefore, whether earlier or later, was devoted to destruction, He had been taught as plainly as possible by the experience of the past year: and this stood, if before none other, yet before his spirit, fixed as a divine necessity. And yet it was, as experience had likewise sufficiently taught, properly only the heads of the existing Church of the true God, or rather, to express it more precisely, only that tendency became dominant in it, which could not endure the undisturbed beginning, much less the happy progress of his work; and which, because it had a dim consciousness of having been by Him wounded to death, began seriously to think of his ruin.

But, in truth, this tendency in it, now wholly dominant, had not thus by accident or temporarily arrived at this absolute rule: it lay of old wrapped up in the incompleteness of the whole ancient Church; but had at length, after so many other changes in this the Primitive Church, as one of those tendencies most deeply wrapped up in it, arrived at its most complete form and attained absolute rule; and now, as the most dangerous impulsive power concealed in it, had become so despotic and irresistible, that its maintenance was the condition of that of the whole existing Church, and its fall threatened to drag down with it the Church of all true religion. If then it was only one particular tendency in the existing Church of the true God, though that arrived at absolute power, which was now threatened with death by Christ's work, and not, properly speaking, that Church itself with its fulness of eternal truths and strength, now, it is true, clouded over and obscured, without which the Messiah could never have appeared and worked: it followed that this his own new Church, when He had to establish it for the living and enduring instruments of this kingdom, must be founded, not without the ancient Church, but in and out of its midst. Only in it were the living stones already furnished, which might form the firm corner-stones and pillars of this new structure; nay, He had already, unobserved, formed them for Himself on this old holy ground, and could now at the right time choose them as they best fitted. When once this as a providential necessity was present to his spirit, the consequence must be that his whole work must take up a new position and tendency. He must now draw about Him a small and very close, but yet large enough circle of disciples; for within this and for this, that work, which was the Idea of his whole life and working, was now to be carried on by Him with, if possible, yet intenser ardour and power. If the world was yet too dark, and the ancient Church of the true God too weak as well, to receive his Spirit immediately into them, He must for that reason work with more simplicity and power, to plant it in full life, and naturalized in the circle of a new Church of the same true God, to be drawn closely around

Him; that hereafter at the right time it might burst forth from the narrow limits in which it must first find refuge, in order to find a firm hold on the earth, and irresistibly spread over the universe.

And hence now, for the first time, the whole activity of Christ developes itself to its full stature and majesty: when thus openly threatened by the world, and in constant view of this declared open opposition, with all the more certainty and clearness does the Imperishable stablish itself, invincible by the whole world; and amid the ever-growing straitening from without and limitation from within, it becomes the most ardent and warm, but also the most mighty and victorious which the world has ever seen. It was, so to speak, by accident that Jesus now took just twelve of his disciples into his constant closer confidence, and formed them to be the foundation of the New Church: He could not have chosen a much smaller number, for in every community, however small it be at first, there must be a certain manifoldness in its impulses and actions, if it is to endure and grow. But always with Him the Spirit's free action and providential necessity are in the most wonderful unison, the one always harmonising with the other; and so was it here.

Among these twelve—a number of old holy in Israel for all peoples and communities, relations and employments, (as is sufficiently shewn in the earlier volumes of the Author's History), a number which naturally recalled the early beginnings and the eternal importance of Israel— there had thus, in the midst of the ancient Church, been laid the smallest and yet the sufficient and firmest ground of a new Church, in which the old itself, though it should fall, could yet rise again with new strength and youth, as it were with the indestructible might of a second immortal life.

CHAPTER XXI.

THE FOUNDING OF THE CHRISTIAN CHURCH.

As shewn above, it might have been late autumn when Jesus resolved to take up this new position. He was then just come back from the feast days in Jerusalem, and now resorted again, first with his older disciples, to the lake country of Galilee. But there was already accompanying Him a constantly increasing crowd, even out of Judah and Jerusalem whence He had come, and out of Idumæa in the furthest south, as well as from the neighbouring Phœnicia in the extreme north-west, and from the regions beyond Jordan. Here He continued his earlier daily work, as it was above described; constantly so wonderfully besieged and thronged, that He commissioned his four first disciples to keep a small vessel ready on the lake, that He, at least for some moments, might remain more solitary and independent. It was assuredly chiefly sympathy with the crowd, which moved Him, after his return, first to give Himself again wholly up to his earlier days' work of ministering to the sufferers of all kinds who waited for Him.

But He seized the first moment suitable to carry out

L

what He had discerned to be his now higher providential work. Even in earlier times, when He would have a somewhat longer time for Himself, He used to retire to a range of hills, which stretched to the west from the lake of Galilee, and which would not be too far from Capernahum. To this quieter solitude He resorted again, but invited this time those twelve to accompany Him, who henceforth were to form around Him the exclusive circle of a community. He doubtless knew these on the whole, at that time, more intimately; and chose, from a much larger circle of those who would have been just as ready to follow Him in all his wishes, these only because they seemed to Him the best adapted for the higher end which He now saw before Him.

The acquaintance and the motives which guided the Saviour in the selection of disciples have already been discussed under many aspects. Many met Him voluntarily, many He encouraged by his own call; no one was kept by Him, whom his own freest choice did not attach to Him. As He became continually better known and more renowned, his cause seemed, at least in some obscure future, to promise imagined benefits of all kinds: many constantly streamed to Him with a request for closer participation in his work; but no one discerned at once so truly the deeper motive of the would-be follower, nor so strictly with the most suitable reply rejected unsuitable requests and their perverted views. The oldest Gospel narrative puts together three examples of this sort, which may serve for all. To a learned man who offered to follow Him everywhere, He shewed the great dangers of following the man who on earth had not where to lay his head; and thus indeed extinguished for ever the too quickly kindled fire of the learned man, who was probably used to worldly honour and comfort.

To another, whose zeal was plainly more earnest, but who asked for leave to first bury his father who had just died, He replied, the dead had their own province, and kind, and care; he might let the dead bury their own dead, but himself at once, without further worldly care and encumbrance, as well as without putting off and delay, be active for the kingdom of God. Here is no death, and no vain care for the dead; here all is living, and that life must be communicated; and thus He certainly excited this good man, who had yet only some smaller scruples to overcome, to the bold venture, the more resolutely to live wholly to proclaim the truth and work for it alone. To a third, who, when asked by Him if he would follow Him, replied, requesting that he might be allowed first to say good-bye to those he had at home, He rejoined that no one who, as it were, lays his hand to the plough and yet looks backward, who thus is a half man at willing and working, is fit for God's kingdom: through this solemn reprimand He was doubtless quit of a follower who would have joined Him, yet not with all his heart.

Thus grew and thus melted away the number of his more independent followers. And if an old tradition fixes at seventy the number of those who adhered to Him more truly, and, though constantly remaining loosely bound to Him, would gladly have followed Him everywhere, the calculation may be approximately correct. But the formation of the number of such disciples, and its somewhat more particular introduction into the Gospel narrative, belongs to a rather later period of this department of narrative and literature. It is quite otherwise with the twelve, whose singularly high importance, as well in the older Gospels as in St. John, and elsewhere in the early Christian literature is so prominent, and first in St. Luke, is thrown somewhat in the background behind those named by him the seventy. These twelve were chosen first from out the wide circle of disciples, and must have been taken more closely than any one else into Jesus' closest intimacy and confidence. To them He would impart his whole spirit and let it overflow into them in most absolute fulness, so far as a living teacher and leader can do this towards his nearest disciples and friends. All the deep insight and peaceful serenity, but also all the sublimity, of the indescribable flight of his spirit should become theirs; all the inexhaustible activity of his saving love should be their sweet life's solace. And because all this can only be reached through discipline and self-trial, He would, as soon as possible, Himself send them out as companions in his own work, that they might learn to advance God's kingdom, as well by preaching and teaching as by the power of active healing and deliverance, and might accustom themselves also even without his immediate presence so to live and to work as if He were continually among them: nay, more, this their mission for working by themselves for God's kingdom must have been in his mind a principal cause of their appointment, so that He doubtless Himself distinguished them from the other disciples by the name Apostles. But, in so far as they before all and in all, whether gathered round Him, or on his commissions far from Him, wherever they might be active seemed to form a closer circle round Him as their teacher and guide, a circle drawn close not only by love to Him and his work but also by fidelity and faith, He formed in them the foundation of a new community, which, small and weak as it was at first, might yet become the irreversible beginning of an eternal Church of the perfected true religion, to embrace the whole world.

The goodness, capacity for instruction, and endurance of the several members of the twelve, was hence in great measure the first point: and the whole of the following history shews how little Christ was mistaken in their selection. He had to select them from the circle of his existing disciples, and this was already provided for Him. He evidently chose in preference his first disciples, whom He had the longest trusted more closely, in so far as they seemed to Him suited for their new difficult calling; and in addition to them, from those who had followed Him somewhat more recently, such as He had noticed as the most willing and able. He looked in this not to earlier position, nor to means and other externals; not even to marriage or celibacy, for Peter had before been married; probably also one or two more, certainly not all. That they were taken less from the learned class, resulted from the then quite perverted tone and position of that class. As the Messiah and his work could least proceed from the then dominant schools, officials, and authorities, only from the deepest soil of the whole ancient Church, which alone had remained freer from the errors of the time and more receptive of the eternal truths and hopes of Israel; so it was in this quarry that He found the first fitting stones and pillars for his new Church. Several of the twelve, as shewn above, had been in the school of the Baptist; another came out of the school of the Zealots, as his second name Kananäos probably shews; and, according to the existing primal constitution of Israel, all its members indifferently had free access to all the deepest truths and the highest aims of the new Church. Of the power and privileges of the old priestly stock, of long time only some remains of little importance for the higher spiritual life had been preserved: the old tribe of Levi itself, never too sharply severed from the rest of the people, had long been almost merged in the rest of the people: yet there were even from the race of the priests (Chap. VII.) some among the twelve. So too the twelve were on the whole without much property, yet some of them inherited (as *e. g.* the sons of Zebedee) comfortable means, and the toll-collector, Matthew, had been as such certainly not a poor man.

Every one from that circle became a man whose name among men has never been lost, and whose memory in after times spread ever more widely in the great world. Yet among them also great differences soon shewed themselves, according as either Christ Himself more distinguished individuals among them, either as being his oldest friends, or also, as the result shewed better, the measure of their activity and fidelity. Thus was formed pretty early, in the age which we have accustomed ourselves to call from them the Apostolic, a definite circle, in which men loved to number the twelve after their names, and in which they loved also to add the second names by which some were wont to be denoted, according to distinguishing names given by Christ Himself. This numbering of the twelve in order remained fixed in its essential features; only smaller differences were allowed in it. At the head were named constantly the two pairs of brothers who were the first disciples, and had besides remained very close friends of Christ. But among these again, Simon, surnamed Cephas or Peter, was put first: by age, calm firmness and decision, by readiness too in word and spirit, distinguished not only among men but also by a peculiar trust of Christ Himself in him, he soon ranked as *primus inter pares*, and continued to preserve this willing deference from his companions in the sequel also. Immediately in connection with him was often named his younger brother Andrew, who also remained constantly in more close union with Jesus and had freer access to Him. Yet it was preferred to insert between the names of these two brothers the other two brothers, the sons of Zebedee, of whom John the younger especially was accounted the Lord's favourite, while he himself gave constantly the precedence to his brother, and both together were regarded as very close friends of the Lord. Both being unmarried, but accompanied by their equally zealous mother (on whom see Chap. VII.), were the most fiery amongst these four; but Christ once stilled their too violent zeal by addressing them with the name, not afterwards to be soon forgotten, of "sons of thunder," instead of naming them after their father who was already dead, "sons of Zebedee": probably it was on that occasion, of which we are informed by the earliest Gospel narrative, when they wished in a village of the Samaritans to bring down fire from heaven on its inhospitable inhabitants. He might then at the moment with admirable truth address them, "ye sons of thunder, know ye not of what spirit ye are?" not, that is, of such a thunder spirit as you are constantly shewing, but of quite another, which I have taught you and which you should better understand. The eight remaining it was early learnt to divide into groups, four in each: and the same Apostle was constantly put at the head of each of these two groups, while the places of the rest in their groups was somewhat uncertain. The four which were constantly placed together after the first group, apparently ranged themselves, in goodwill and other excellence, next to the first four. Philip, who is constantly placed at their head, was likewise among the earliest disciples (Chap. XII.), and is mentioned elsewhere, also as distinguished, although as somewhat slow in his conceptions. Bartholomew, who is always named in the second place, and is the Nathaniel described at greater length Chap. XII., was added as the first born of the disciples on Galilæan ground. Matthew, who here occupies the third place, is only somewhat better known to us through the Gospel named after him: he was according to this a publican, and his calling is told so similarly to that of Levi son of Alphæus (Chap. XVII.), that his name was actually inserted in the Gospel named after him in place of the corresponding account of Levi; doubtless because the last composer of this Gospel was well instructed as to his position, and thought it worth to be principally attributed to him, somewhat better while to make the readers also of that Gospel, which is acquainted with his circumstances. The man of honour, but somewhat hard to convince of higher things,— Thomas, or as his name was translated into Greek Didymos, who in the old lists closes the group of these four, but after repeated revision of the whole list of the Twelve goes up to the third, nay, even the second place, —was from many evidences one of the oldest disciples.

We know, comparatively, least of the four of the last group, amongst whom Judah, Simon's son, commonly called from his birthplace "the man of Karioth," as the subsequent traitor, occupies the last place. Where womanly forethought and help were wanted, several women were glad to render them; some, relatives of the members of the company, some, more independently connected with them, but all giving their services quite freely, simply as led by the higher love to the one common object: among them some were plainly better off, who joyfully offered their whole worldly substance to the higher cause of Christ. But neither the brethren of Jesus nor his mother formed part, even of a less intimate band of the community, though they also did not

CHAPTER XXII.

The Higher Teaching on the Kingdom of God and His Earthly Community.

When we now survey all which was done by Christ, in the course of perhaps a year and a-half, towards his present great object, as it is told us by the most exact accounts we can command, we must admire not only *what* He did, but also *how*, and the gradual way of his doing it. We are, it is true, now little able to distinguish in detail the many discourses and teachings, as well as the rich abundance of deeds and adventures found side by side with them, so as to describe each in its exact order of time; although we shall see that even here we are not wanting in all data for knowing as a whole the course in time of this manifold activity of Christ in its intensity. But it may safely be assumed that the behaviour of Jesus to the twelve, as well as his deeds and experience, in this period, sketched roughly and as a whole, developed itself in its connection as St. Mark first attempted to describe it. So soon as Jesus saw Himself surrounded by the twelve, his first business must be to communicate to them in respect of both the inner and the outer side of God's kingdom, that more definite and higher instruction which alone was capable of accustoming them gradually to work aright for God's kingdom. It was necessary that there should be a time in which this higher teaching in such smaller circle should become his most important daily work; and He, in the midst of his other working, with most pleasure and most necessity, took every opportunity for this: this was however the first time—this time of his greater intimacy with the twelve—in which He could venture to let them also take a more independent share in his life-work. More express instruction on the nature and the duties of the Church of the perfected religion, was thus, now again, the first and most necessary point. This Church He was fully resolved to found as soon as He chose the twelve, and it was already existent so soon as they followed Him as their Lord and King leading them to God: only in such a community could the richest seed for the Kingdom of God grow up and promise fruit. What the perfected true religion is in itself, and especially in its relation to that then taught in Israel, and which pleaded in its support some passages from Holy Scripture, and what it demands; and secondly, what virtues are the right means of maintaining the high spiritual life demanded by it,—these must be the two great subjects of this instruction, as well as the way of applying these to such disciples as had advanced above the lower stages of knowledge, and were resolved themselves to work with the Messiah Himself more immediately for God's kingdom. When Jesus accordingly took with

Him the twelve whom He had chosen up the "Mount" with Him, whither He had long preferred to resort alone, it is quite probable that He here also immediately gave Himself to the instruction of the new community on such fundamental truths, and continued some time so doing. The "Sermon on the Mount" has accordingly its true historical meaning, to which is due the peculiar importance given it in the Gospel narrative; it contains although with something of artificial animation and structure, yet certainly an abundance of such truths as sounded then for the first time, and could not afterwards be heard again. It treats, strictly speaking, of the double subject only, spoken of above, but is introduced like a true address of welcome, and concludes with a short pregnant glance into the future with its temptation and trial. St. Mark had given it at this place, as we have the strongest reason for believing, though perhaps, as usual, more briefly; but unfortunately at this very place in his Gospel the great hiatus has been left by the last editor which we now cannot restore (chap. iii. v. 19). If however it stood originally quite at the beginning of St. Matthew's collection of discourses ("Sprachsammlung") we can the more easily understand how the last composer of the present first Gospel could give it a place so prominent, that it appears the first express saying of all which Jesus uttered; which can only be explained by the fact of people having gradually accustomed themselves to look on the whole period with the choice of the twelve, in which certainly Christ's activity culminated as almost the whole of his active life. Just as (Chap. X.) the memory of the first of the three periods of the entire public activity is almost totally lost in the Gospel of St. Mark, and by St. John first was again more clearly separated; so too the second of these stages in Christ's history (Chap. III.) began to be obscured and mixed up with the third as the principal period: this is very noticeable in the present first Gospel, whilst St. Luke has escaped much better from this mixing up of facts.

This explains the fact of this discourse, which as delivered, at least in some of its principal sayings, can only be intended for the closer circle of disciples, or (to speak more precisely) for those only already ranking as members of the new community, appearing in the present Gospel of St. Matthew (Matt. vii. 28) and similarly in St. Luke, as one heard by the whole multitude; so that, in short, it was quite in keeping when St. Luke describes it as delivered after Jesus had descended from the Mount, "upon a plain," when many hundreds might easily hear it. When once the community of the perfect religion is in existence, God's kingdom is already constantly preparing itself within it with much greater power than when his King (Messiah) first walked quite alone on this earth, without having around Him any fixed close band of adherents and companions. If the Saviour had, immediately on the first commencement of his public working, to proclaim at once the speedy coming, nay the actual commencement, of God's kingdom upon earth; now that a more definite way was opened for sharing in it, and a more intimate experience of it was possible, He could discourse on it with a zeal quite new, and declare its nature. And He had to speak on it continually to the multitude as well; for He must at the commencement speak to them of the same subject—it was, in fine, the one great subject on which He had constantly to speak: He could then, when in the already existing community of the perfect religion a firmer commencement had been made for advancing it on earth, speak of it with more exalted plainness, joy, and hope. But God's kingdom was with Him, even after the true and enduring beginning had been made, only one continually in formation though tending to its completion; never occupying the whole Present, because before all spiritual and heavenly. Thus Futurity and the ideal engrossed his spirit, in its striving to express in thought and speech more accurately what only the spirit's eye can behold, but which it must seize with as much certainty as though it were present to the eye of sense. But where this domain of the inner sense predominates, there the spirit, deeply drawing it in and with beautiful clearness and easy abundance applying it, transforms its several intuitions into the most admirable images and pictures of actual life; and just so did Jesus love to represent his intuitions on the toilsome beginning, often disappointing, yet not to be entered on in a murmuring spirit, the after all joyful progress and the inestimable value of the Kingdom of God, representing it to the multitude in parables just as true as attractive. We cannot say that the Saviour composed these parables merely for the sake of the multitude; rather, many of the truest intuitions, can be no otherwise expressed so shortly and truly: but He was fond of speaking to the multitude on such subjects in rich abundance and attractive graciousness, if perchance many a one might be attracted by the parable to think deeper for himself on the hidden meaning. But that this hidden meaning was to be revealed to the disciples, whether they themselves asked for it or not, need not be said: with them it was all-important that their conception of the truths themselves should be sound and correct on the basis of which alone such intuitions and images can be raised, and none of them was to be left without an independent insight into these simple truths. The beauty and completeness of many simple parables which Jesus had uttered, doubtless led on and attracted the disciples later, as they recalled them, to exhaust more completely their sacred meanings, and explain them in Christ's own sense: we still see this from those preserved in the Gospels. For a string of such parables—seven in number, of some length, which the Saviour once, speaking from a vessel in the lake of Galilee, had delivered to the people in St. Matthew's "Sprachsammlung"—has been admitted as a counterpart of the Sermon on the Mount: but although St. Mark, and still more the last composer of St. Matthew's Gospel, drew primarily from the same source, yet the parables and their meanings are given in the two with considerable differences. Between the flow of such lessons on the building up of the Kingdom of God in the community, and the actual first founding of it, an interval of some length must however have elapsed. For could discourse on it with a zeal quite new, and declare its nature. And He had to speak on it continually to the multitude as well; for He must at the commencement speak to them of the same subject—it was, in fine, the one great subject on which He had constantly to speak: He could then, when in the already existing community of the perfect religion a firmer commencement had been made for advancing it on earth, speak of it with more exalted plainness, joy, and hope. But God's kingdom was with Him, even after the true and enduring beginning had been made, only one continually in formation though tending to its completion; never occupying the whole Present, because before all spiritual and heavenly. Thus Futurity and the ideal engrossed his spirit, in its striving to express in thought and speech more accurately what only the spirit's eye can behold, but which it must seize with as much certainty as though it were present to the eye of sense. But where this domain of the inner sense predominates, there the spirit, deeply drawing it in and with beautiful clearness and easy abundance applying it, transforms its several intuitions into the most admirable images and pictures of actual life; and just so did Jesus love to represent his intuitions on the toilsome beginning, often disappointing, yet not to be entered on in a murmuring spirit, the after all joyful progress and the inestimable value of the Kingdom of God, representing it to the multitude in parables just as true as attractive. We cannot say that the Saviour composed these parables merely for the sake of the multitude; rather, many of the truest intuitions, can be no otherwise expressed so shortly and truly: but He was fond of speaking to the multitude on such subjects in rich abundance and attractive graciousness, if perchance many a one might be attracted by the parable to think deeper for himself on the hidden meaning. But that this hidden meaning was to be revealed to the disciples, whether they themselves asked for it or not, need not be said: with them it was all-important that their conception of the truths themselves should be sound and correct on the basis of which alone such intuitions and images can be raised, and none of them was to be left without an independent insight into these simple truths. The beauty and completeness of many simple parables which Jesus had uttered, doubtless led on and attracted the disciples later, as they recalled them, to exhaust more completely their sacred meanings, and explain them in Christ's own sense: we still see this from those preserved in the Gospels. For a string of such parables—seven in number, of some length, which the Saviour once, speaking from a vessel in the lake of Galilee, had delivered to the people in St. Matthew's " Sprachsammlung"—has been admitted as a counterpart of the Sermon on the Mount: but although St. Mark, and still more the last composer of St. Matthew's Gospel, drew primarily from the same source, yet the parables and their meanings are given in the two with considerable differences. Between the flow of such lessons on the building up of the Kingdom of God in the community, and the actual first founding of it, an interval of some length must however have elapsed. For the first lessons presuppose the commencement and the growth of this in a definite, sometimes smaller, sometimes wider field; and already speak, from a fulness of the most varied experiences, on the nature of this higher manifestation only seen in flashes of intuition. Christ must, further, continually return as soon as possible to the wider circle of his full activity, and work on in it with all his power. It is then quite in harmony with the development of the whole history, that St. Mark, between these two grand divisions of the higher teaching on the inner nature, and its fundamental condition (i. e. how the perfect religion is to rule in the true Church), and on the sublime history of God's kingdom, inserts a more narrative portion, in which we see Christ, after his descent from the Mount to Capernahum, at work after his earlier manner: for St. Mark likes in such cases, by stringing together narratives alike in idea, to lay before us a picture of an entire portion of the great manifestation true to history.

CHAPTER XXIII.

THE RELATION BETWEEN THE LORD OF THE NEW CHURCH AND MEN AND SPIRITS.

ST. Mark's design in his way of grouping incidents together is particularly observable in the picture he presents to us of Christ's doubled energy, power, and esteem in the world, and at the same time of his re-doubled exhausting activity in it with all its suspicion, and its good-natured perhaps but unworthy, on one hand, its malicious notions on the other: for now, just at the commencement of his new position, his activity must be most intense and powerful. His spirit being now doubly active, doubly energetic, and doubly powerful, the evil spirits fly, it is true, more helplessly from before Him; but so much the more mysterious and obscure does his own spirit also appear to men of the most various descriptions and most different positions towards Him. The first half of this double truth, which the history of Christ collectively had taught, and which was to be continually proved most strongly during this period of his activity, is taught us in the account of how the evil spirits, who tormented the son of a heathen centurion in Capernahum, fled from before Christ's presence, when He came down from the Mount where He had been founding his Church. We saw however that this particular story in St. John's more exact recollection falls properly at a much earlier time; a time, however, when Christ likewise, after a longer absence and driven as it were by a spirit of higher experience, was returning to Capernahum. But when once in the narrative the story had been shifted to this later date, to a time when the community had already been formed; then, quite in keeping with the exalted state of Christ's spirit, there was appended to it very appropriately the words in which Christ's spirit, delighted at such belief in a heathen, had divined that heathen as a whole rather than Jews would come to God's kingdom. If the Church of the perfect religion is in existence, it stands, rising as it were in the midst of Israel, and at first only capable of forming itself out of it, yet already face to face with the whole world, and so also freely offering itself to it; so that before it, all older distinctions of various forms of religion vanish: a truth which could become plain immediately after the founding of Christianity, and doubtless was early enough expressed by Christ. With yet more certainty does the narrative of the increased activity and energy belong to this period. When Christ is again at home with his disciples, then appears at once such a crowd of people asking for help of every sort, gathering about him and the twelve, that they did not even find time and room to refresh themselves with food. The less is it to be wondered at, if

He Himself, in the midst of the most stupendous excitement and exhaustion of these days, to those who without rightly knowing Him noticed only his outer behaviour and the violent struggle of his spirit therein visible, his becoming as it were raving, He appeared to be approaching from frenzy, a collapse of mind, and to be only acting and suffering as it were spasmodically. And this appearance in so unwonted a case had produced most opposite effects on the wider outside circles. The report had already spread in the town that He had gone raving mad from exhaustion. When his kindred (i. e. his brethren and his mother) hear this report, they hasten to look for Him and bring Him home, but find his house closely beset by crowds, and for a long time they cannot come near Him. They were quite strangers to all his present exaltation of spirit, yet feel in this unexpected distress human compassion, and think they must help Him somehow. But while these are gradually coming to look for Him, in the room itself, or at any rate close to Him, and perceptible enough, there has broken out quite another kind of commotion. Some scribes from Jerusalem, come down with a bad intention, have at once adopted eagerly in their own sense the idea of his mental state which has gone abroad, and find in this his condition a confirmation of their long-cherished suspicions, that He was possessed by the supreme spirit of evil diseases (Beelzebub), the same through which He works his miracles,—casts out, that is, the demons of others. But if so malicious a reproach, and that too proceeding from such wise rulers from the

Capital, might bring others in such a case to complete despair, it only furnishes Him with the occasion of exposing the absurdity of the charge, and at the same time of so discussing the whole subject that the reproach falls back on the heads of those who thus thought and spake evil; and this all the more, the more perversely, in course of the dispute kindled by them, they wish to tempt Him further by the demand for a miracle to be wrought before their eyes. The discourses which the "Sprachsammlung" (though it is true on another occasion composed for the confutation of such reckless reproaches and demands upon Christ, in their wonderful elevation are not inferior to all the rest, and lead us up to an elevation where we feel not too far removed even from the surpassing sublimity of St. John's reports. Meanwhile He has become the centre of all who are listening to his wonderful sayings. Then comes to Him the information that his mother and brethren are standing without seeking Him.

But if He is engaged at a work before whose divinity all the lower relationships, thoughts, and cares of the previous life vanish, how much more must He at this moment, in such high employment and such blessing on his work as Head of the Church, hold those for mother and sister and brother, who like these are crowding around Him attracted by his words! And how little need has He, whilst drawing in, instead of exhaustion and weakness, only new strength from his sublime work, of the help however well intended of those who do not yet understand Him, and are not yet labouring with Him at that which never exhausts!

Another time He made a similar reply, when a woman, carried away by the unsurpassable truth and power of his discourse, having blessed her who had borne Him, He applied her words to bless rather those who heard and kept the word of God. And if He at this time of highest excitement and effort, standing already as Head in his Church, in spite of all such misconception and hostility, yet knew such sublime experiences, we the more easily understand how He from the disquiet of the town, taking refuge again in the freer bank of the lake, could *there* utter to those who sought Him out such still brighter pictures of the commencement, of the growth, and of the value of God's kingdom which was touched upon above (Chap. XXII.). It was thus He tasted the firstfruits of his activity, now at its zenith, and which his spirit clothed in refreshing lessons amid the labours of the sultry noon.

CHAPTER XXIV.

The Practical Education of the Twelve.

I. THROUGH TRAVEL WITH THEIR MASTER.

But He was soon to prepare for Himself far sweeter fruits of this sort. After that the Twelve had received higher instruction enough for the commencement, it was time to practise them more directly in their life-work. Their great life-work falling to them as the first members of the community, must be the announcement of the Gospel in the whole world. He resolved accordingly to take them first for companions on a new round which He Himself wished to enter on to proclaim the Gospel. They were in the distant country to collect more experience than they could in the one town; were to share with Him the dangers of such a journey into unknown regions; were to hear how He proclaimed everywhere a varied and a new, and yet everywhere the same Gospel; and to see how He everywhere also actively helped and healed where it was practicable to help, and a higher compassion called Him thereto.

That such a prentice journey was undertaken by

Him for the practical preparation of the Twelve for their own journey, needs not be added. We know not now very accurately at what period of the year it happened; but from the criteria, to be explained below, it may have been undertaken in the late autumn of this year.

To extend it very far was objectless, and could not be intended: yet it must also through its variety be sufficiently instructive, and so indeed may have lasted a full month, or perhaps somewhat longer. We still possess through St. Mark a somewhat more minute representation of it, since here too He brings forward, in a course of several pictures, the most prominent features in it, and those which remained most fixed in the memory. The very commencement of this journey might serve for a new lesson to them. As St. Mark tells us, Jesus—on the evening of the very day in which, on the western shore of the Galilæan lake, He had been setting before the people still brighter similitudes of God's kingdom—started on a voyage towards the eastern shore. He had on that day, as we read of his doing at other times, discoursed from the high prow of a vessel to the people crowded on the shore: He now commanded the Twelve with Him in this vessel to steer towards the other shore: He had not provided Himself with victuals or other stores for the journey, still He wished to commence the journey, and the Twelve were ready, after dismissing the assembled people, to thrust forth with Him into the lake; other vessels also accompanied them on the voyage.

Then there arose a great hurricane, and the waves beat over the ship so that it was already almost sinking under them. But He Himself was meanwhile sleeping in the stern on the cushion brought here to him: as though even the most violent turmoil in the world could not awake Him. We think here naturally on the similar situation of that ancient prophet, described in the book of Jonah: but what a totally different result appears here! When they venture at length to awake Him, not without a gentle reproach for want of care for them, He commanded stillness to the wind and the sea; and when, unexpectedly and to the astonishment of all, suddenly a great calm comes on, He censures the unnecessary fearfulness and want of faith of the twelve. Thus appears, at the commencement of the journey, how much they were wanting in the highest trust in God and quiet self-possession amid outward turmoil. But their trust in his Messianic majesty was not a little increased. On the south-eastern shore they came into the region mostly occupied by heathen, which was denoted the Ten Cities (Decapolis), because it belonged to the province of the Ten free towns (Bd. iv. s. 518) in the north-east of Palestine. A region less occupied by Jews it was hard to go through; it is significant then that Jesus did not disdain even such for his present purpose, or rather chose it designedly. Here now, not far from the lake, He found in the mountainous district belonging to a town Gergesa a man possessed, the most terrible being conceivable: he felt himself tormented by countless evil spirits, and hence named himself with the Roman word, then new in Palestine, "Legion," raged and raved against all men, but had with it all a wild strength so untamed that he had continually rent all sorts of fetters with which it had been attempted to bind him; he had accustomed himself to the lonely dwelling in the tombs on the mountain before the town, and lived here like a naked animal, crying, striking himself with stones, as if to be freed from the torture. Yet even such a hardly human being had the Saviour, should He approach him, power of love and saving mercy sufficient to release. And in fact, as all possessed feel a secret desire to be released, he was seen to hasten from a distance to the Saviour: but when he heard how Jesus commanded the unclean spirits to come forth out of him, the apprehension of the violent pains of this coming out overcame him, and when come quite close he falls at his feet and begs Him not to torment him. But Jesus leaves him not, rather probes him with questions still more deeply, as though He would evoke and drive all the thousand evil spirits the more irresistibly to make themselves known and trust him. And already these feel, and the man possessed with them feels, that they cannot longer resist his mighty word; but both the man and the demons feared to die at once and have to go to hell, and they beg at least to be treated as gently as was possible, and not to be sent away into the distant deserts: and as if the unhappy man, doubtless originally a man of Jewish belief, before the fixed severe and yet loving gaze of Christ, ventured at last to remember again the nobility of his Jewish descent, and in doing this to quite recover his reason, he begs Him to suffer the demons to go forth into a herd of swine feeding there quite close by, as though such were the only place meet for them. But so violent was (so the story soon shaped itself) their leap forth into these, so soon as Jesus allowed it, that they forthwith drive the swine into the wildest flight, and hurl them down the precipice into the lake; the swine thus perishing carry these unclean spirits themselves, however sorely against their will, into hell with them, whilst the man, set free from them, comes at once to his long-desired rest. This narrative—one of those given at the most length, and in its kind the most instructive which St. Mark gives us—furnishes the deepest insight into the notions then in vogue on the evil spirits and the possessed, and was doubtless among those most frequently repeated. That the district was heathen, the mention of the herd of swine also shews; but the representation could only ascribe to one possessed, who was not originally heathen, the desire of the evil spirits to go into such a herd. Further, that the herd perished is a certain fact preserved in memory; the possessed man, by his last most terrible convulsions and violent motions, might easily come into closer contact with one of the herd, and one become unruly easily takes all the others after it: thus, from the place and manner of it, men might easily see a closer connection between this event and the last convulsions, and hence with the immediately following healing of the possessed. But only the Jewish popular wit, in the midst of the agitation of the notions on unclean spirits and their pleasure in unclean swine, could combine so closely, and thus connect into one narrative these two ideas. The owners of the herd, moreover, and the rest of the inhabitants of the town, although naturally vexed at the loss of the herd, do not bring Jesus to account, as though He had been the immediate cause; but, as the story concludes, astonished at it all, and not least at the possessed now healed and become quite sane, whom they themselves had been so unable to tame, only desire Jesus to leave their district. On his embarking, the once unfortunate man, actually as a new convert, begged to be allowed to accompany Him; but the Saviour bade him rather in his own country, and so in the midst of heathen, proclaim the praise of the true Deliverer and of God, as one of the most speaking living witnesses of divine deliverance. In this also Christ was great, that He did not, as we might have supposed, seek to count among his companions one redeemed from a heathen land and the worst superstition; whilst yet He took none the less interest in the fate of the "children of Abraham" scattered among the heathen, nay of the heathen themselves, and helped them, when salutary, individually, just as He did his own countrymen. Of other events of this journey on the eastern shore we now know nothing. When He returned over the lake into the neighbourhood of Capernahum, immediately a multitude again assembled about Him, so that He staid some time on the shore. Then came one of the elders of the synagogue, named Jair, out of the town, with the equally reverential and instant request, that from compassion to his dying daughter of twelve years old He would hasten to his house to heal her. Whilst on his way there and accompanied by the throng, there pressed in a woman who had been a great sufferer from an issue of blood for twelve years, had spent in consequence her whole substance under the treatment of many physicians, and yet only became constantly worse.

She had probably come here from far, and knew none who could commend her to Jesus, of whose healing power she had heard; but she had so much faith in Him, that now hardly had she touched trembling the fringe of his garment trailing behind (die Alterthümer, s. 265), when she felt herself already relieved and healed. But yet it was in no wise his mere garment which worked the cure; and, though the woman might think so, *He* feels and knows it to be otherwise, and may not let such a new superstition spring up. So He turns round to see who had done it, asking who had touched his clothes? His disciples do not understand his meaning and the purport of his question, as in such a throng it was not surprising that his garments should be touched; but He feels more truly what must have happened, and repeatedly looks round with severe look; and not until the woman, feeling herself found out and timidly hastening to Him, had acknowledged the whole truth both of her action and her belief, does He with reassuring word confirm the healing. During this unexpected delay, tidings arrived from the house of the elder of the synagogue, that his daughter was already dead, he should not further trouble Jesus: but as though the Saviour had not heard this He exhorts the father only to have firm belief: He hastens forwards with his three most intimate disciples, enters the house, full on one side of flute-players who were playing the established death's melody, on the other side of bewailing kindred; He utters words of hope, enters alone, although laughed at for it, with the elders and his three disciples into the upper chamber of the house where the child lay by herself, and quickens her through taking by the hand and a mighty appeal. He then bade take care of the restored child, but wished, as usual at this period (Chap. XXII.), that not much should be said of his help.

It is quite likely, as the old account here continues, that Jesus now, without further stay in Capernahum, took again his twelve on a tour with Him towards the south-west. But here they were to have just the opposite experience. In his own town of Nazareth, which He likewise visited in this tour, He appeared teaching one Sabbath in the synagogue, but found by experience that the people here, the greater the power of his word, and the report of his miracles which had preceded Him, would the less believe in Him; because, led by small-minded criticism and mean envy, they preferred looking at what was best known to them, the human side of his descent and earlier history among them, and of his relations still living among them, rather than on the pure and divine side in Him: the evil report of (Chap. XIX.) his exclusion from the synagogue might here be spread abroad from Jerusalem, and eagerly turned to account by his enemies. This was not unexpected by Him, as this world goes, for He knew how such envy on the part of one's town and kindred has ever been strong in the world: but yet again he had most cause to marvel at their unbelief, as nowhere certainly in the world had this been so groundless as here. Neither could He—as this old account, with great truth, from correct reminiscence, has no scruple in relating, on account of this very predominant unbelief among them—accomplish among them any mighty work worthy of remembrance: only He healed some sick by the laying on of hands and other means generally used by Him.

This rejection of the Gospel in Jesus' own town of Nazareth formed always certainly a very prominent reminiscence in the older Gospel narrative; and much more, besides that above touched on, was related about it. The latter town thus gained a particularly ill report for Galilee—and rightly, for Christ first appeared in it at a time when a higher respect should have met Him even in his own country, as one long approved, nay already surrounded by many honourable disciples. For, that this was the first time in which He visited Nazareth appears by all analogy, and the way of speaking of it by the older narratives: He had doubtless, as He knew them so well, good grounds for not giving them such a trial earlier. The small-minded envy of towns seems to have had an effect on other Galilæan towns, Capernahum for instance: this was, probably at least, the principal design of the "Sprachsammlung" in having shortly touched on the circumstance, and put together some discourses with reference to it. He asked from them repentance and faith; they on the contrary asked Him first to shew such miracles as they had understood He had done in Capernahum: if He wanted something from them, so did they too from Him, and so the old proverb was good here, "Physician, heal thyself."

Then He shewed them this truth, that higher works and divine blessings may not be had at command; just as the old great prophets had not received their mission to help all the many who probably expected it in their bodily needs, only specified individuals. He knows for the rest, and any one may well know from ancient history that the true prophet is nowhere less acceptable than in his own town. Such truths were in fact appropriate here, and in this particular case were sufficiently dwelt on: the saying also about the prophet in his own town, as remarked (Chap. VII.) according to old reminiscence, was traced back to Christ. But a later author held it right that Jesus should have appeared at the very commencement of his public ministry in the town of his youth, Nazareth: He there, after his wont visiting the synagogue on the sabbath, had presented to Him the Holy Scriptures for the lesson and the lecture; He then, from the prophetical book of Isaiah, read the very passages which most minutely touch on the first appearance of the Messiah, nay, seem to evoke and at the same time to attest his claims; and amid the most intense interest of the hearers He delivered an exposition, which at first called forth the highest astonishment at such gracious words; but then, when at length with severer words He had called for true repentance and amendment, in fact called on them to forget their earlier human relations as his fellow-citizens, He excited them to such displeasure, nay, towering rage against Him, that they drove Him from the town and to the brow of a hill, to throw Him down from thence; yet He safely escaped, going through the midst of them. And doubtless the tradition (Chap. XIII.) was not without good reason, for informing us that such fate of extreme contempt and danger of life befell Him at the first time of his appearance: so again that He once took for his text those prophetic passages, sounds like quite true history. But that this all happened in Nazareth, and thus early, nay, that his whole public appearance commenced from thence, is contrary to the older accounts and recollections, and seems to have been first brought by St. Luke, so far as he thought he could, into more close connection with these older accounts.

But He did not allow Himself to be checked, through the contempt experienced by Him and his disciples in Nazareth, from pursuing everywhere in the neighbourhood, in the company of the Twelve, his great life-work. At this time too may be placed the help which, moved by deep compassion, He rendered to the widowed mother of the only son who was being carried to the grave: this happened in the little town of Nain, south-east from Nazareth, on one of the southern slopes of Tabor. But we now only have the account preserved by St. Luke, and from indeed a later source, where doubtless it was only very shortly related: a closer view of the circumstances of the event, as we see them always sketched so instructively by St. Mark, is wanting here: and thus much only can we say, that the burial here spoken of, in those times followed usually very soon after death.

CHAPTER XXV.

THE PRACTICAL TRAINING THROUGH THEIR OWN MISSION.

WHEN the Twelve, through such experiences in their wanderings with Himself, as well as by the earlier more express instruction received from Him, were prepared more minutely for their last life-destination, He might now venture to send them out themselves to learn to further the kingdom of God through their own activity. The time was thus now come for which He Himself had so longed. For to accustom them to work as early as possible at an independent work of their own for the kingdom of God, must be one of his highest endeavours; and no one could more than Himself wish for their readiness and reliability to grow and ripen. No one too knew better than He, how much the infinite domain itself which was the region of his activity needed the most varied labourers, and how in that domain even the smallest labour, if only rightly begun and rightly continued, brings its own infinite reward. They were now to learn so to advance the kingdom of God, after the great example He had set, and on the firm foundation

He had laid. As then with Him teaching and preaching were the first steps, but corresponding active helping and healing were equally important: so they were to learn to proclaim the near coming, nay, the already successful commencement of the joyful kingdom of God, with its earthly community and their duties in the world; and at the same time also, by their own helping and healing, in all right ways to advance the great salvation of the kingdom of God. The latter part of their mission must be most closely connected with the then most necessary and salutary acts for helping and healing, as may be seen (s. 217 ff.) in the case of Christ Himself. It is hence plain that, before sending them, He gave them a closer knowledge of the means of healing and relieving the many wants of the time which He Himself (Nach s. 224) used as outward means in his works of healing, so far at least as they could well be imparted and applied by beginners. Nothing can be more historical than that such a mission of the Twelve was once appointed by Him: He might send them forth from that very journey on which He was then engaged, as the old narrative gives us pretty plainly to understand. But it is equally certain that He had to use a certain caution, in order on this trial journey not to bring them into too great difficulties. We know, for example, that He commanded them to enter no heathen or Samaritan province: the management of such provinces was in itself much harder; and if He Himself on good grounds (Nach s. 237 ff.) limited his working almost wholly to Israel, He might now still more require of the Twelve this self-limitation, since many questions would here have come before them which they were as yet quite unable to solve. He probably wished them to limit themselves to the province of Galilee, which was generally best known to them, and where at present they could most easily begin their difficult work.

It is equally certain that He gave them before their mission many more particular instructions and exhortations, such as were particularly appropriate for this new work: but none could be so weighty and important as those on the proper spiritual means which they had to use for their purpose, and on the reception which they were to expect in the world: higher glances also could not be wanting on the whole Messianic work and fate, as well as predictions on the development of all Messianic effort, wherein they themselves were now to take a nearer part. The "Spruchsammlung" had put together at this point all which Christ spoke in reference to the mission of his disciples and their reception in the world: and although into this whole, for the sake of convenient connection, many particulars may have been admitted which Christ did not till a much later time, in the clearest prospect of his speedy death, utter to his own; still these golden sayings belong, taken altogether, to the deepest and most important which have been preserved from his mouth. For a great part of the deepest feelings which moved his own breast, as that of the very first evangelist and ambassador of God Himself into the world, and which governed his whole Messianic life, must find utterance in those words wherewith He encouraged his disciples to the like life-work. He may have then given them many more particular counsels at that time, and much necessary only for this particular purpose may have been settled: for example, how long their absence was to last; when they were again to meet with Him; and what directions they might severally best take. That they were sent out in pairs must be an old recollection. The journeys of the Twelve might certainly begin and end the very winter, as each two, in one month or two months, might see and experience enough. Yet it is certainly possible that some such prentice-journeys were repeated also in the following year, although we have no information on this. That Christ sent forth the seventy essentially as He had sent out the Twelve on prentice-journeys, is a somewhat later view and account, which St. Luke from one of his manuscript sources has admitted into his history.

CHAPTER XXVI.

THE DOUBT OF THE BAPTIST, AND HIS END.

AT this period falls one last closer contact of Jesus with the Baptist, and the closing of the Baptist's earthly career could not remain without influence on the more speedy development of the history of Christ. For the remembrance of this in many respects very important event, with its most immediate consequences, we are indebted to the " Spruchsammlung," out of which one of the most beautiful and also most historically instructive portions on this has been preserved. The Baptist lived (Chap. XIV.) over a year in prison; and though outwardly spared by the Tetrarch Antipas, nay, receiving considerable deference, might, considering the arbitrary character and caprice of this man, be hourly contemplating his end. No wonder that this long imprisonment gradually somewhat subdued and clouded his spirit: the grand hope of his life that the Messiah, if the right way be prepared for Him, will speedily come with power, had not been fulfilled in the way he at first expected; and Jesus, on whom he had then laid all his hopes, as on Him who would soon prove Himself the promised

Messiah, whose first steps He had Himself helped forward, so free from envy and with such success, had not within the space of two years and a half appeared as such a Messiah as from passages of the Old Testament he had expected. With intense interest he followed his steps, and might be, not a little, partly surprised and partly rejoiced, that Jesus, who was carrying on a life-work akin to his, was allowed to work freely: but though no more offended with the lowliness and desultory character of his deeds of healing and other miracles than He had been with the freer and more cheerful rule of life to which He accustomed his disciples, yet these were not the works which he had expected as the final works; for if he looked on them as the proper beginning of Messianic deeds, he yet thought that the Messiah could not stop at them; and it seemed to him at length time that He should display openly a greater power in the world. But now the Saviour's day's work remained uniform, or at most made progress such as seemed to the Baptist little glorious, and the whole Messianic salvation seemed to him strangely delayed, notwithstanding, as he had hitherto supposed, the Messiah being already come. It is not then very surprising that he, in his present state of continued anxiety, and in the only too certain prospect of his speedy end, wished to receive from Jesus Himself a future beyond that which he dimly foresaw. Doubtless also he was much driven to it by his disciples, who had not gone over to Jesus. How one of these, before the Baptist's imprisonment, fell into a dispute with Jesus' disciples, we saw above (Chap. XIII.);

but after this captivity they must have become much more uncertain in their whole position, and doubtless pressed in to the master to learn from him decidedly whether they should go over to Jesus. Thus might the noble-minded man, pressed and subdued by all this, resolve to send two of his disciples to Jesus, to learn from Himself whether He were really the expected Messiah, or whether He with his disciples should hope for another.

In this embassy lay no faithless doubt, rather an encouraging invitation to Jesus to become at once in its full scope *that* which he had once expected of Him and was still not disinclined to expect. But a doubt of Him as the complete true Messiah lay certainly therein: *that* John, who (Chap. VIII.), once conquered by the first sight of Him, firmly trusted at once to have found in Him the future Messiah, was no longer he who thus enquired in doubt; and we see in this at one glance how things had changed since to the two men, and how little the elder, simply because he had remained where he was, had really followed the development of the Saviour, consistent yet ever forward, and striving to mount ever higher on the only right way towards the goal. The doubt, humanly excusable as it was, must have inwardly pained the Saviour as a providential indication: for it was only the same doubt, which in a harsher form sounded in his ears from so many other quarters: but that He was rejected even by *him* who had first called forth the whole Messianic movement of the time, nay, who had himself once discerned in Him, with joyful trustfulness and encouraging appeal, the future Messiah, and even for long after had admitted no doubt of Him,—this must the more sensibly touch Him; and surely at no moment of this year did the whole picture of the checkered part of his whole history, since that meeting with the Baptist, come so freshly before his spirit as it did then.

But it was not fitting to give utterance to such pain and dejection, however well warranted, before the ambassadors of the Baptist, nor even to let him be publicly informed of it: no one in the keeping back of well-founded depression was greater than He. So he calmly shews them his incessant and uniform daily work; how those needing help of every sort, even the most extreme in body as well as in spirit, are relieved and benefitted by Him—*that* is his office and his business; and how far He was from working at it in vain they might readily see; the further development is not his alone, but also God's work: but blessed is he who finds in Him no offence, and does not, in consequence of the unobtrusive commencement of God's kingdom, doubt of its presence and its mighty movement. This they might report to the Baptist, and in this He had said all which He had here to say, and on which the Baptist with his disciples might further reflect. Yet, after the departure of the embassy He could utter before his closer friends who then surrounded Him, as well as before all others, the painful thoughts which stirred his deepest soul: and we yet possess from the "Spruchsammlung" the gist of the words so admirably pungent in the thought, and at the same time so transparent in their picturesqueness, which unquestionably belong to that time, and are for us the brightest mirror of it. Who the Baptist is, and how men behaved to him and to the Messiah, once and now? When men once in great troops went out to the Jordan to the Baptist, what should they have seen and looked for in him? a doubting man like a reed shaken by the wind? at that time he was not (as now) a doubting man! but no more would they have looked for in him an effeminate luxurious courtier, which he is not yet, he who in any case even now in his doubt was an honest man, who was a prophet, nay, as the mighty pioneer of the new Messianic period more than one of the Old Testament prophets, and might in truth be accounted the returning Elias promised in the Old Testament; but who yet, on the other hand, as one doubting of the actual appearance into the world of the kingdom of God, stands far below even the least of those who do not doubt in it, and because they believe in it may already be true members of it. For this is now to be discerned as the true distinction between the Old and the New, and in this the Baptist forms the bridge from the one to the other, that now the Kingdom of heaven, with all its powers and blessings, stands free to every one to conquer it, and as it were takes possession of it, (for without such boldness and spirit no one can win its blessings). But if it were now unavoidable that the Baptist with his followers, the more the Kingdom of God proclaimed by him developed itself according to its beginning, should meet it with all the greater doubt and be rooted where he stands; what is to be thought of the wisdom of the children of this world, who will neither have the Baptist with his rough severity, nor Messiah now come with his gentle cheerfulness; will give the harshest accounts of the one equally with the other, nay, who actually admire their own wisdom in censuring and rejecting both, different as they may be! Truly the divine wisdom which sent both men, and which these her wickedly wise children would censure for sending both, is by this very censure best justified; in that these with their wisdom do not themselves know what they wish, playing like children with the most solemn subjects, never satisfied, and in their continued frivolity only becoming ever more unhappy. Oh, for how long and how earnestly He wished in the most varied ways to save this generation, if it were yet to be saved, and not rather wholly devoted to ruin! With such words He spoke of all the various human efforts and sects of the time; going in his sorrow over the Baptist's doubt now become apparent. What he said then to his disciples when the Saviour's reply was brought to him, and what advice he gave them, we know not from these old and most reliable accounts; but we can easily conclude from the course of the history. In truth, the Saviour's short reply was not capable, was not even designed to overthrow his doubt; and he might have himself made earlier that deeper reflection which it was designed to call forth. He remained, according to the best conclusion we can form, persistent in his waiting and doubting. But his days were numbered. Certainly soon after this, the fate already mentioned (Chap. IX.)

overtook him in the prison; but unjust and horrible as this was as regarded its human instrument, it can hardly be said that as regards its providential side it happened too soon. For that which was truly new and creative in what the Baptist was called to establish, lasted and worked on for long even without his own further human working; and what was really divine in his effort and work, nay, what was a necessary and in itself infinitely important element in the development of all history of the true religion, even now in its strongest effort towards completion, *that* like a true hero of God he had striven for and won. The day when his work culminated was that in which he baptized the Saviour; and the deepest discovery made by his penetrating eye was his discernment in the Saviour of the only one who could become the Messiah. But because he did not discern the only right way, in which He might actually become and did become what he hoped from Him, the paths of the two from that moment must separate ever more widely, though slowly and without the least fault of the Baptist.

The doubt which grew in him during his long suffering he certainly did not retract in the few days yet left to him: otherwise his disciples would not have continued his work and his whole manner of considering the future, as they nevertheless did (s. Unten). Thus he died, only testifying for us in his late-born doubt and in his death, how hard it was, practically, even for firm faith to rise to the elevation of Christ; and in truth this was then infinitely harder than it is now, or even than it was in the later Apostolic age.

His disciples took away his body, after his death in imprisonment was known, to render it the last honours: many disciples remained true to his teaching and his hope, though they gave up the particular hope in Jesus. And after that his outer work was finished, might his disciples with all the more decision again assemble and agree among themselves what was now to be done to continue his work after his views. In the whole of Israel his memory lived on (s. 52) in high repute. But no one before his death judged him so rightly, and brought forward what was divine in him so simply and clearly, as He of whom he doubted at last, and whom he troubled by this doubt; and what was of imperishable nature in his work, that could but survive in Christianity undisturbed for all times, and it has thus survived.

For the rest, important and instructive as it is that we should thus, through the precious remains of the "Spruchsammlung," have such complete information on this last phase of the inner life of the Baptist, it is equally certain that this gradual darkening of the now setting but once so brilliant star of the Baptist, had no higher importance for the pure truth of the now completely risen light of Christianity, nay, could exercise but little influence on its further development. It is the dark side of the Baptist, important for the complete historical narrative, instructive in itself, as everything connected with so great a hero of humanity must be, better for the simple Christian friend and admirer of the Baptist to be left in obscurity and passed over in silence. Hence we cannot wonder that the Baptist's former disciple, the Apostle John himself, in his Gospel neither touches on the death of the Baptist, nor on this, as it doubtless seemed to him, slight darkening of the Baptist's mind. He does not deny what the earlier Gospel writings contain about it, but will not speak of it in his own, and prefers, at greater length than had been done in the earlier accounts, telling all that was Christian of the Baptist; for the disciples of St. John at that time recalled most gladly those good words which the Baptist spoke of the Saviour after his baptism, and only some of them lingered at his last gloomy words.

CHAPTER XXVII.

The Return of the Twelve, and their new Practice.

Not very long after that painful experience from which Christ was not spared, He was to have a joyful one quite calculated to throw a far penetrating stream of sunlight into the whole boundless future of his life-work. The Twelve returned, and gave Him an account of all which they had seen, learnt, and done: they were greatly rejoiced at the good success of their work, particularly at their having begun to learn even to cast out evil spirits in the manner and in the name of their Master. But He could not allow their joy to pass without enlightening and warning them. It was like that of novices, and might well prove dangerous to them. For of long time He was beholding Satan fall like lightning from heaven; who fallen can no longer hurt nor is longer to be feared: this is the true meaning of God's Kingdom, that the power of Satan is broken, and that he has fallen to the earth as if from the sky, where he mysteriously and by pure surprise could hurt man, he is now where, being as it were visible, he can be easily seen and avoided.

Christ Himself quite differently and far earlier experienced this subduing of Satan's power, nay, *He* has first made it possible: in so far then is the present joy of the Twelve over their power that of novices; but every such joy, however justified, is to novices so much the more dangerous, because it may rouse their human pride and make them too confident. Therefore should a man rejoice and take courage, not in victory over the power of the enemy, but in this, that he knows himself by faith a member of the Kingdom of Heaven, and feels sure in his spirit that he does not stand as an enemy against the forces of heaven. With such words and corresponding images He subdued at that time the first overflowing joy of the Twelve, as He always did in like cases, and thenceforth more constantly as they began to work more independently. So soon however as He has parted with the Twelve, and sees Himself more alone, then breaks forth more freely the bright sun-gleam, with which the experience of the commencing independence and joyful working of the Twelve for the kingdom of God must fill his spirit: and as though He gave now, without design, an example of that pure joy before God, which, as He had just said before the Twelve, is allowed to men, He exulted in deep spiritual emotion and in bright clear gaze into all futurity, praying to God, thanking Him that the truth of the kingdom of God on earth being actually begun, misconceived as it was by the wise and prudent of the time, and even by the Baptist, had been by Him revealed to those who, like his disciples, might have counted before as the infant souls of the time, only that they had a spirit simple and guileless enough to be receptive of pure truths and become true members of God's kingdom. The older have no purer joy than to watch and see how the first germs of the higher divine thought and action exult in their struggle to come into being: but yet purer and brighter must have been the joy of the Saviour, when He found how the seed of the kingdom was springing up in his disciples; his own spirit would become young again in theirs. Against all the petrified errors and inveterate perversities of the time, to preserve that spirit and make it receptive only for the truths of God's kingdom on earth, and able and strong for working in it; that they should face this world as innocent children, but for God's kingdom be unyielding industrious children, this only had been his endeavour for them at this time: He saw now the first-fruits ripen of his purest wish and of his culminating activity, and could thus the more easily comfort Himself for the mistaking even of such men as the Baptist; and beheld in spirit more steadfastly the whole future development of his eternal lifework. And let none ask how such joyful overflowing utterances of his thankfulness to God and his deep presentiment (as given here from the "Spruchsammlung") could be heard by others, and thus ultimately written down: his spirit was not so divided between God and men; nor was his most secret thought and speech so concealed from his most trusted disciples, that it could have remained dark to them also; and that too when it touched so immediately and firmly, as here, the basis of his whole earthly working.

XXVII.] FURTHER INSTRUCTION OF THE TWELVE. 195

But in spite of this first so joyful success, which the Twelve's own activity achieved, the Saviour perhaps did not think it opportune to send them forth again on new conversion journeys, in the view of drawing as soon as possible all He could into his circle. Rather He gathers them again closer around Him, as they had yet so much to learn of the higher matters of belief, and of the right behaviour in the difficult situations of life. How He now, at this elevation of his whole public life, worked both for the Twelve and for the whole multitude, and how He then was regarded by them—of this St. Mark, in the more connected history of one or two days, has again sketched a picture similar to that which he gave us of the previous period (Chap. XII.). But St. John wished here to explain one of the more remarkable expressions which the Saviour uttered on occasion of the most important of the events here related by the older Evangelists: and it seems, in fact, as if on reading the older Gospels, or rather only one of them, namely St. Mark's, he placed himself intentionally back most vividly amid the whole state of things of those days, in order to be able to give the more certain account of the grand saying of the Saviour on that occasion. Thus at this place the two principal channels of Gospel narrative again meet, to flow on even fuller of the whole public activity of Jesus, but each with its own living stream. St. John adds here too, by way of supplement, and to throw a bright light on the whole temporal course of things, that at that very time the Passover was near. As we may now somewhat better from the two sources understand these events, they might have taken place somewhat as follows.

When the Twelve met again round Jesus, He wished to be able to stay and converse with them in a more lonely place, because the people, who went in and out seeking help from Him at the place where He had now been staying for some time, formed such an immense crowd, that He could here do nothing for Himself with the Twelve, nay, the Twelve found hardly even space here to enjoy food with Him. He accordingly embarked with them on board the vessel which stood always ready on the lake for such voyages, in order to seek a more lonely part of the coast: but those from the multitude seeking help and instruction had, at the first sight of them starting, soon guessed the place, hastened thither quickly on foot, and were actually there to meet Him on disembarking. So St. Mark tells us, and doubtless this place, which is nowhere named by him, would naturally be supposed to lie not far from Capernahum, as we might well assume that Jesus gave his Twelve instructions to meet Him here at his former usual fixed place of resort. But He might have grounds for not staying long just now in this same Galilæan neighbourhood of Capernahum, as we shall again see. When then St. John here at once assumes a situation at the further side of the lake of Galilee, he may have supplied this from more exact memory, which we have no ground for wishing to dispute.

Even here then He could not be much alone with the Twelve; and taken with compassion for the "sheep which have no shepherd," He devoted Himself even here, in teaching and healing again, to the wants of the multitude.

Approaching evening surprised Him as well as the crowds hanging on Him: and the Twelve remind Him in this lonely place to let the people depart in good time, that they may go into the villages round about and there buy themselves food. But He who had been satisfying them with higher food, so that they hung on Him as if they forgot place and time, would fain, in this unexpected need, give them the lower food as well, and enquires of the prudent Philip whence bread could be bought for them: but Philip thinks, hardly could enough be bought for a great sum, sufficient for the five thousand. When meanwhile Andrew finds at a refreshment dealer's in the neighbourhood five loaves and two fishes, the Saviour holds even this small store sufficient to feed the great crowd in this solitude; He bids them sit down, takes the food, with believing glance up to heaven divides it and gives thanks; and not only are they satisfied, but there remain over the most abundant fragments. Thus does He still, infinitely more than the Twelve hitherto understood and supposed, supply the wants of the needy: and if the power of his spirit surprises, it must all teach the true disciples how much they were yet wanting in the higher belief; that belief which in genuine love despairs the least where the need is greatest, and under whose sway in cheerful giving and imparting all doubles itself, and suddenly in place of want there is superfluity.

We have here a narrative like that of the marriage feast: only that here the miracle is greater in proportion to the growth of Christ's activity since that its first beginning, and already it embraces many thousands. And here we can also shew how old and enduring the narrative is. For St. Mark again inserts essentially the same narrative, varying only in some accidental circumstances of small importance, in another somewhat later place in his narrative: but it is here also (which is very important and a sign of its true origin and great antiquity) placed in the same lonely situation on the further shore, and agrees so entirely with the first account in everything which concerns the Twelve and their yet weak faith, that we cannot possibly allow in the vulgar view that the event originally happened twice. And this reminiscence, belonging certainly to the older stock of Gospel narratives, early received a more settled form, but was soon repeated with such variety of circumstance, that a collector, who like St. Mark found two somewhat divergent forms of it, could at once so take it as if the event had been repeated and suitably divide it into two groups of facts. We cannot now state with more accuracy in particular, what furnished the first occasion to a narrative, which, in addition to that said already, only teaches us how the Saviour, with the smallest outward means, but infinitely more through his spirit, his word, and his prayer, satisfied in the most miraculous way even the bodily wants of all who came to Him on that evening, as to the father of the family; and how easily the spiritual blessing may be followed also by the bodily. The peculiar form of the tradition was doubtless naturally affected by the sense of infinite blessing drawn from the higher satisfying with the bread of life, which the disciples ate after Christ's resurrection, as broken and distributed to them by the Lord Himself; and recalled how once He Himself on earth had broken to a great multitude such a miraculously satisfying bread of life, and distributed it with accompanying blessings.

But it is not surprising that, after such a day of most unexpected and most intense work, He wished in the evening to be alone by Himself: to this desire contributed, as St. John tells us, the excitement of the multitude, who would seize on Him and " make Him a king," and thus lower the Messiah in Him from his pure elevation to the vulgarity of the temporal life of the time; so seductive is experience of bodily benefits. But only the more eagerly does He withdraw from them, sends the Twelve alone to Bethsaida, dismisses the people, and goes into the mountain for solitary prayer. But towards morning He looks down on them from his height with his watchful eye, battling with a contrary gale in the midst of the lake. To see this and to help them is all one with Him, and over the midst of the lake reaches his helping arm of love. But his approach and his approaching help was so mistaken in the dark night, that they thought they only saw a ghost in the figure hastening on over the water to their help, nay, almost passing by them; and instead of meeting Him half way with the higher faith, they were only frightened at Him. How little then were they even yet, in spite of all their earlier experience, accustomed to the higher faith when in great mortal dangers! Not till He had come on board and spoken words of assurance to them, did the wind, according to the older narrative, calm, and their dread of the storm dissolve into a yet greater dread of the power of their Master.

Into the somewhat later narrative, as the present St. Matthew's Gospel shews us, was interwoven a notice of the behaviour of Peter towards Christ in this great mortal danger; and generally from this time this peculiar bearing of one to the other is often touched on, and in a way which leaves no doubt that Christ, from His present exalted position towards the Twelve, directed His view especially to Peter's behaviour as the most remarkable and strongest of the Twelve, and laboured above all to raise him to a truly rocklike faith. With this view we are also told here that Peter recognised before all others the nearness of the Lord approaching over the lake to help him, and desired, for the confirmation of his own belief, to walk with Him likewise on the waves of the sea: but when this permission had been granted to him by the Lord, he nevertheless in the midst of the danger becomes afraid, and only in the Lord's extended hand is help found.

A most speaking picture also of the whole later behaviour of Peter. But, evidently with fuller understanding of the original meaning of the tradition, St. John tells us in conclusion, quite shortly, the Twelve would have taken Him into the ship; but swifter than an arrow, with the wind suddenly become favourable, the vessel flew on to land. Thus favourable is His mere proximity: and how little need has he of human help! And thus assuredly this narrative, just at this place, has no other lesson than this, how the Twelve were to learn, even alone, to meet fearlessly the greatest danger in the world, they having been taught in their earlier journey (Chap. XXIV.) the same lesson of faith when His bodily presence was with them. The older narrative goes on to tell us, that when at length after such anxieties in the night they came to shore, and land, they find themselves driven south to the land of Gennesareth, which thus appears somewhat south of Bethsaida, the spot where they should have landed. But hardly have they landed when He is recognised even here, and in the renewed streaming of petitioners of all sorts, hours and days slip by Him, even in walking through these regions. Thus closes the more connected series of pictures, wherein the older narrative sketched the daily movements and occupation of the Saviour at this period. But St. John's aim was, to build up on a great saying, which he indisputably had once heard the Saviour declare aloud before all the people, an express exposition of the great truth, as to what in Christ's mind and saying is the eternal food, in contradistinction to such bodily eating and bodily food, and how man should receive this. He therefore goes on to explain that the people on the eastern shore had, greedy of further such benefits, remarked to their astonishment, that one boat in which the Saviour had come with the Twelve is there no longer; while yet He was not be found on this shore, although He had been seen to retire in the evening to the mountain: hence, as accidentally other vessels from Tiberias were not far off and were going to return, they shipped in these to the west coast, and sought for the Saviour in Capernahum: on their asking Him however, from curiosity in bewildered astonishment, when He arrived, He, in the well-founded misgiving that they wished merely further to enjoy his bodily benefits, and for this came so eagerly after Him, turned the conversation at once to the true bread of life, and afterwards, when they were offended, Himself continued it in the synagogue at Capernahum. This grand discourse is itself distinguished from the earlier like great ones in St. John only by its subject, which is fitting for this later period of elevation of soul in the Saviour's public activity. Not till the Messiah has, with His whole spirit, His word, and His work, so given Himself to the world as now in this advanced stage of His work, can He assert that his word, as He had already imparted it wholly to the world, nay, He Himself with his whole life and being, effulgent as it had appeared in the world, is, if received in faith, that truly satisfying food, which, unlike that bodily food then sought by the people from Him, gives eternal life and immortality: the discussion before us only carries out this truth in all its aspects; whilst here also, after St. John's usual mode of representation, the short questions and objections, the doubt and bewilderment of the men, serve only for the ever stronger assertion of the great truth even in the most pointed assertions; and every interruption of the discourse serves only to carry on the subject to its highest sublimity. The eternal food must however be won in the way it is now offered to the world, namely, through faith in Him who gives it (John vi. 28 f.); that belief which, without asking for sensible miracles, knows that this alone is the bread of life, which coming down from heaven in quite another way than the manna (vv. 30, 33) gives life to the world; and that this bread of life is the Messiah Himself truly and rightly understood (vv. 34, 40). If this seem too incredible or too lofty an assertion, that the Messiah Himself is this bread of life; it must, on the contrary, in logical sequence, be maintained (and on this the discourse goes on, as in a second higher advance to the declaration of the mystery of the sacrifice, as the Apostolic period saw it completed in Christ) that, if the true Messiah only proves Himself the true Messiah by giving his flesh and blood for the life of the world, this very flesh (vv. 41—51), nay this blood alone (vv. 52, 58), is the heavenly food which gives immortality, without eating and drinking from which, no one can receive the true life. But because the thought of this discourse thus naturally passes on to the time when Christ has already in fact given his life for the world, and thus must be hard of comprehension to the hearers before that time, it takes somewhat of a turn, through the question, whether men would doubt of its truth when Christ has been already glorified through his death and resurrection, and when belief in the vanishing of all corporeal substance will be much harder, but, because the highest conceivable miracle shall then be completed, be also far more inexcusable. Only he whom the Spirit impels by faith can at any time conceive this (vv. 60—65): and the Twelve at least, with Peter at their head, are prepared for this faith—although He Himself knows better than they do, how difficult in its actual realization this faith is even among them. Thus does this discussion, because it falls at this period of such intensity of activity in the Saviour, lead us already to that highest pinnacle of all knowledge and intuition of Him, where the firmest and highest faith alone is enabled to abide, and for this very reason, where unbelief lurks so close, even in the circle of those who would raise themselves up to Him. And freely as this grand discourse and discussion has been here repeated by St. John, the older Gospels support him in this, that from henceforth all now turns upon belief or disbelief in Messiah now almost sufficiently manifested, but especially upon that higher belief which must be no passing visitor in the circle of the Twelve, and in all who like them come closer to Him, and which is yet quite different from that of the first beginners and of mere petitioners.

CHAPTER XXVIII.

Increased Frequency and Extent of the Journeys with the Twelve.

But whilst the formation of the Twelve into the stem of a true community of the perfected religion was continued by the Saviour thus incessantly and with ever-increasing success, as his great daily work at this period, the sultry clouds of the deadly storm were gathering ever thicker over his head. For however He sought in the time yet allowed Him (see above) to confine Himself to the education of the Twelve, and to take from the world all pretext for working against Him; yet this world saw ever more plainly, how even his most peaceful and silent working threatened their whole structure with the most open danger: and though, when called on to define this danger more minutely, it might float very vaguely before them, they naturally felt it all the more, since everything which proceeded from Him, both the smallest and the most helpful to suffering humanity, proceeded immediately from a quite different spirit to that which possessed the ruling power of the time.

No saying expresses the whole situation, as it gradually shaped itself, more briefly and plainly, than that which, according to St. John, He Himself uttered at this time to those who stood not as his downright enemies, but yet indifferent and unsympathising towards Him. "The world cannot hate you, but me it hateth because I testify of it that its works are evil." This He need never have testified aloud: his whole life and working, and every gentle innocent word from his mouth, gave testimony to this. It was about this time that the nearest prince, Herod Antipas, first was troubled in his spirit about Him. He had doubtless heard of Him for some time: not so much his doctrine as his works of mercy had long spread his name everywhere: but it is also not at all surprising that the multitude judged very differently of his proper nature, and sought in a variety of ways to solve the riddle of his manifestation. The vulgar popular understanding sought at any rate for something uncommon and miraculous in Him: but that He is the very Messiah was the last conclusion they arrived at (Nach. s. 231 f.). But every one might easily know that He and many of his most intimate disciples were from the Baptist's school, or at least that his design was somewhat the same, and that his works were greater than John's. Many therefore thought he was the promised Elias; others that he was at least Jeremiah risen again (Bd. IV. s. 194); others were satisfied to look on Him simply as some prophet, without seeing in Him the resurrection of one deceased. But the most terrible idea about Him was fixed in the mind of Antipas: he feared that in Jesus, the Baptist murdered by him had risen again, and therefore he possessed such wondrous powers. Thus the bad conscience from his guilt fastened in his mind on the vague superstition of the time: and what a short step it was, from this tormenting view of the Saviour to the command to put Him in prison and execute Him, like the Baptist shortly before. If he did not at once do this he deferred it certainly only for a time, from a vague fear, as from the same cause he had so long let the Baptist also alone. But at least he now tried a fox-like trick to get Him out of his province: some Pharisees feigning good will must advise Him to be gone, as the Tetrarch would kill Him. The reply He made to "that fox," who had not addressed Him openly, has an unmistakeable resemblance to that in which He replied to the last message of the Baptist: He shortly declared what was then his duty in life, and how He would not let Himself be disturbed in it, although the Divine Voice told Him that He would soon enough have to leave Galilee, not from fear of Antipas' threatenings, but on quite other grounds.

In fact there was an enmity against Him far more deadly at the centre of the existing spiritual power itself, with its proud position in Jerusalem, and its troops of Pharisees and other schoolmen dispersed everywhere, whose enmity burned ever more deeply because their pretended religion felt itself ever more oppressed by his perfect true religion. His call was not like the Baptist's for a mere preparation for a new better time: He called for entry at once into the duties of the Kingdom of God; and it was not by single blunt remarks that He irritated the wrath of the rulers of the world, as the Baptist had done; He worked like a king in his own kingdom—in the world, yet floating above it. And thus was there kindled against Him, not as against the Baptist, a partial, calculating, and well-defined animosity: the spiritual power itself, as the great centre of the true religion in the form it had then become petrified in the world, with all the abuses which adhered to it, felt itself most immediately and powerfully attacked by Him, and could not, if it would make head against Him, coexist. The opposing power was the spiritual might of the people of the true religion, that is to say, the most exalted power of the whole world at that time, as it had risen up furnished from its armoury of the most exalted truths, and, proud of a history of many centuries grand beyond compare, was willing to overlook its own offences: this power it was which now felt itself within these last few years oppressed by the Baptist, and then far worse by this Galilæan, and sought in the destruction of this man, which seemed as yet so easy, to annihilate from out of the corner of Galilee his chiefly Galilæan followers. The rulers had already adopted a milder measure as they might suppose, if only a temporary one, against Him apart from his followers: they had, as stated above (Chap. XIX.), put him under the lesser excommunication; and it seems that they extended the same punishment gradually to Galilæan synagogues, as they henceforth threatened with it his open followers ever more bitterly, and in part actually applied it. As however this punishment served them in little stead, they caused Him and his most intimate disciples to be watched more closely, in order to find matter for new charges. This storm, which, in spite of all his innocence and all his reserve, rose ever more fiercely against Him, might have long been foreseen by Him: He had known from the first what He and what the world would have; and since He had laid the foundation of his Church, the most cruel sting had been taken from their fury and their wrong. But yet He had to avoid the world's enmity as long as possible, in order to continue as long as possible the difficult work which He had begun in the formation of the Church: for it had long been apparent how much, after the first favourable beginnings, was yet to be done; as also, how hard it was for the higher belief to find here an abiding place. But, with the suspicion and hatred of his enemies ever on the increase, He found nowhere a resting-place for long: henceforth then He undertook with the Twelve the more frequent and distant wanderings even to the remotest borders of the ancient Holy Land, and could the more easily, among the many unforeseen accidents of every day, accustom the Twelve to that higher belief and that firmness of their whole spirit which was yet wanting to them, and at the same time give help to more, who were worthy of his loving help; it seems, indeed, as though his spirit had driven Him to calmly visit all the chief places in the whole land, which it was his first business to invite to the perfect true religion. But the nearer his life-work was to its completion, the nearer insight must He give to the Twelve into the whole virulence and true nature of the enmity of the world in its then ruling powers, and also into the necessity, to Him alone clear, of his near death; and if for this short glimpses in deeper lessons sufficed, these must be given more explicitly on every opportunity. We find from good proofs that the warnings of Christ, on the perversity of the dominant Schools, did not reach their greater frequency, directness, and sharpness, till towards the end of his whole active working: it was when his work appeared in the world more complete and distinct that this enmity also met Him more decidedly; and then the Twelve had been sufficiently prepared to understand more completely this antagonism, and more rightly to comprehend it.

CHAPTER XXIX.

THE DISTANT JOURNEYS IN THE NORTH.

THESE journeys occupied at least the whole summer of the last year, and of them we know from St. Mark many particulars; only that his peculiar mode of narration must here not be overlooked. Christ preferred staying in Galilee, and journeyed through it with the Twelve to the most varied quarters, so that He visited besides Decapolis (IV. s. 51 f.) the north-easternly neighbouring countries, which were then still ruled by the mild Tetrarch Philip; his residence in Galilee under Antipas became at the same time constantly more insecure. The repeated voyages over the lake of Galilee, and the constant journeys towards the three different provinces abutting on it, shew how fleeting his foot must already have been on earth; and there assuredly lies in these constant cruises on the lake a good portion of certain reminiscence. Once more, when He was staying in the district of Gennesaret (described Chap. XXVII.), some Pharisees and Scribes just come from Jerusalem reproached Him with his disciples not being sufficiently observant of the laws of bodily cleanliness. But He seized this opportunity to establish not only in their presence, but in the presence of the multitude and especially of the Twelve, the true view of all which is clean or unclean for the spiritual man; and also to shew the whole perverseness of the Pharisees, and in general to lay down moral regulations. He went from thence north-westernly to the borders of the ancient city of Tyre, and went into a house intending to stay some time, but wished to remain here quite unknown. There soon however hastened to Him a woman of Greek education, but born here, to beg Him, as the Messiah of whose power she had heard, to heal her daughter possessed by an evil spirit. At first He would have nothing to say to her, but so much the more anxiously did she hang on the Twelve assembled before the house, so that even these, moved with compassion, beg Him to give her a decided answer. Then He informs her, He had not been sent to the heathen but "to the lost sheep of Israel," who had a nearer claim on his help: but as she succeeded in putting aside even this hindrance, through her meek humility, He gives in to her petition, moved by so much true faith. So little then will He reject even heathens from sharing in his gifts, and hence in his kingdom (for the kingdom is where his gifts work), if they, as is fair to ask, with stronger faith break through the stronger barriers which separate them from it. It seems even as though He would designedly give a plain example of this, as He was visiting countries where the heathen population predominated. The journeying extended further north even to the ancient province of Sidon, as far as any

members of Israel had ever settled in these quarters—
soon again to be principally occupied by heathen. From
thence He turned back in a south-easternly direction,
probably crossing the Jordan north of the lake of
Galilee, then eastwards from this into the midst of the
province of Decapolis, and so among a predominant
heathen population. Here He healed a deaf man who
stammered, by a mode of healing touched on somewhat
more minutely (oben 224): but in vain did He charge
most earnestly those who had brought the deaf man for
healing, not to speak of it; they could not refrain for
astonishment.

At this time and place is fixed a second feeding of
the multitude of which we spoke above (Chap. XXVII.).
From the eastern shore of the lake He crossed over to
the province of Dalmanutha, by which probably is meant
the south-west of Galilee. The Pharisees left Him no
rest even here: they demanded of Him a sign, but only
to lead Him into temptation. He decidedly refused to
accede to such demands of unbelief appearing under the
pretext of belief, and declared at that time, with special
meaning, what was generally to be thought of such
askers for a sign. The Spruchsammlung, and still more
St. John, intimate very clearly the meaning of his answers
to such demands: but no expression of this sort from his
mouth took naturally deeper hold, than that only one
great sign would be given to that generation, very much
against their will, but all the more surprising and crushing,
that of the old prophet Jonas. As he returned from the
depths of the sea in order to speak with all the more

force by his own person and his fate, witnessing for the truth of his words; so would He, after his apparent defeat, return to this generation speaking with words all the more potent. This prophetic intuition, the truth of which we shall see marvellously fulfilled, was long and deeply rooted in their minds.

Vexed at such perverse demands, He withdrew again over the lake to the eastern shore: and the old narrative preserved from this journey a remarkable saying of his. They intended to visit again that twice-mentioned lonely district on the eastern shore: but the Twelve had, at their hasty departure, taken only one loaf with them; they had forgotten all other stores, their absence not being remarked till they were on board. Then He spake to them of the leaven of the Pharisees and the Herodians, and how they were to beware of it: so full was his heart yet of displeasure with those perverse demands, which only shewed an impure heart; whereas the members of God's kingdom must keep their heart constantly as pure as though they were continually keeping the Paschal feast with pure food, after careful putting away of the old leaven. But they thought He intended merely to warn them; as they had forgotten the bread, to take no leavened bread from the Pharisees; and for the third time they need the solemn reminder to dismiss such lower considerations and cares. For plainly this narrative was intended to complete the course of lessons begun with the two above: even one small loaf suffices easily for them all; and to forget too anxious care for the corporeal, is better than forgetfulness and misunderstanding of higher things.

It is plain that they now staid at this lonely place for some time. When they went later on the eastern side of the lake district, into a small town whose name is now somewhat doubtful to us, there was brought to Him a blind man whom He healed, but strictly charged him, in order to avoid notice, to remain at home and not let himself be seen much in his own place. From hence, keeping constantly east of the lake and of the Jordan, He visited even the extreme north-east of the Holy Land, pressing on till He reached the place, where, below mountain peaks rising ever higher towards the north, near the then newly-built Cæsarea Philippi, poured forth the sources of the Jordan; without however visiting the capital, He staid some time in the smaller places. Thus far had He now been persecuted and driven away even to the furthest mountain peaks in the land, and that, if not openly yet plainly enough, by the rulers of the people of the true religion: the providential fate determined for Him revealed itself in its inner development ever more plainly to his Spirit's eye, and He had long been prepared for all; but He felt equally sure that it was high time to make gradually plain before the Twelve even the worst and most painful which He foresaw as to his own position in the world, in order to point out to them what, in this respect also, are the duties of the true members of the Church of the completed true religion. For the first time He now purposely started in the circle of his Twelve the question of his own nature: the various views formed of Him in Israel had been repeated, when Peter expressed solemnly, in the name of all, his rock-firm conviction that He was the Messiah. It is here certainly to be noticed that St. John (vi. 69) connects this solemn utterance of Peter with an earlier occasion: but there might well be several such moments, in which this conviction thrilled more strongly through the hearts of the Twelve, and sought even in open speech an inspired expression; though the several Evangelists might have different opinions as to which of such moments was the most sublime and least to be forgotten. The present moment had this peculiar to it, that the Saviour Himself called forth this confession of belief without any external occasion; but the great question must at some time become the subject of solemn conversation, and at the right time He had occasion enough within Himself to bring on the subject. Doubtless at such a free cheerful confession his own Spirit deeply rejoiced: He experienced for the second time that pure joy which (Chap. XXVII.) once before the joy of the Twelve in their life-work and his had prepared for Him; but if then they might rejoice at their success in their first attempt, it was here rather the pure belief embracing the whole future, the first condition of all higher joy, which was here uttered from Peter's inspired mouth. Only where this is present, is there actually present the foundation for an inexhaustible working for the kingdom of God; and hence likewise is there laid firm as a rock the foundation for an unspeakably fruitful working in his Church: and when this rock-firm faith met Him from the midst of the now long founded community of the perfect true religion so freely and cheerfully, there was given to Him again one such a moment of purest joy, nay, of the most blissful looking forward into the whole boundless progress of the Messianic life-work. And yet, according to the Spruchsammlung and the older narrative, He now strictly forbade them to speak of Him as the Messiah in such unrestrained joy; rather He shewed them at this very time the destiny, deeply painful and yet providentially determined, which was before the Messiah in the world: and when Peter, directly He gave this unexpected turn to the discourse, whispered He had better be silent on such things, He was so little to be checked from uttering clearly and completely all that was now to be said, that He all the more repeated, quite openly before all the Twelve, the same painful presentiment according to its hidden truth, and shewed the duties which God's kingdom lays on every one of its members for this as well as for every similar crisis. So little then had He proposed that question on what He really appeared and was esteemed in the world in order merely to elicit that confession, and so closely joined in his mind with the joyful presentiment which it called forth was the painful likewise: but He shews *this* just as plainly, and prepares his own to meet the dangers with the right weapons. And so too in St. John's account of the joyful exclamation of the disciples (John vi. 70), no thought is to his spirit so immediate as that of the black destiny of betrayal which lurked among the Twelve. But the Twelve can now at most hear such painful intuitions and solemn admonitions in silence: and thus is seen a constraint from the contrast between that their joyful faith and these so troubled forebodings of his. No former experience of theirs is able to explain this contrast: yet to the pure faith, that faith which had now at least in some of them become firm as a rock, it is possible to overcome even this contrariety. Faith already penetrated by the heavenly truth, and again directed simply to this, is enabled to see, just as surely and certainly as if they had been already realised, the transfiguration and victory of that divine life-work, which the gloom and sufferings of time yet cloud over. But now at that time the earthly life-work of Christ with the rock-firm foundation of his Church was all but completed, although its conclusion, its outer veil, so to speak, was yet to come: that foundation once laid, the whole inner glory and transfiguration were there: and although the outer glory could as yet be seen by no eye of flesh, yet the spirit's eye was enabled already to see it; and though not yet clear and not yet permanently or by many with equal clearness, still already it could be seen by some chosen spirits in moments of higher intuition: and if everything spiritual can at first be seen only momentarily quite clear and shining as in heavenly transfiguration, wonderfully surprising indeed and inspiring is the first moment of this glory, when mortal man, so far as he may, is surprised for the first time by the glorious picture irresistibly overpowering him, and what his spirit inwardly sees as certain comes before him radiant also from without. This is the great and eternal importance of the history of the Transfiguration, which is rightly inserted at this place: now the three most trusted disciples at least, on a high mountain whither the Saviour had led them, suddenly see Him transfigured and conversing with Elias and Moses, and hear Him out of the cloud, which again removed these heavenly visitants, declared aloud to be the Messiah. A second exalted moment since the Saviour's baptism is possible for Him on earth: but if at his baptism heaven opened for the first time, it opens here much more gloriously to pour its light on the earth. Elias and Moses most naturally represent not only what was most exalted, but also what was most enduring in the Old Testament: with them is now linked the Messiah: not till his transfiguration do they appear again on earth, but only that the earth may hear again from heaven not only "This is my beloved Son," but also "hear ye Him." This is all, for the present elevation of the Messianic history, not too high: we have in view at once the whole course of this development from that moment of the baptism, and see here at once, as in a prelude, the eternal glory beginning, hardly held back by what was first to be completed on earth. Thus the most exalted will here put on intelligible form, the unutterable exhaust itself in words: and everything lower, which perhaps might have given occasion to this reminiscence and representation, is lost here in the purest shining sublimities. The narrative belongs also indisputably to the oldest Gospel fund of narrative. But should we, after 2000 years, form fancies of building huts here, the whole shining manifestation would at once again escape us, and nothing of it be left save the "to Him shall ye hearken" (Deut. xviii. 15). It is further expressly told us that the three did not tell of this glorious sight till *after* the Resurrection. But further, how easy it might be to the inspired glance to see the return of an Elias, the old appendix to this narrative in fact informs us. For when the three, as it continues, asked the Saviour how then about the tradition of Elias preceding Messiah? He allowed indeed this view after its inner truth, but declared that if the Messiah must, according to the Scriptures, suffer much and die, and that this was now speedily imminent; so must his predecessor, who had already come, be a like sufferer, the Baptist namely, whom on other occasions He likened to Elias. Thus surely did all the older ideas and hopes, under the quite new creative ardour of Christian experience and intuition, readily flow into a new mould, and took naturally new forms. And further, the thing itself teaches us, that all such heavenly words, though Old Testament words, yet sounded now with such divine truth and power as was never heard before in this world, and whose new truth must for the first time thus powerfully impress itself. And yet, in truth, how far the Twelve, excepting the three, at least in harder cases, were yet behind what they should be, was here shewn in an example given at some length. When He returned to them He saw them surrounded by a crowd, and in violent dispute with some scribes. His appearance (as though He had been long expected) put all at once into violent commotion, and they hastened towards Him with greeting. On his enquiry into the cause of so violent a dispute, one tells

Him he has brought to them his deaf and dumb son, suffering from the demon of the falling sickness, that they might heal him; but they had not been able to heal him: we may readily imagine how the scribes now attacked the disciples, who hardly knew how to defend themselves. Then deep pain seizes Him, not so much on the disciples' account as for the whole unbelieving and perverse generation, in whose perverseness however the disciples shared more than was reasonable. His own treatment which He then at once begins convinces Him indeed of the peculiar difficulty of this case, and on further enquiry He learnt from the father that his son had suffered from a child of this sickness: yet from compassion on the father, who willingly declared the right belief in his healing power, He made preparation to heal him undisturbed by the increasing crowd, which after considerable labour completely succeeds. To the disciples, who afterwards in the house asked Him the cause of their failing, He shews them how they are yet wanting in the whole magic power of entire belief; and how nothing hard can be successfully accomplished by *that* kind of men who always (as perhaps the Pharisees) go to work with fasting and praying, and think they thus possess all the divine means of strengthening the spirit. In this reply, as applied to the case before them, lay only the reproof that they had too hastily remitted believing zeal for their healing work, led astray by their own doubt and by the perverseness of the opposing scribes: fasting and prayer are not, as taught by the existing schools, everywhere sufficient means to strengthen the spirit in difficult work. Thus arrived then the last days and weeks which He could spend in the north. He wandered much with the Twelve through Galilee proper, wishing to remain as far as possible unknown; and his chief care was to accustom the Twelve ever more firmly to the thought of his approaching earthly end.

He visited in the concluding period specially Capernahum, as though He felt most difficulty in parting with the very place where He had once the longest unfolded his higher activity. Here too it was, where, according to the Spruchsammlung, He seized every opportunity, in those last days, of shewing both by his own example and by the instructive saying, in what manner the members of the community of the perfect true religion must behave in questions on rule, rank, and honour: the Spruchsammlung at least makes use of this crisis to put together all the marvellously deep utterances on such more complicated relations of life. And doubtless it was in the somewhat later times of this period that He spoke most and most decidedly about them, although He continued even to his earthly end everywhere to treat of the same higher moral duties here discussed. For the community needed first a firmer foundation and longer duration, before these duties of the higher Love could be profitably taught in it: now however, after that He Himself had, in the midst of his Own, everywhere proved the power of the higher Love to be inseparable from that of the Truth, it was easy to teach this harder duty in plain examples and words as well. We propose here, merely for the sake of meeting its difficulties, an example somewhat harder to comprehend, which He gave of the dealing of Him and of His towards the existing authorities. When He again visited Capernahum with the Twelve after a longer absence, having Himself gone, somewhat the first, into the house which was here ever open to Him, the collectors of the yearly temple impost, who had probably long waited in vain for the Master of these Twelve, who was still properly a citizen of Capernahum, fell in with Peter, and asked him, as the recognised chief of the disciples, whether his Master does not pay the double drachma. It might be supposed that, as the Messiah, for which He was taken by many, and as the opponent of the scribes and the existing spiritual authorities, as He might be regarded, He would probably not pay the tax; and the Master's precedent would then bend the disciples also. Peter said "yes" to the question, but had first to get the Master's decision. Christ however asked him first the question, whether in his opinion the taxes of a kingdom ought to be exacted from the king's relatives or from strangers. As they serve for the support of the existing order of things, and so fall into the hands of those who maintain the established order, the king and his immediate ministers; it follows that those who exist merely to rule, and in ruling must get their livelihood, need not themselves pay taxes. Thus among the people Israel the Levites paid no taxes, because, as standing according to the original constitution as Jehovah's immediate representatives, they had to keep up the established order; and the Romans paid no taxes as having become the lords of all other countries, and having undertaken for them the care of the government. Hence, also, Christ, as Head of the true Kingdom of God and of the new Israel into which the old had passed, and with Him his highest officers, should be free from taxation, and need trouble themselves no longer about the old order of things. But in order to give no offence, He will with his people pay the taxes, and respect the existing authorities so far as they were only demanding obedience in temporal matters: and how easy it is in truth to find such worldly possessions as are needed (for *e.g.* paying the required taxes)! In the mouth of the first fish which Peter takes, on casting a line at the Lord's bidding, he shall find a stater, equal in value to four drachmæ—sufficient to pay the tax for both. That this was done and the tax paid in this way, we are not told: the expression originated from well-known though very rare examples of such supplies found in fish: but how the blessing of the higher religion rests even on such temporal employment is often dwelt on in the Gospels (compare Chap. XVI). Such then were Christ's views on the relation between Him and His and external rule. (Compare Matt. xxii. 15—22.)

CHAPTER XXX.

The Feast of Tabernacles in Jerusalem.

UNSETTLED meanwhile as was Christ's foot more and more, and continually as He wandered in the north with the Twelve; He had no desire, since his last visit to the feast in Jerusalem, and since the founding of his Church, to go thither again. The Passover had passed this year without his having appeared there; and the Feast of Tabernacles now approached without any apparent symptoms of his journeying up thither. And why should He needlessly and prematurely visit a place, which He had already known by experience, and constantly newly experienced, to be the focus of all the hostility against his life-work? He had constantly, in the education of the Twelve, and the completion, so far as possible, of the rest of his daily work, work infinitely more important to do than contending with the leaders and supporters of the spiritual authority and the laying bare their nakedness. Yet it could not have been his intention to avoid for ever the centre of all existing true religion and its authorities, nor evidently ever was it. Rather, if his life's work, present as it ever was to his Spirit, and daily as He was advancing it in the world, could have conquered for all time and all nations without a fatal conflict (and the possibility of this He can never have quite given up, still less in his human will rejected it); it must have conquered from this centre; and in any case He needed to have strength and courage enough, once more freely and openly, at this high centre itself, to offer it for their free judgment to the heads of the people, when it was already nearly completed so far as He could now complete it—would they make it their own or not? He must once more appear openly before them, just as He was, as He taught, and as He worked; to see whether they would let Him thus be and teach and work; in fact, lay no intentional impediments to the advance of the complete true religion, or would they not?

When now in this year the Feast of Tabernacles approached, and He (as we must assume) was just come to Capernahum, his brethren living here (who were not indeed downright hostile to Him, but indifferent and lukewarm towards his doctrine) proposed to Him the question, if He had Messianic powers and works, why did He not appear quite openly with them in Judæa? Galilee, in which alone for a year He had moved, was held, as compared with Judah and Jerusalem, a country in which one only works, so to speak, in the dark; Jerusalem alone is the high illustrious world in which He must reveal Himself. To such words, reported by St. John (John vii. 2—5) with remarkable honesty, He only replied "his time was not yet come;" *He* must put up with much suspicion and hate, of which they now knew nothing; they might go up, He would not go up yet. So they went up without Him. He had however, in thus replying, only refused to go up in the usual manner, namely in the public Galilæan caravan, in order not to enter before the feast into the Holy City in a festal procession: He would thus have been at once known there, and would have, as if intentionally, excited the notice of the authorities, which now He earnestly wished to avoid; for He still felt that his life's work was not to be broken off through his own impetuosity; and He had still cause to be eager for every hour, in which He could continue to devote Himself to the Twelve and to other sufferers. There was however in this matter another course open to Him. He might go up some days later: He thus avoided the public festal entry, and yet, as the feast lasted seven days, and had too a concluding great day in the eighth, could come into the midst of the throng, and discover how people in Jerusalem, amid the concourse of such numbers, were disposed towards Him and his work. This course must seem to Him, in fact, to offer many advantages, irrespective even of the needless great dangers which the earlier entry would have occasioned. For it was far more moderate and forbearing to appear in this great centre, where in any case his cause must be ultimately decided, once more making indeed no denial of the Truth, yet otherwise seeking all quiet reserve and peace; in order to gain all the more leisure for the complete exposition of his cause, and to try all that could be achieved by the deepest self-negation and quiet on his part. It may even be said it was a providential duty of love not to make the disturbance of his work too easy to his enemies; and, with all the honesty and boldness which the work itself demanded, still, so long as possible to keep out of the way. He did not then enter Jerusalem till during the week, but "as in secret," avoiding purposely all notice, far differently from the time when He entered for his final Passover: He was however accompanied by his most trusted friends. His enemies had long waited for Him in vain, whilst the judgment of the multitude, always so loudly expressed on feast days, was divided about Him: but at the same time, from fear of the lesser excommunication with which the spiritual authorities had already threatened his followers, it was a good deal suppressed.

Yet He appeared in the very middle of the festal week, in the colonnades of the outer sanctuary, teaching; and actually escaped all more violent interruption among the people, as well as the snares of the enemy, longer than He usually did in the capital. We must indeed, from the reports before us, assume that He actually remained till the feast of the dedication of the Temple in December (John x. 22. Bd. IV. s. 356 f.), if not always in the capital itself, still in its neighbourhood, and in Judæa.

In this quarter of a year He had thus time and opportunity enough to learn to know most completely the settled feeling of the multitude, and still more that of its spiritual rulers towards Him and his work; and to shew them sufficiently, though with all self-restraint and foresight, what manner of man He was at the full maturity both of his doctrine and his activity. And certainly this quiet and yet perfectly plain revelation of his entire being, at the decisive centre of the spiritual power, during the meridian height of his public working, belonged so essentially (so to speak) to the duties of his Messianic office, that it would have been much missed had it been wanting. Thus only could and must be finally decided, whether his work on earth were to conquer peacefully or not: for here in Jerusalem were bound so singularly close together, all the treasures of science, and all the motives and means of action, as they had been nowhere else: and that the final decision was prepared with such entire quietness, originating in the deepest necessity and without the very least violence of surprise and appeal on his part, was no small advantage to the good cause itself: so that in this, as in everything else, we must not a little admire the heavenly, clear, and sublime view, which urged Him now to act in Jerusalem as He did. We must hence also feel very grateful to St. John, that He in his Gospel has described these encounters much more definitely in time and place than had been done in the earlier accounts. The older accounts tell us likewise, that the final decision in Jerusalem followed after a solemn general battle against all the tendencies then dominant: but in their characteristic manner some only of the most prominent points of the dispute are put together, and these again are accumulated on the last two days of the last festal journey; nay, this whole crisis, as decided by a journey in the autumn, and a final Passover journey preparatory for the final end, is there lost sight of. But we shall be able to speak more at length below, on the more minute events of this last journey.

In St. John's manner of painting the events of the last stay but one in Jerusalem, he brings forward, in his peculiar manner and in the freer repetition usual with him, many characteristics of what he wished himself to recall, but nothing except what most intimately concerns the grand question of this very period of the public life and work of Christ. Will the Saviour at length, in Jerusalem itself, on that brilliant elevation from which He now shines forth into the world, and in that entire unreserve of his language which He now uses, in spite of his forbearance, by the rulers or even by the multitude in the necessary way, be recognised and accepted? That is the grand question of this stage of the development of the history. How much was there to speak for Him in Jerusalem! and even if the opinions of the rulers, with very few exceptions, had already turned too decidedly against Him; the multitude was however freer from prejudice, and, less bound by mere scholastic views, might yet decide for Him. But the way in which the multitude, after long wavering and uncertainty in the strife between the most diverse conceptions and opinions, was at length carried away into the general rejection of Christ, nay, his persecution to the death,—this is here most vividly described: and the way in which all the several considerations on which it all turned in this long fluctuating strife, through Christ's merit carried on tolerably quietly, are portrayed—with such truth, though only with the slightest touches; *this* is the most instructive lesson in this narrative. And as in this manner all the characteristics are here related, yet only so far as they are important for enabling us to see before us the last great event which the history of these three months had taught; so the whole narrative of these days is subordinated to the proper treatment of one single subject, which, once entered upon, proceeds through a hundred changes in word and in action on its shifting course, till it arrives at length at its final conclusion. We shall give here a slight sketch at least of it, as from it we get the clearest insight into the reasons why Christ's cause could not conquer even in the multitude as it was; and here, as nowhere else, can look into the confusion of the strife about Jesus' true character, which one time, before and after his death, was to be debated with such animosity.

When He appeared teaching among his enemies, the doctors object He is not a learned man worth listening to. This is a first reproach then, which is not without weight with the unlearned mob. But He shews how surely it is a question of something else than school learning; it is the question of doing the will of God, that is, the complete true religion necessary alike for all men, the same which He preaches and for which they would kill Him (John vii. 15—19). When the multitude think this cannot be so, and are inclined to look on it as an exaggeration of his fancy, He shews how wrongly the

Scribes condemned Him for his former work of healing in Jerusalem (Chap. XVIII.), in which the multitude were not guiltless: the people then are surely in danger of ill-treating Him still worse, doing Him even fatal wrong. They have no fitting reply to make to this; so the popular favour inclines towards Him; they cannot help also thinking that the rulers, who say nothing to Him, probably had already recognised Him as Christ: only that He is of such well-known descent perplexes them; to meet which He shews how little important earthly parentage is here. But when He, on this, touches on his heavenly descent, the maintaining of which long before seemed to the rulers blasphemy, they wish to arrest Him at once; but the multitude rather incline to the miracle-worker, and the rulers do not venture to take Him. The rulers now, in consequence of this favourable feeling of the people towards Him, only send spies to take Him, if perhaps the people might again become disinclined to Him: but a kind of unintentional scorn sounds in his last public saying for the day, that He will go soon enough from thence; but this too is miserably misunderstood by his enemies to mean that He would go among the heathen, of which they have secretly greater fear than they will allow. On the eighth, the great concluding day of the festival, He spoke with unusual emotion to the assembled people on true faith: the Apostle here, in breathing new life into the sayings of Christ, proceeds from the two fundamental conceptions, the most exhaustive of the true notion of the Messiah, and on which also the perverse judgments of men were sure to take most offence; because it became now more and more essential to have right notions about Him. These conceptions are of life and light; only that Christ here (as doubtless the Apostle remembered), on account of the peculiar ceremony of the day, instead of speaking of life generally, spoke of the water of life. Then were many much moved and inclined to account Him the Prophet, the forerunner of the Messiah, or Messiah Himself; while others had doubts of the last, as He was not from Bethlehem, of David's stock; others were even inclined to take Him prisoner; yet they did not venture, held captive simply through the power of his words; so that the officers returned to the rulers having done nothing: among these rulers, indeed, only very few ventured to remark on the great wrong they had been on the point of doing (viii. 21—30).

When He then next proceeded, from the notion of light, to speak of right faith in order to cling to his manifestation, the Pharisees, fettered by their low earthly thoughts, raised their ever returning objections; but sought in vain thus to work on the people. Nay, when on another day, an ordinary sabbath, in view of his speedy departure—in spite of all the constant, almost intentional misunderstanding on the part of his enemies— He called with increasing emphasis for true faith, He found thereupon many inspired by such faith. But when He now would speak to those very men who would believe on Him of the higher duties and consequences of true faith, and would convince them that only the truth to be won by faith can procure them the freedom they desired; their national pride took offence, and they became gradually more bitter against Him, the more decidedly He defended his expression and followed it through all its consequences; so that they would actually have stoned Him, had He not, preventing the full outburst of their fury, got quietly away from them out of the temple.

But that same day He healed, according to his wont, one born blind: when this got abroad, forced as they were to admit the truth of the miracle, they pretended to have found in Him a great sinner for having done this kindness to the poor man on the sabbath; they persecuted in consequence the man restored as well as his parents: and when he rejected (as no sound arguments) their advice to regard his benefactor as a sinner, they put him under the lesser excommunication; but could neither prevent the blind man becoming even more deeply rooted in his faith, nor their being by him denoted, as they deserved, ever more plainly and openly, blind leaders; disagreeable as it was to them to hear it, and much as many of the people were influenced by it: thus a great inclination began again to arise in his favour among the people. But when at length He appeared publicly at the feast of dedication in a rather numerous assemblage, and there to the passionate demand He should at length, if He were the Messiah, openly shew Himself such, and put Himself accordingly at their head as an earthly king; He only replied, they should first have the true faith, in order to see that with

Him is eternal life and salvation, and that He and his work and word are inseparable from God: their fury breaks out again against his imagined presumption towards God, and they are so little to be softened by his most true representations, that He has to hurry away to escape from their full fury.

Thus then had it been decided by this so long-suffering and patient long-continued stay in Jerusalem, that even the multitude, in spite of its pitiable condition, and in spite of the sparks of a less corrupt, better spirit which at certain moments flashed forth to the shame of the hardened leaders, was yet incapable of actually taking hold of the true salvation when it was at length brought near to it; because at last, even when otherwise they had not been wanting in willingness, some too firmly rooted prejudices of various sorts blinded their eyes and made them miserable tools in the hand of their blind leaders. When this attempt had also been in vain, Christ might mourn, as according to the oldest Gospel writing He did mourn towards the close of his manifestation: how often had He laboured in vain to gather like a hen the chickens of Jerusalem under his wing; but they themselves would not be so saved by Him! Of other events during this stay in Jerusalem and Judah, we know nothing certain. Yet this is the probable date, when the Saviour was staying so long in the capital, and tormented by the schoolmen with all possible tempting questions, at which we may place the story about the woman taken in adultery, which was inserted quite early in St. John's Gospel at this place where it probably seemed appropriate. It is assumed in it that He had by night his lodging on the Mount of Olives. When then He had one morning returned to the outer court of the temple, and sat down to teach, the Scribes and Pharisees brought to Him an adulteress taken in the very act, in order to enquire of Him, whether He would apply to her the punishment of death by stoning appointed by the old Mosaic Law for such adulteresses. Without doubt they long knew the gentleness of his judgment on such sinners among the lower orders whom the spiritual rulers condemned most deeply; whilst hypocritically they avoided in their own case rather the appearance than the essential part of the corresponding sins. But He made as though He heard it not; stooped down, and with his fingers wrote on the ground, apparently in spirit only busied with Himself, while He doubtless began to write down the same as He afterwards said aloud, and thus meant at the same time to make those present, who so forgot their own characters, mutely attentive: but as they did not stop asking, He looked up, and called on him who felt himself innocent among them, to first cast the stone at her; He then stooped down and quietly wrote on for Himself. Solemnly however as the embassage from the Sanhedrim— the oldest at its head—had come to Him, they shewed little solemnity in leaving Him punished by their conscience, the eldest first: when the last of them was gone, He dismissed the woman with the solemn command not to sin again. This narrative belongs in truth, in its whole character, to the later narrative stock; and it is hard to say, how far in its several features it is historical: yet in its final purport it agrees very well with the rest of the narrative, which shews us the behaviour of the Saviour, and that of the equally proud hypocritical spiritual rulers of that time towards the sins of the lower orders.

CHAPTER XXXI.

THE STAY ON THE EAST AND ON THE WEST OF THE JORDAN.

DECISION OF THE SANHEDRIM ABOUT CHRIST.

WHEN the Saviour, as above related, resolved to depart from Jerusalem, He resorted to Bethany on the other side Jordan towards the north, to the same place where he had, under the Baptist's hand, felt the first moments of his Messianic mission. The choice of the place just now is as remarkable, but also certainly just as intelligible, as his having for the last time visited Capernahum (Chap. XXIX.) He foresaw how soon his earthly daily task must come to an end: and where could He more suitably prepare Himself for this end, than at that place where everything reminded Him of the first consecrated moments of his public activity? For the end must be not less divine and great than was the beginning.

Then met Him likewise here at this place, where the Baptist had so long worked, many believers, finding that all which the Baptist had expected and prophesied of Him had actually been fulfilled in Him (so far, that is, of course, as it could as yet be fulfilled). He might have staid here not many weeks, when He received very sad news from a household very dear to Him in the other Bethany, which lay not far from Jerusalem on the eastern slope of the Mount of Olives. This was the comfortably off household of Lazarus, whose hospitality He had often enjoyed in his wanderings: the two sisters of the head of the house also loved to listen to his words; and in no house did He feel so much at home as here. Martha was probably the younger, while Mary managed the house; Lazarus was probably younger than both; Simon the father, surnamed the Leper, appears to have been dead at this time, but to have been living at Jesus' first public working. It used to be told, how in earlier time, on a visit once of Jesus to this house, the sisters had at the same time busily attended on Him, but in very different ways: Martha waiting on Him, and feeling she could not shew loving attention enough; Mary engaged in silent listening to the Master's word, she too feeling as if she could never be satisfied with listening. When now Martha, unwearied in bringing external comforts of all sorts which she thought would please the Saviour, came to Him and asked Him to bid her sister help her also in such offices of love; in loving anger He reproved her too great care for such things, and added, one thing only was needed for every one—care for the higher divine matters; and that was the good part Mary had chosen which could not be taken away from her.

The brother and sisters had probably been converted

to the higher faith, when Christ in earlier times used to stay much with their father since dead, when he, whether agreeing or doubting, had discussed much with them the new Master. The sisters now sent Him word that his friend Lazarus was dangerously ill: and as they sent this message a long way to Him, they plainly wished Him to come and help them.

He certainly was not lacking in good will to help his dear friend: but He had to reflect that a return into the neighbourhood of Jerusalem might at once be fatal to Him: this the Twelve also knew, and they certainly spared no pains to keep Him back from such a project, of going thither again and that so soon.

He overcame however this hesitation, and saved the friend already deceased. So St. John tells us; and nothing can be more historical than this event, the only one of much importance which he tells us, belonging to this last period before the Paschal journey. For that it is omitted in the older accounts is not of much importance: the events of this last period, from the departure out of Galilee to the last procession to Jerusalem, are not in them so accurately separated; whilst St. John supplies with most obvious intention this defect: and, like everything else which he tells us, this particular event also fits in most perfectly into the true course of the whole development, as was touched on at greater length above (Chap. XXVIII.) But it is at all events plain that St. John, in giving us a most vivid picture with even unusual interest, starts in his narrative from the same general view of Christ's earthly being and working, which is the spirit and the spring of his whole Gospel. We cannot even fail here to detect a certain art suitable to the general design of the Gospel. It is in fact observable, that St. John, in his whole Gospel, gives only one example of each of the principal "works" of Christ, but a satisfactory and sufficiently pregnant example: and so this is the only example of raising the dead which he instances. But as he delights everywhere to set forth Christ's life and light as the true life and light; so it seems to him, since this eternal life must extend even into this earthly life, that a raising from the dead is the best illustration of this great truth. And since now the earthly period of the shining of this single light in the earth's darkness must soon come to an end, he evidently thought it worth while to shew that in this last act also the same miraculous power of divine life revealed itself as in all earlier miracles. Thus no narrative of the Apostle is warmed by such a deep ardour and bounding vigour as this before us, where he attempts in one grand picture to portray the palpitation of His life for the life of the friend, as also His fight with the darkness of the world, and amid all, His calm of victory and His joy of victory shewing itself from first to last. These burst forth amid all the yet higher notes of the consciousness of the Messianic glory and this mighty proof of it. So soon then as He hears of the sickness, He exclaims at once with sublimest confidence, that the sickness would not lead to death, but to God and Messiah's glory; and remains quite quietly two days more at the same place. On the following day, as though a deep feeling said to Him suddenly, the sick man was then at the point of death,—as not a moment more is to be lost, He calls quickly his Twelve to go again with Him to Judæa; replies to their hesitation, "We must work as long as it is day," and then tells them more particularly, "Lazarus is fallen asleep:" on their understanding this of the ordinary sleep only, and consequently not being inclined to go with Him, He tells them at length plainly, as though only the more deeply convinced of it by their opposition, "Lazarus is dead," yet He would be glad to go with them to him that they might learn to believe on Him; and finally is least of all to be kept back from going by Thomas's somewhat cynical unbelief. But when they, coming down the eastern bank of the Jordan, and then crossing the river, arrived at Bethany on the fourth day from the moment of death, they learn he had been that long laid in the rock-hewn grave; and find many mourners assembled about the sisters. Nevertheless, Martha, who, at the news sent in advance of his coming, receives Him without the village before her sister, is clear in her faith in his Messianic power; Mary, who was sent for by her sister, came followed by the rest of the sympathizing friends, who thought she was hurrying out to weep at the grave. Then, while He sees all weeping, the moment comes for Him to act; and as though He must by repeated sighing, in deepest emotion and weeping, gather together all the deepest powers of love and compassion, He begins his work; bids them shew the grave, goes up to it in sight of the mourners, some of them perhaps angry with Him that He had not come earlier to save; He bids roll away the stone, while Martha gives her opinion that the dead "by this time stinketh;" He looks up in prayer and thanksgiving to his Father, full of divine assurance of victory, and with powerful voice calls forth the dead yet wrapped in his shroud; thus strangely refuting all the various doubts. And who, on reading this long, deeply inspired story, does not feel, from its whole manner of telling and construction, that boundless joy of victory beam forth, with which the first Christians contemplated the death of Christ's friends, and his own appearance in due time to give them new life? It is only the glance forwards, even into the great future, which could fill the Apostle's recollection of that great incident of the past with such heavenly joy, and shed a halo round his words here; and he misses the most beautiful part of the story, who fails to see or denies this. The Saviour's return into the neighbourhood of Jerusalem, and the recommence- ment of his work of all sorts so close to them, must have at once put the chief priests of the capital into greater disquiet. They had expected indeed He would not lightly return to Jerusalem or its neighbourhood again, and meanwhile would be left in the more remote frontier provinces, more and more forsaken by his fol- lowers who had been already excommunicated: they were disappointed soon enough by the occurrence in their neighbourhood, at which so many Jews in autho- rity were present; and hence resolved to lay the matter before the Sanhedrim, in order to arrive at a plan for the future. We know not now what Pharisees and other ecclesiastical chiefs were the first and most active enemies of the Saviour: as his cause advanced upwards from below, some time might elapse before the acting high-priest Caiaphas took closer notice of it. But if these enemies would now be no longer satisfied with small penalties against Him and his followers, but would induce the Sanhedrim, under the high-priest's presidency, to a measure of more complete destruction against Him, they must first of all think of a satisfactory pretence against Him; and such they could hardly fail to find. The deepest ground of the opposition lay, as has been remarked, in this alone, that on the one side the complete true religion, in all its rock-firm certainty and insurpassable splendour already in full action in the world, incarnate in the Saviour, met in the spiritual powers, on the other side no proper inclination; nay, not even the proper first condition for its reception was present in the great majority of those who would have preferred letting wither the true religion, which they thought they had in their hands and defended; and just when it was in greatest need of its proper completion, had no conception of the only right way in which this could be achieved. Had now this completed true religion come before them in an outwardly brilliant form—for example in that of a great conqueror over the Romans—they would have readily joined such a Messiah and accepted his innovations of any sort: but as every truth, still more the highest truth, must commend itself purely by its own merits to men; nothing then was more necessary than that the completion of true religion should offer itself in the least imposing forms to those who had to be first prepared as individual members of that community, in which alone they could arrive at its correct knowledge and cheerful acceptance. The ecclesiastics were from their whole education and position quite incapable of this: and as they despised the Saviour's doctrine, so they despised his works also, blinding themselves to its true nature with all manner of pretences. It was then inevitable, that as they would not accept the truth which presses them so close, they must become from step to step its most implacable enemies, and fall into the delusion that they could crush it likewise through the outward destruction of its Founder. Accordingly, if they would now overthrow Him through the accusation of heresy, they must take care to charge Him with nothing from which, as they well knew, He could easily defend Himself, for example, that He obstinately broke the sabbath: such a complaint moreover could not have brought about a sentence of death to be confirmed by the Roman procurator, as was then the custom. But there was one question from which the fatal blow might be more easily brought to bear, even his assertion of being the Messiah. This must have been now notorious, however He had striven to ripen the belief in Him as the Messiah among those alone with whom this belief served only as the incentive to the completed true religion; and it might easily have been most shamefully misinterpreted, however great the effort to steer clear of every injurious misconception. But if the wish were not to go into the ground and meaning of this fundamental tenet, but merely use it as a pretext for his bodily destruction, none better could have been found. For even the name and idea of a *king* at those times of subjection to the Romans, and the experiences of the times of the later Maccabees and of the Herods, had power to spread abroad a paralysing terror. The most timid might tremble at the thought, that if the people should follow further this *king*, a rebellion might arise against the Romans yet more terrible and destructive than the former: the fear at least of such a spectre might easily be spread everywhere, but nowhere more widely and successfully than in Jerusalem and the Sanhedrim itself. And those who wished to act with true acuteness and finesse in the matter, might, through such an accusation of the man to the Romans, think even to gain especial credit with them and praise for their vigilance and foresight.

Such sort of man was the acting High-priest Caiaphas. When the question about Jesus was debated in a sitting of the Sanhedrim, and many thought with a sigh, if He were let further seduce the people, the Romans would come to destroy both land and nation, and overthrow the already so much endangered sanctuary; Caiaphas suddenly broke in, as if a new higher light had dawned on him, almost ridiculing the others: he sees here no danger, but on the contrary a great advantage which might be gained for the people; the death of the one might bring advantage to the people, namely, gain for it anew the favour of the

Romans; let them reflect "what a gain it is for them that one man should die for the people, and that the whole nation perish not." This maxim was of course at once sufficient to lead them to a conclusion: it is at the same time equally intelligible, that the Christians afterwards, after that the Lord had fallen in quite another sense for the nation and for all mankind, found in that saying the truest prophecy, which the high-priest had uttered as against his will, and only as moved by the higher spirit of his priestly office. And so many another man prophesies the truth against his will, especially in a crisis of such importance: and it is a witness only to the very guileless thoughts of the first Christians, and St. John especially, that in such an answer of the high-priest they found something divine, and only in so finding were satisfied. The Sanhedrim resolved now, after this preliminary inquiry into the matter, that Jesus must be had up before their court, and hence any one who knew where He was staying was to shew the place. But even in the Sanhedrim He had a friend, Nicodemus: it is not impossible that He was now warned by him. It would indeed have been rashness, had He now at once, and as if to brave them, gone to Jerusalem, to shew Himself to his mortal enemies. He knew his time to be not yet come: He resorted therefore with his Twelve, not indeed beyond Jordan, but to the waste district on the north-east border of Judah, not far from Jordan, to a town named Ephraim. The Paschal festival was already not very far off: and from that district where He was now staying many people were already going to Jerusalem to attend it; such, that is, especially as before taking part in the Paschal festival had first to bring offerings of purification, lepers for example, who had been healed but not pronounced clean by the priests. Such, on meeting each other beforehand in the Temple, wondered that He had not yet come; nay, they imagined He would probably not yet come this time to the feast at all: for that the greatest danger here threatened Him must have been pretty generally known. But He had come in his own mind to quite another resolution.

CHAPTER XXXII.

THIRD ADVANCE.

Christ's Temporal Fall and Eternal Victory. His Resolution to meet the Crisis.

Though Christ saw clearly that the world was firmly resolved to crush Him and his work on earth so soon as possible, it was no longer his first necessity to escape from their blindness and fury in the way He had often done before, and had to do for the sake of his own work. For already his life-work, amid all the difficulty of the time and all its discredit with men, in the founding and educating of a church of the perfected true religion, was so firmly grounded that it might stand against all storms; and his spirit, which is itself the spirit of the perfected religion, had found in this community such a possibility at least of becoming vital in it and working on for ever, that He had no longer to fear He should quite vanish from this earth when He Himself must bodily leave it. We have seen this above in the development hitherto of his unrivalled history; and he knew it then better than any one else. For, while his life had been all the more laborious and difficult since He had drawn around Him the compact circle of a new family of the perfected religion, and had joined with his care for the whole world the particular care likewise for this little world now nearest to his heart, yet He had felt in this last period moments also of the highest and purest joy, and could now have a taste of his whole future majesty which was here to commence. And if He had already so far carried on the great work of his life that He could leave it to itself and Him in whose Spirit He had founded it, He had at the same time left nothing untried in any quarter to advance its existence and work in the world. His work was the revelation of the perfected true religion, its establishment upon earth through his own work in it and for it alone: and to shew that inexhaustible patience in commending it to that people, or rather that great community, and bring it home to them in every way which they were best prepared and called upon to understand and receive; what He, as an individual placed at that time and in that body, with all human and divine labour and love, could do for this work, He had perfectly done; nay, already in the midst of the great ancient church of the true religion, there stood a new one of that religion perfected, small as it was, all the more invincible, and little formed as it was, yet with a kernel all the firmer, and capacity for more infinite development.

In this state of affairs and in this confidence He had, accordingly, no longer to fear, as He once had, even the most deadly encounter with the chief priests and the people so easily led by them (Nach s. 63 f.): for this people in Jerusalem, dependent on the enjoyments, pleasures and advantages of the ecclesiastical system as it had formed itself in their midst, was certainly as much to be feared as the few rulers themselves who urged on his destruction; (just as, to quote similar instances, no people are more wretched than the populace of Rome, dependent on the papistical pleasures, enjoyments and feasts; and no people in the sixteenth century were more relentless against the Reformation than the Parisians under the rule of the court of the Sorbonne and the Jesuits). It is a consequence of the whole position of such capitals, that everything which most concerns the Empire, however remote may have been its origin, must always be decided in their midst; and there, where with the highest spiritual effort the highest truths can be proclaimed and the most widely effective salvation can be won, may just as easily the most extreme misconception and blindness rule, and the most unutterable woe be accomplished in wild passion. Even the ancient Israel, under the kings in which the noblest prophets worked, was counted the most unnatural mother of her own children, and as the worst persecutor of the prophets: it was all the same with the modern Jerusalem, as Christ Himself once exclaimed. In it now was to ensue the great decision on the cause of Christ, greater than any one of the earlier great decisions: He could predict the issue of a now repeated new visit to this city, and in his human nature wish to avoid it; but from the divine view of his cause He needed now neither to fear nor avoid it. But it would have been just as unworthy of

Him to bring about such a final decision through appearing in Jerusalem without reason, and thus sharing in the sin. The feeling of human justice and honour might have led Him, just because the people there wished to destroy Him, to appear under his enemies' eyes the sooner and more openly: but his cause and his character alike were raised infinitely above all human irritation and human bravado. If, on the contrary, a duty independent of the will of man brought Him there, then He could as little hesitate about going there as He had, shortly before, about going to Bethany or the Mount of Olives: it was further due to the position He took at that time, not to appear this time, as at the former feast of Tabernacles, reserved and silent, but freely and openly, although without courting observation. The higher duty was now ever before Him—in presence of his enemies, the more bitter they had become, all the less to draw back in fear and forgetfulness of his life-work; when now there was added a particular occasion in the path of duty, the higher duty combined with the lower, and nothing could hold Him back from going into the midst of the most threatening danger.

Such an occasion now arrived in the Paschal festival. Every man of the people of Israel was entitled, nay, bound to share in it in Jerusalem, although this obligation allowed of exceptions and excuses: nothing was looked on as more meritorious than the festal journey, nothing more impious than to disturb the festal joy of any one in Jerusalem. He resolved then to go this time to the Passover in Jerusalem. And He wished this time, like every one else, to appear with the Twelve freely and openly, without the reserve shewn at the previous festival, the cause of which was now wanting. In so doing He considered his life-work already all but finished; He knew into what danger He was going, and had a clear presentiment of what was impending: but He knew yet more certainly that here also He was only following his higher duty; He prepared then quietly for the festal journey, and resolved not indeed to court notice, but also not to oppose any public recognition of an innocent nature which met Him voluntarily; prepared even now in Jerusalem itself, and upon the journey thither, to proclaim only the same truth which He had always brought so home to the people, and although prepared for everything, yet neither in misanthropic ill-humour nor seeking death, nay, not driving from his breast the never-failing hope. He had ever followed the divine will in everything; He followed it even in this, as He felt clearly, last earthly crisis of his cause, represented as yet in a bodily form by Him; ready to suffer even the last extremity for it; and yet as surely hoping even to the last moment of his earthly life for the divine help and grace. It is the same wonderful mingling and reconciliation of human free will and complete human feeling with the devotion to the higher will, which marked his course through life, only more strongly and clearly the more the history rises to the highest crisis, and the more completely accordingly all here lived in the memory. For no portion of the chequered public life of Christ has come down to us in such completeness, even in its apparent trifling occurrences, as all this last period. It was rightly thought, that nothing from the first times of the Apostolic age was so important to know correctly as the last conclusion of that single history, even in all its little details: and although in the effort after most exact reminiscence some trifling variances nevertheless resulted, yet nowhere does the stream of this narrative flow from all its various sources so full and so smoothly as here. Even St. John found just here but little to tell of more particularly; but this little is, considered carefully, assuredly important and instructive enough.

CHAPTER XXXIII.

THE LAST FESTAL JOURNEY.

IF Christ at the taking this resolution staid (see above) in the north-eastern corner of Judæa, supposing He had wished to take the most direct road to Jerusalem, his journey would have first been towards the west by the great highway from Galilee and Samaria to Jerusalem. But then He would not have passed Bethany on the eastern slope of the Mount of Olives, past which, both according to St. John and the older account, their journey took them. This very route, stated to us so distinctly by St. John, has an unmistakeable connection with the direction past Jericho, which according to the older account He took on this last journey: and we have every ground for supposing à priori, that the recollection of the older narrative would have been of the greatest possible exactness in respect to these very events which universally seemed of such extreme importance, and consequently that they must be looked on by us as the most reliable possible, where St. John does not contradict them, and where we know no grounds for doubting their contents. The journey from the north-eastern corner of Judæa might indeed have passed Jericho, but it would doubtless have been some way round; and a direction past Jericho points rather in itself to a journey from the country beyond the Jordan. When now the Saviour, according to the older account, on his way to Jerusalem, arrived first at the borders of Judæa, journeying beyond Jordan, and so approached the capital past Jericho and Bethany, we have every ground for finding in this traces of more exact reminiscence. In fact, there is no reason why Christ should now have taken the shortest route: rather—now that his whole life had become continually more and more an unsettled wandering; now too that He had so many followers scattered about; since too the districts on the two banks of the Jordan especially had, as the places of the earliest Gospel working, become so dear to Him—we can well imagine that He resolved, on going up from the north-eastern border of Judæa (Mark x. 1), first to cross over Jordan, then cross back again over the river to Jericho, and so on to Jerusalem.

We may hence assume that the several occurrences on the journey, which the older narrative has preserved for us as especially memorable, now actually took place. They were doubtless not in themselves more memorable than a thousand others which have no memorial; but as having occurred at the very commencement of this last journey, they appeared, as did later everything connected with it, worthy of more particular notice and more exact reminiscence. As He would this time, like every one else, make the journey quite publicly and solemnly, many gathered about Him before the journey, in order from various motives to give Him one last word: for we may assume that this time, many besides the Twelve joined Him for the journey. Then it was some Pharisees proposed to Him the question "tempting Him" as to his judgment on the question of divorce when desired either by the husband or wife. These Pharisees had doubtless long heard how strictly He judged of divorce: besides at that time the case of the marriage (s. 51 f.) of his country's prince Antipas was much canvassed, in the meshes of which the Baptist had already let himself be caught: it might be supposed that He also would, like the Baptist, be caught in the obscure mazes of the difficult question: this was only one of the temptations into which his learned hypocritical enemies had repeatedly led Him. But He solved the question so decidedly and yet with such extraordinary truth, that they could meet Him no further in this quarter. When they brought to Him (as if to say farewell) some children for his blessing, and the disciples would have kept away from Him this interruption, as they deemed it, He the rather gave Himself lovingly up to the children, and taught on this occasion how the childlike temper must also continue in those who would be the most perfect members of God's kingdom. He had already started to continue the journey, when there hastened to meet Him a rich but in truth rather young man, to ask Him, with signs of high veneration, what he should do to obtain eternal life. His conversation with this man, as He tested his knowledge and still more his good will and receptivity for the duties of the true religion, and the way in which on this occasion a like conversation began on the highest duties and the blessed hopes of the true confessors of Christianity—all this must have correctly survived in memory more than many other things, as it happened at so peculiar a time and concerned some of the final and most difficult moral questions of the new Church. It may readily be supposed, and it is also expressly mentioned, that the journey this time passed with unusual solemnity. He walked Himself in front, in good heart, with the most unbroken trust, at the head of the Twelve and of the rest who this time accompanied Him: but some heavy sadness and evil misgiving seemed already to have fallen on his companions, and many followed Him walking under a kind of vague fear. From the Twelve themselves He never concealed the fatal dangers which He already foresaw He must encounter in Jerusalem. But He well carried it all through; and could not give up a particle of the genuine hope for the cause of God's kingdom one day to conquer even visibly. It is then no way surprising, that on this journey, leading of necessity, as all dimly saw, to some crisis, a certain dispute about rank and honour broke out among the Twelve. The two sons of Zebedee were always closer to Him than the others (although He valued not less the energetic Peter and his brother, nay, wished to see Peter first of all in every action): the two were probably of better family and richer than the others, and had wholly offered up their goods for the cause of the rising kingdom of God; in other respects also, in all decision and devotion, they competed with the best; they were also now accompanied by their mother Salome, now a widow, who had constantly shewn no less markedly the purest devotion for Christ's cause. They probably had for some time been looked on among the Twelve as the favourites of Jesus; and were themselves of fiery spirit enough, in return for the highest sacrifices, of which they felt themselves yet further capable, to expect the highest honours in God's kingdom when perfected. It was however, after a more exact reminiscence, only their mother immediately who ventured, on this journey, to speak a word for them to Christ: whilst, indeed, that such a matter was discussed at all between them and the Lord aroused the envy of the others, as they deemed themselves all alike zealous, and might for the most part rightly so deem. The marvellous penetration and truths which Christ revealed on this most delicate occasion, and the noble wisdom with which He stilled such emulations, form the most beautiful appendix to the conversations on rule and power among men which mostly fell in these last times, and in these first appear in their most profitable place.

But when He, having come over the Jordan to Jericho, was leaving it amid the large escort which accompanied Him throughout the whole journey; a blind beggar, who had discovered his presence, besought Him as the Messiah for healing, and would not be kept back from persistent entreaty, in spite of all who desired him not to interrupt the journey. So Christ, willingly interrupting his journey, came to the assistance of his firm faith. This occurrence also, as delineated by St. Mark in his graphic manner, would hardly have come down to us so accurately, had it not occurred at this last most important time: the older account, as we have it in St. Mark, had, as is quite unusual, preserved the name of the blind man who was cured—Bartimæus. And no doubt, as the story intimates, he remained constantly after that a well-known useful member of the new Church.

But a story was current of another conversion in Jericho on this last journey. A rich Jew named Zacchæus, who as chief publican of the city was no favourite, wished to see Jesus as He entered; and as he was little of stature, mounted a low mulberry-tree standing by the road at a place outside the town where He had to pass. The Saviour had scarcely seen him, when He bade him come down, as He would that day be his guest; and He did, in spite of all the murmuring, lodge with that unpopular man. But his hope of opening even to this son of Abraham the way to his salvation was at once most beautifully fulfilled: that day brought salvation to him, converting him into the most warm and honest member of God's kingdom. Thus beneficially worked now, as much as at first, the mere nearness and virtue of his presence. St. Luke takes, in conclusion, this little reminiscence of Zacchæus, who doubtless worked on long afterwards in the Apostolic Church, from a later Gospel narrative; and in placing, as he does, the adventure with Bartimæus before that with Zacchæus at the entering into the town, he probably followed likewise therein the order of this later account. From Jericho lay the direct road to Jerusalem, past Bethany, which lay to the east of the Mount of Olives: here St. John resumes his narrative, partly because on Lazarus' account this place seemed to him of such peculiar importance, partly because he finds here in the old account something to complete and improve. According to the older account (Mark xiv. 1—11), the Saviour, going thither as usual from Jerusalem for the night, on the second day before the Passover being at Bethany "in the house of Simon the leper," whilst He was going to the table, there came a woman with a valuable flask of genuine ointment, and breaking the flask poured it on his head. Some however of the Saviour's company took this amiss as waste, and thought it would have been better to have sold the precious ointment flask for a good sum, and given the proceeds to the poor; deeming, in thus judging, they would have met the Saviour's own view, who had always enjoined on his own particular regard for the poor. But Jesus reminded them to offer no reproaches to the woman; she had done a good work on Him: for they had the poor with them continually, but *Him* they would soon lose, and they might imagine she had anointed in advance his body for the burial: as her work had proceeded from pure love, so would it (especially as shewn by her at such a time when the love of all the world would turn from Him) be everywhere mentioned in the world in the Gospel with the Gospel itself for a memorial to her. Thereupon, as the older account tells us, Judas Iscariot went to betray Christ to the chief-priests; though here it is not expressly said that the traitor was of those who murmured—it is for the reader an obvious conclusion, and indisputably lies in the purport of the whole narrative.

But in this account the woman who shewed such love to Him had not been more clearly defined: and when the narrative became more circumstantial, a very different occasion of their censure might naturally have been thought of. We have seen in the example of another somewhat later narrative (that of the woman taken in adultery), that, at the time in which the Gospel accounts were talked of with ever livelier interest, Jesus was reproached with excessive consideration for women's frailties: the Pharisees moreover became looked on more and more exclusively as his incessant detractors and spies; as we see also from St. John's representation. Thus the account of the woman who anointed the Saviour appears to have been gradually drawn over to these favourite objects of the general Gospel narrative, and when inwoven with the earlier times of the Saviour's active working, to have taken a more generalized form. Thus it was told, that when Jesus, invited to the house of a Pharisee named Simon, would have sat down to table, a woman living in the town, but known for her loose life, came with a flask of ointment, and, moistening his feet with her many tears and kisses, had so to speak dried them with her hair and finally anointed them; when the Pharisee only wondered in silence how He, if He were a prophet, could be ignorant of the woman in her earlier life, He contrasted with the Pharisee's fancied justice, leading him to unloving harshness, the sacrificing love of this woman springing from the candid acknowledgment of her sins, and the great longing for redemption from its burden, and finally forgave her her sins. This is one of a hundred similar stories, as they kept ever forming themselves anew from the material at hand; so that not the particular purpose, but only the varied and beautiful composition and form of these stories is new. And this very later account it is which St. Luke admits in place of and to the exclusion of the earlier, and interweaves it with the earlier part of the Gospel history. But if St. Luke himself, through this proceeding of his, intimates to us that he looks on one of the two accounts only as a kind of duplicate of the other, we have the less cause for doubting its origin.

It seems now as if St. John had read both the earlier accounts, and endeavoured to amend what was defective in both, or was to be further carried on by the more exact history. Thus he mentions first of all, that Jesus came on the sixth day before the Passover to Bethany. As now (as will be made clear below) the fourteenth of Nisan (or the Paschal month), on which in the evening the Passover was eaten, being on that year a Friday, was looked on by him as a half-working day, in which, especially in the morning, any business could be performed, whilst St. John (John xiii. 1) at the same time accounts it the day of the Passover; it is plain that he looks on the thirteenth as the proper first day of the feast (which began in the evening), and consequently the sabbath as that sixth day in which Jesus came to

Bethany. He could, on account of the sabbath, travel over no long journey on this day, and had probably early in the morning arrived here from a place quite near. Secondly, St. John tells us it was Mary the sister of Lazarus, in whose house the Saviour took up his lodging, "who anointed his feet and wiped them with the hair of her head, so that the house was filled with the odour," while Martha waited upon them and Lazarus sat at the table: and in fact this is what we should imagine as probable. Thirdly, he expressly names only Judas Iscariot as he who had expressed his censure on the waste of the costly ointment: but we learn also from him the truest cause which might lead him to such an opinion: as the pursebearer of the company he thought he had a special call to make such a frugal remark, even though he had not been at the same time a thief and spent the money entrusted to him for his own profit, and so made the remark from an evil intention. Christ however then merely answered him, according to St. John, Suffer her to keep this for the day of my burial, as if He would fain have this day looked on as the day of his burial, on which such a custom was fitting; though on other days it would not have been fitting nor approved by Him. This day He staid in Bethany: but as this village, separated from Jerusalem by the Mount of Olives, was situated in a generally very thickly populated district, we see without difficulty how, as St. John tells us, the same day in the evening many came into this house to see Jesus and Lazarus at the same time; that the chief priests also in the Sanhedrim itself, as they had outlawed Jesus, were very spiteful against his host Lazarus, and sought to destroy him, as St. John tells us, was all consistent. The now rapid concourse of events made them quite forget the hospitalities received from Lazarus.

CHAPTER XXXIV.

The Entry into Jerusalem.

For the very next morning He meant to enter into Jerusalem, and prepared quite openly so to do: and soon enough were the proud but withal timorous chief priests to see Him as close as possible at work. There is no doubt that the ensuing entry into Jerusalem was, even by his own desire, to come off as a royal entry: He had no longer cause for hiding Himself either from the multitude or from the chief priests, as *Him* who He actually was and whom He felt Himself to be. Cheerful, showy processions were moreover, according to old custom, always permitted to those entering for the feast, and on these occasions much was overlooked. Further, a good number entered some days or weeks before to keep the feast in Jerusalem. And so for Him there was to be one day of exuberant and loud joy, such as sounds on the king's entry into his kingdom. He would at least no longer interfere with the conviction and hope of the world freely offering itself to Him; and both the conviction that his kingly work on earth was accomplished so far as He could carry it, and the cheerful courage in face of death, raised Him this day to a festal frame of mind, the direct opposite to that on his last entry. A misuse of the present public Messianic appearance was no longer to be feared: it might now be pretty clear everywhere in what sense He wished to be King and Lord; or if a new misunderstanding arose about this (Luke xix. 11) that might now be easily removed by Him, as He pointed back to his past and always uniform working. The people of the ancient true religion, as it was then on earth and had its centre in Jerusalem, were now to see Him coming quite openly as He who, if they joined Him with the honesty and love belonging to the perfected true religion, alone could save them; his destiny was in short all but finished on earth; but it would have remained unfinished, so far as He Himself had to work at it, doing and trying everything, if He had not tried this the last resource which could proceed from Himself. Yet it did not proceed from Him as something designed and undertaken by Him with long-continued cunning design: He only now allowed free play to the open joy of his followers; just as He, the day before, had only not checked the unwonted testimony of love in his host's house in Bethany.

The only part which He Himself took in the matter was, that He mounted an ass's foal for his entry: to appear publicly in this way and thus enter into a town was quite unusual with him; this was generally known, and consequently this resolution of his was regarded afterwards with peculiar attention. The older narrative in simple faith found, in the very way this ass's foal, at

Christ's command, had been sought, found and brought to Him as the rightful Lord, one of the symbols, consecrated of old, of the favourable commencement of a kingdom and a kingly procession. So the account appears in St. Mark, and quoted from him in St. Luke. In this older narrative it is further not distinctly said that He spent the last night in Bethany and started from thence in a procession: rather it is here stated quite generally, that when He approached Jerusalem and had already come to Bethphage and Bethany, He sent two of his disciples into the village lying over against them to fetch such an ass's foal. By this village is, according to all appearance, intended not Bethany, but the village lying somewhat further back, and not yet discovered, Bethphage—probably the same from which the day before He arrived at Bethany, and where also He was of late well known. Even then, though Christ never said at the time that He had chosen to enter on an ass's foal in consequence of a Messianic utterance of the Old Testament, which seemed here peculiarly appropriate, it is in itself probable, and we can hardly help so concluding. The oftener these recollections were followed up, the more certain must have seemed this regularly formed design of the Lord in the choice of this animal. The last composer of the present St. Matthew's Gospel inserts the Messianic reference; but, much more accurately, and in a certain respect with admirable candour, St. John mentions that the disciples at that time had not known Christ's intention in it, but afterwards, on later recollection of this time and this action, had correctly seen its importance from the Old Testament prophecy. Some of the assembled followers covered at once this foal with their own garments thrown on it; others, going before the procession, threw, according to old custom in such royal processions, their garments as a carpet on the road to make it even and decorate it; many plucked off green palm branches from the trees of the gardens close by, likewise according to old custom, to do honour to the procession; but all who went in front or followed behind sang a short Messianic hymn, which came suddenly into being in the exalted spirit of this moment, and which may be named the first song of the new Church, and from many tokens it was for long often chanted in the early times of this Church (Matt. xxiii. 39). As soldiers accustomed to victory and filled with the hope of victory address their general with inspiring words and pray Heaven for him, so are the winged words of this short song, glowing with the spirit of the early Christian hope of victory, true rallying words, around which the first squadrons of the Messianic faith took their stand: and we cannot doubt that they resounded that day for the first time, but afterwards were words never to be forgotten. St. John indeed touches on the events of this procession only briefly and in passing: for, from his less regard to the behaviour of the people to Christ, this popular occurrence might not have seemed to Him very important as compared with others. But the occurrence at the time was certainly an unusually imposing one. The whole capital, the older account tells us, was moved by it; though most of the people would only acknowledge a prophet in Him who rode in. And equally certainly did this jubilee among the people, and this triumphant excited expectation of the closer followers, last on some time into this week, as even the little boys loitering in the streets began to sing that inspiring song: when some on the part of the ecclesiastics pointed his attention to this, He replied to them, in Old Testament words, that God Himself loves best to be praised by the mouth of infants, or, according to another account, should they be silent the stones would cry out. But St. John, as generally, from the reason above given, he lays such stress on Lazarus' history, informs us how especially Lazarus' history, testified to by so many now entering and loudly repeated, had drawn on Him the general attention in this whole march.

CHAPTER XXXV.

THE LAST PUBLIC WORKING IN JERUSALEM.

THUS then had the Saviour come face to face again with his deadly enemies, appearing earlier indeed at the festival than they had expected Him, and certainly far more publicly and solemnly than they had imagined. They might now have been able to carry out at once their earlier resolution of taking Him prisoner, the more as He had now shewn Himself quite openly the King of Israel: but the multitude of his followers frightened them not a little, as, besides his closer friends, the multitude seemed for the moment not altogether indisposed towards Him, and looked on Him as at least a prophet and a benefactor to sufferers. They let Him then at first move and work freely, but everywhere sharply observed his conduct, and hoped soon some favourable circumstance would occur to second their desire for his destruction.

He now recommenced his usual work at once, even in the capital. That ruin and death threatened Him at every step, He could not fail to know; but after that moment of higher joy and shouting of the crowd, He only worked quietly on in his usual manner: He again healed sick of all sorts, and especially He taught, if possible with more power and authority than before. His nights He spent at first with his friends in Bethany on the other side of the Mount of Olives, later in a garden on the slope of the hill on this side. From early in the morning He was constantly in the temple. The days and the hours were more indispensable than ever, every moment yet left to Him infinitely more precious.

He had done now, literally, all which He could humanly do and attempt. After that He had openly shewed Himself at the high holy centre of the people of the true religion as the "King" of the completed true religion embracing the true kingdom of God, it was now the business of the people, lower as well as higher orders, to decide for Him equally openly; with simple honesty and heartiness to lay hold of, that is, the completed religion which He had exhibited, and as whose living illustration and result He Himself stood in their midst. Thus He could only go on as He had begun: but He did not weary of laying this religion before the multitude, even after that moment of more public manifestation only more plainly (if needful) and more urgently. It is in many respects not unimportant to remark, that Christ now, after the public tokens which He had Himself given by his entry, could not find it becoming to his position to give a new sign of the sort, and so in fact He gave none. He could not, consistently with his higher duty, look on his active working as at an end with his public entry, and wait accordingly in quiet on his part for the people to join Him of themselves and remain true to Him: what He offered was too unusual and too little accompanied with earthly power and outward splendour; He must work on as He had begun, in order to bring what He brought yet more home to men; but a new public sign was neither necessary nor useful. The older narrative places indeed at this period a temple cleansing; and this would now have, as accomplished after the solemn entry, a far more important meaning and purport than it might have had in the first days of the Messianic inspiration: it would have been not merely an act of authority of Him who had been now declared to be King, but also a token that his kingdom had actually begun with the entry, and a warning that now his disciples also, and the rest who had already joined Him, ought at once to apply their hand with equal violence to reform the existing state of things. But to judge from the other tokens, not the least action was now done by Him, which the enemy or even his own disciples could look on as a deed of violence; rather He kept off even the first motions towards it: for we observe that even the older narrative knows nothing of a participation of the disciples in that temple cleansing. St. John however, who is evidently intentionally silent about it in this place, has doubtless on good grounds put it at a far earlier period, entirely suitable for it on all internal grounds.

But the great final decision pressed on in these last few days quickly enough. He had not turned out of partiality to the lower orders or those least capable of judging, still less had recourse to any deed of violence, or even taught in any way that outer violence should be used. And accordingly his call and his appeal were addressed at first most powerfully and plainly to those only who in any way would be guides and teachers of the people, who were publicly honoured as such, and were responsible to God for the power which had fallen to them in the Church. That his words and his rebukes were specially directed immediately to them, and necessarily wounded them most severely, had, as above remarked, been long noticed by them. Now He once more appeared amongst them at the very place where all the most varied forces of the time converged most intensely, and from which they produced the strongest reaction in all quarters; once more was the divine truth brought close enough to them, but only that they might immediately once more and for the last time unite most shamefully against the One, to follow whom they had long made themselves incapable. This is the great historic truth which the oldest narrative, preserved in St. Mark, expressed in this place most clearly, in painting the way in which at that time all the spiritual powers in Jerusalem, differing as they did otherwise in their earlier history or present position, yet combined to tempt the Saviour in the temple, proposed to Him captious questions the best each could, but were by Him refuted and taught a better lesson; and yet in truth would none of them be taught and improved by Him. The Sanhedrim, appropriately, had Him asked questions as to his authority for all his actions: He silenced them by representing his life simply as it was, as the proper sequence of the Baptist's, whom yet they would not allow to have been an impostor: the Herodians and Pharisees, otherwise at enmity, wished, united at least in this matter, to snare Him, simply through popular captious questions, but only succeeded in bringing forth yet more plainly his all-sufficient wisdom: the Sadducees wished to annihilate Him through ridicule and wit, and only helped thereby to make themselves ridiculous: a proud Doctor wished to injure Him through subtle pedantry, and only succeeded in making conspicuous here also the Saviour's all-surpassing insight. Thus the attacks of all had the opposite effect to that intended; and unhappily He had to conclude with the most just condemnation of the behaviour, habits, and position of the spiritual lords of that time, wholly perverse as it was. Even though of the disputes and sayings which this oldest account and other older and later accounts crowd into this crisis, many may have happened originally at other times: yet the purport of the whole composition succeeds well enough in giving ocular proof, that neither in an earlier nor in this last and decisive period could deliverance proceed from any one of the spiritual powers such as they then were. And thus then would, with these spiritual powers, the whole existing Church have been at heart wholly rotten, and in the Messiah's eyes lost irretrievably, had not his eye caught, as it were in its recesses, even in the temple itself one of the most touching examples of that truth and uprightness in homely life, which ever remains the most indestructible basis of all true religion.

Thus beautifully and inimitably does the whole of this narrative close with the picture of the poor widow, who, unnoticed by passers-by, but not by Christ, threw more in proportion into the temple treasury than all the rich. He had certainly long discovered that at the heart of the ancient people there yet rested a sound germ, from which could grow the Church of the completed true religion when the beams of the true Sun should fall on it: from this germ He had already selected his Twelve. But when all the ruling powers of a people have long become past improvement, as in these few days was completely decided, it is as though one met a carefully fenced and tended fruit-tree, from which fruit is yet in vain hoped for, and whose improvement is thus hopeless. It is not surprising that such thoughts, which had long been moving Christ's heart in reflecting on the fate of the people, in these last days specially engaged his mind, and rose to a flame which had never so flared up in Him; nor need we wonder that He gave free utterance to these feelings on every opportunity which offered itself to Him. Thus there passed into the oldest narrative the touching story, how, when He, the morning after the entry into the city from Bethany, again was going into it, He hurried, being now hungry, to a fig-tree which promised a luxuriant growth of fruit, but found it without fruit, and so uttered a curse on the tree which so long had been false to its promise. The next morning, in passing by again, the tree was found completely withered. It was surely a far higher thought than that of a mere fig-tree, which then so deeply moved

Him, and elicited from his mouth a hard saying never to be forgotten. That over the people of Israel the sudden fall was now irrevocably impending, *that* was the frightful thought, which oppressed Him earlier but with special oppressiveness in these days, and which found its most mild discharge in the curse on the fig-tree. He shewed also no reserve in his forebodings of the speedy end of Jerusalem, as the oldest reminiscences in various ways let us know. The history itself will soon teach us how little He was mistaken, and how frightfully his ill-omened word was fulfilled. And thus it seems, as if in the first Apostolic times before Jerusalem hurried on the ruin prophesied to it, in noticing the unexpected early withering of that fig-tree, a token had been found of the fulfilment also of that much more solemn prophecy; and that in this way the history of the fig-tree came to be so often repeated. For there were indeed in Jerusalem, even among the members of the Sanhedrim and the rest of the more or less influential members of the ecclesiastical body, both at that most critical period and afterwards, many very honest individual members, who could not quite reject Christ's cause, as St. John in particular plainly enough intimates: but they also, the more threateningly the danger gathered about the head of the purely heavenly Champion, became more fearful, and let pass what they thought they could not hinder; or at most, after the fall of the dreaded blow, shewed some compassionate interest. But they acted as if they were entire nullities, and by their timid half-and-half nature only furthered the grand downfall. If the chief of the people thus hung back, He did not on that account appeal to the passions of the crowd, although it had cheered Him on this time in the first hours with so unwonted joy and hope. It is this his final bearing towards the various parties of the crowd, which alone St. John brings before us, in the manner of its decided enough disclosure on that day of the solemn entry. For how his position towards the rulers in general had been decided, had been clearly represented by St. John on the occasion of the last entry to the feast of Tabernacles, so that He tells us nothing further of importance upon it: on their part, as we there saw, the most deadly enmity had been for some time threatening Him; of this He was aware, and therefore no public dispute of importance arose with them. The populace on the other hand, although at the last feast, led astray by the chief-priests, they had in the end declared against Him, had yet remained less prejudiced, and had once more received Him well: it was yet a question what form at this final period their nearer attitude would take; and from this view that day of the solemn entry had also, according to St. John, its high importance; it became indeed the grand concluding day of the Saviour's whole public working. And as St. John likewise indicates all the most prominent summits in the Gospel history, in the way the earlier Gospels had described them, but paints them at the same time quite independently more after his peculiar style; so here He sketches unmistakeably, in his own style, the picture of that heavenly Transfiguration of the whole earthly work of Christ, waiting suddenly to burst forth, described partially by the earlier Gospels (Chap. XXIX.) but by them shifted to another earthly scene. St. John here sets before us only some few majestic features which complete the whole picture of the public working of Christ (St. John xii. 20—36).

There were, it is stated, present on that day (as we can well believe) a good number of Greeks arrived among the visitors to the feast: by these Greeks St. John doubtless intends Greeks by nation, Jews by faith, so born, or proselytes from the heathen. All Jews living among the Greeks and other heathen in the Roman empire were then looked on (Bd. IV. s. 290 ff) as freer thinkers and less fettered by popular prejudices: some might early divine that Christianity would spread much more easily among them than in the Holy Land, as the history of the Apostles was then practically teaching; and so St. John especially, when He wrote this, had long known by deep experience. In an earlier passage St. John had accordingly expressly told us, how some had so misunderstood an expression of the Saviour's, as though He intended, disgusted with the Jews in the Holy Land, to go to those among the heathen, in order to bring them over to his Messianic doctrine. Now on this day some of these Greeks wish on their own impulse to learn to know Jesus more accurately; they apply accordingly to Philip, who does not venture to inform the Master of their petition until he had taken with him Andrew, who was on more intimate terms with Christ. And if He had acceded to such a petition, and now devoted Himself wholly to the Hellenists, what an entirely new state of things might He not have introduced even at this last turning-point of his whole working, what disquiet in the land, and what unforeseen difficulty been able to make for the chief-priests! We can, in fact, from the history of the Apostolic period rightly appreciate this; as, in general, none more eagerly took up the Christian doctrine, nor more faithfully held it fast, than did the Hellenists. Thus this became (as we may quite correctly suppose) a last temptation for Christ in this final period: but not for a moment was there doubt of what was here to be done.

Not thus,—through uproar among the people, or through help from without,—could, as He saw, the great cause, which He had hitherto borne alone, win the victory. He had now been for some time resolved to die for it, if need were, and felt that only thus would it conquer: and though the thought on death, the nearer it approached, must be all the greater shock to Him as a man, He yet would not pray the Father to save Him from this hour, but only that His name might be glorified through his death, in the certain prospect that so at last the Messianic cause itself and the Messiah Himself in his divine side, instead of being destroyed, would be glorified for ever. And as He thus intimated to them that He had now no longer time for such new human acquaintances and connections, and concluded with the highest and purest possible prayer to the Father in the extremest emotion, there came also, St. John tells us, from the Father the true response, and a clear heavenly voice announced to the earth this response: just as temptation overcome constantly leads to higher transfiguring and glorifying. But when the people (St. John goes on) thought to have only heard thunder in the voice—others would at most see an angel's voice in it—He shewed them that such a voice served not for Him principally (as if He had much need of strengthening and attestation) but only for them, to strengthen their faith; He knows Himself how the whole spiritual issue is already decided, and in spite of his outward fall, or rather in consequence of it, that the time for glorifying his whole cause is beginning. But as they were not able yet to comprehend this, He advised them to make use of at least the short time, during which He was to be visibly present with them. As St. John's representation may be compared in so many places to a bird, which boldly rises to the highest heaven and flutters there till it gently drops down again, so especially is it with this short but most sublime passage. With the boldest flight the thought here rises at once from the immediate occasion to the sublimest truth and the highest wish and prayer, seeking not in vain from heaven itself a response: but should any one mistake the nature of this heavenly voice, then at the same elevation its true end and its own proper meaning are further declared, and at last in the gentlest condescension it is declared what must without fail be done by every one.

What was decisive at last, according to St. John, was that the whole people of the true religion of that time, taking them as a whole, did not find courage and resolution enough to follow Him truly and honestly, blinded through obstinate prejudices of all sorts. The populace cheered Him on, it is true, for a short time, but became again directly more reserved when they did not see immediately the outward fortune, which was strictly all that they sought through Him, and saw themselves only met, as they thought, by his severe demands. And finally, even in matters of outward success, fortune, and welfare, all the several efforts and sects of any nation are dissipated in it again when as a mass it remains behind its duty. Great as were the faults of the existing chiefs, had not the people themselves of long time allowed themselves to be thus moulded? and did they find at last, at the final hour, the right means to improve the spirit of their chiefs? As all special efforts and sects first proceed from out of the people itself, so also the errors and failings of these wound the people itself as a whole. Israel should have known as a people, that the purely divine, so far as it can appear in human form, with all the infinite saving grace concealed in it, appeared in this inconspicuous form of Jesus of Nazareth: that they did not know it, is in fine its one great fault. And this very utterance is, according to St. John, the last decisive saying which the Saviour makes on the whole behaviour of the people towards Him, though only in those general truths and sentences which go beyond all which is merely national, and therefore may strictly be applied to every nation and every individual in it. (John xii. 44—50.)

CHAPTER XXXVI.

The Betrayal. The Bodily Death and the Eternal Hope. The Bodily Separation and the Eternal Presence.

According to the older account also, the kind of outward interest of the multitude, dreaded by the chief priests in their long-formed deadly plans against Christ, in the course of these few days soon went to sleep again. The multitude saw nothing of the sensible majesty realised, such as they had principally hoped for on the day of the entry; so its warmer zeal soon cooled again, there was even an entire reaction against the Saviour: and though the chief priests continued not wholly free from fear lest an arrest and condemnation of Christ might, in the impending feast-days, most liable to outbreak of popular tumult, call forth a dangerous disturbance among the multitude (Mark xiv. 2), they yet saw clearly that the interest of the multitude since the day of the entry was at least not on the increase; and thus might they soon again expect to attain their end, if any favourable accident should befall in aid of their continued watchfulness and vindictiveness. But it is the most beautiful token of the insurpassable goodness of Christ, and of the spiritual majesty of his cause, that they, with all their own industrious espionage and with all their most entire and decided hostility, in spite of the fast growing lukewarmness of the multitude, ventured on no fatal step against Him, till treason from his own circle came to their aid. So surely is it established in this greatest historical case, that a cause wholly good in its deepest foundation and pure origin can be really injured only by treason from its own midst. The only important point then here is to discern truly, how such treachery was possible even in this community, then in its first commencement and under Christ's own eyes. Treachery in a good cause, when it appears, is always only the outburst of indecision and perplexity long existing in the community, although perhaps very inapparent and imperceptibly infecting it; this only accidentally, so to speak, gathers on an individual member, and through his particular guilt leads to a violent blow.

We saw however (Chap. XXI.) how certainly Christ's cause, in spite of its original purest goodness, must, through the firm stablishing of the community, descend to the casualties and weaknesses of this earth. Everything earthly, if it will put itself under rules, subsist, maintain itself, and advance, must form itself within definite limits, ranks and numbers. As the first firm stones and foundations of his Church, so far as this is and must be in some degree temporal, Jesus chose his Twelve, after a number suitable but established and almost necessary. He surely chose the Twelve as the best whom He could choose to fill the number, and no one *in order that* he might be his betrayer. But we may say of the first choice the same as Christ (according to St. John xii. 18) said at the end of his earthly history, "He knew whom He chose," that they, that is, in consequence of the general variety in human spirits, would not of necessity, without exception, even in respect of the great cause itself which should unite them, be all alike; that rather, just because of the singular elevation and difficult task of their new life, the most varied modification of their particular efforts might find place, even possibly to arrive at the entire misconception of the most certain truth, if perchance special new temptations should supervene. What calls forth the most strenuous and truest activity of the human spirit needs also the highest freedom of motive and resolve: not in order to take this from them did Christ choose his Twelve, when once He had to fix and fill up a fixed number of his closest disciples. Judas Iscariot was entrusted with the money affairs of the new Church,—for these at some time must be specially taken in charge by some one member. Thus, when the thoughts of all should be turned simply to the things of the kingdom of heaven, this man must busy himself with such earthly things, for they too were indispensable. In this lies for him a peculiar temptation: to collect all the money, keep and increase it, may gradually become too attractive; and if at the same time his spirit is greedy, self-seeking, and thievish, he can easily find the excuse that his office compels him to bring and keep together as much money as possible: the temptation, indeed, thus to protect himself against all the probable emergencies and changes of life may become the stronger even the more as the possession of treasures of this sort is despised by the rest, or the non-possession of them even required by one of the laws of the society. To this temptation Judas Iscariot succumbed. We are indebted to St. John's more particular account for the knowledge of this, and this his last conduct would otherwise in every way be historically far less clear to us than it now need be. His growing inclination to money might, in the course of this year and a half, have remained unnoticed and artfully concealed by himself: although however Christ never yet had said anything severe to him in reference to it, the half reproof which He had given him (John xii. 7f.) shortly before might have hurt and annoyed him. When now, being in such a frame of mind on the following days, he also found that the kingdom of God he hoped for—from which with his ruling propensity he must have hoped for special outward treasures and advantages—would not be realised in the way he had secretly hoped for; further, that the people as a mass remained almost indifferent,—might not the desperate thought suddenly have seized on him to have one parley with the high-priests, who as he knew had already set a price on the head of this Messiah? might he not have amused himself with thinking it might be a good plan sometime, at least to have some conversation with them? For we may safely assume that, probably some days before his final separation from the Lord, he had been negociating with certain chief-priests (Mark xiv. 10 f.) : that these represented to him the enterprise, if he would undertake it, as highly meritorious, and on their part also were every way urgent with him, may well be assumed. That the money promised for the betrayal, with the further temporal advantages which might be shortly pointed out as to follow, had also much attraction for him, is only what we might have expected from him: on the other hand, to the chief-priests nothing could appear more agreeable and advantageous than the opportunity offered of taking Jesus as a prisoner in the sight of the world, and that through the treachery of one of the Twelve.

Accordingly, as will likely be the case in all more important decisions which originate in evil motives, two causes combined to determine Judas Iscariot to this step. Mere covetousness would hardly have impelled him to the horrible deed; the amount of money which the chief-priests offered him was indeed small enough. Neither would the fear of the discovery of his covetousness and its possible punishment in the circle of the new Church have been able alone to drive him to it: it had not been much noticed hitherto, and certainly he had not been reproached by Christ in a way he could not get over. It is indeed quite clear, that afterwards, among the first Christians, covetousness alone was ever thought of as the only motive for so horrible a deed: it is plain also that this Iscariot subsequently received the reward of his crime, and bought for this money, with probably other which he had saved, a field in Jerusalem (Acts i. 18 f.): this had been hitherto, from some cause which we now know not, called the "Potter's field," but the Christians named it after this, on grounds we can well understand, "the field of blood." He did not however long survive his crime: he died, as some related afterwards, through a fall as from a precipice, others said it was by self-strangling. The last account is however connected with a particular notion which likewise grew up in the Apostolic age: that so soon as he saw Christ actually condemned, he wished from compunction at once to restore the money to the chief-priests, but when they would not take it back, threw it down to them in the temple and hanged himself: they had however not dared to put it into the treasury, but bought with it that field to bury strangers in. We cannot allow of any other supposition than that the field afterwards actually served for such an end; while the story of the immediate repentance of the traitor was probably merely devised by Christian charity.

But neither can we mistake the fact, that the singularly disturbed atmosphere in which the spirit of the new Church had now to breathe, and the cruel crisis which in these days awaited the whole cause of the completed true religion, supervened as the other occasion which quickly ripened the seed of the traitor. Now was the time when, in the Church hardly founded, everything temporal and eternal, earthly and heavenly, must be violently parted, and this young Church at once undergo the hardest possible temptation. All hope of an earthly kingdom must be plucked up from the roots, the visible Head of the Church arrested, nay, humanly most deeply disgraced and killed; thoughts must be turned away from the Messiah bodily present, and turned towards the heavenly Messiah alone, to appear, it might be, from heaven again. As this danger pressed on ever closer with that issue, which was to the common mind quite unexpected, he who would yet remain faithful in this Church, must make his own an intuition and a hope such as he had never been familiar with or needed before. It is certain indeed that Christ Himself was not in the least surprised by this danger, nor in his entire spirit the least bent by it: we see Him, although in no wise seeking for death and all its horrors, and at the very last prepared for another issue, if God preferred it, yet in the sublimest calm and blissful peace admitting even the hardest and most painful thoughts, and rightly discerning and rightly executing all that was yet to be done on his part. If He behaved towards the great world, to the last moment, as has been above for the most part described; we have cause for the greatest wonder here, at the way wherein, in the gradual advance of this last crisis and finally in the crisis itself, He behaved towards his own so long as He was still free to deal with them.

He saw his earthly end approaching more closely; He spoke in the circle of his own ever more definitely and at length, of his intuitions and hopes of the future of the true kingdom of God, even after his earthly decease; He expressed them in the most striking forms, in the most admirable pictures and instructive parables, setting minutely before their eyes what the eye of flesh had

U

never seen and yet was certain, sometimes in shorter inspirations and regular prophecies; and He always added thereto the right counsel and the truest comfort. If He had earlier (Chap. XXII.) at the right time explained, not only to his own but to the multitude as well, the essential nature, the right beginning and value, and the eternal meaning of the true kingdom of God in figure and in teaching in the sublimest manner, He now completed this whole course of prophecy and instruction by the equally insurpassable true intuitions and prophecies on the nearer and more remote future of affairs after his return to his Father: but as then He had only sketched the grand features of all true insight into the nature of the completed kingdom of God, for the purpose of at once exercising his own in their corresponding duties; so even in these last times He revealed none of his many intuitions on the development of its whole future, without wrapping up therewith a corresponding counsel or comfort for his own. And in what fulness He imparted these last clear glances and intimations to his own we may see especially from the valuable fragments of the Spruchsammlung, which placed the most copious exposition at that time when once, in these last days, leaving the temple He had sat down with the Twelve over against it on the Mount of Olives to reflect and teach (Matt. xxiv. 3). St. John passes over most of it, because at the time when He wrote it had been already in great part fulfilled, and at that time there was much else more important. Nor for us is it the right place to enter into the particulars of it, as the discussion of it belongs rather to the history of the time when it had its greatest importance—the Apostolic period.

If however He now with the greatest clearness discerned the utter and deadly hatred of his enemies, and that He, if He would not abandon the cause of his Messianic calling, could not escape from their fury; He must above all reflect, that He must be constantly ready, gladly and joyfully, should God ask for it without his guilt, to give up his life. And in nothing does He appear nobler than in this, that He nowhere and in no wise, seeking death from despair as one might think, nor in anywise through his own human guilt drawing it on Himself, rather as a man drawing back from the pain and the horror of death, yet the closer the bitter necessity advanced towards Him the more calmly submitted to the divine will, should it demand from Him even this sacrifice. Doubtless indeed He was from the commencement of his public course prepared for even its hardest issue in what concerned his own life consecrated to the divine call: but in all its plain necessity and its actual terrors, this bitter necessity had gradually come before Him ever more strongly. But although since that first bright commencement of his Messianic activity He had already run through the most varied stages of this activity; yet even at that stage which He now occupied He might humanly have very easily drawn back from his calling and avoided all danger of death. Not one charge which could be named rested on Him: and how gladly would the chief-priests, if He would now have submitted Himself to their will, have let Him escape with probably a short imprisonment even after the betrayal of Iscariot! But then He would not have been Christ, that is, not the leader in the kingdom of the perfected true religion: and if we cannot conceive in Him any actual wavering in the two earlier stages of his Messianic activity in all the chief crises of his life, how much less could He now, after He had gathered about Him the community of the perfected true religion, and had laid in it the immutable ground of all completion of the kingdom of God—now, when the eternal salvation of the souls not of the Twelve only, but of all who at any time and in any place on the earth desired this salvation, depended on Him as on no other in history! He now belonged no longer merely to Himself nor even to God alone; He belonged entirely to that community to which from the beginning He had given Himself with his whole immortal Being: and He knew what consequently was his duty, as the Head of all striving for the divine salvation, and as the true Shepherd of his flock, and could foresee how in the divine pleasure even his innocent death might help to bring about the final and most violent shock to the existing world, and the beginning of a complete breaking up of all the hardened and lifeless guilt of Israel and of the whole world.

But if He had this higher devotedness and firmness not only always before, but now yet more in view of the immediately coming black destiny; what deepest pain must it again have caused Him, on the other hand, to see how all Israel and the rest of mankind, and especially his Twelve, must forsake Him! How much would He have preferred humanly further devoting to them all his most immediate love and care, and how well He knew how much they needed to human view his entire nearness and ever ready help! He gave then to his own during these last days not only the brightest hope and the warmest comfort in the light of his intuition of all futurity; He gave away also at last *Himself*, as far as He could, with his whole love, nay, as it were, with his whole life in body and soul, so completely that his outward separation from them might become the most abiding spiritual presence. A divine sacrifice, or, according to the ancient consecrated conception, an offering for all who wished for his light and his salvation, and especially for those who stood closest to Him—such had been in truth, hitherto, his whole Messianic life and effort: and never in the same way as He, has any mortal being sacrificed his whole work and life as the purest offering to the divine will and the eternal salvation of all men. But now, in the last moments of his visible existence, when He foresees the near doom, and best knows with what difficulty the perfected true religion can become at first, even in the circle of those standing closest to it, an inseparable possession and a blessing working on with ever greater might, it is all the more urgent on Him to give Himself away with all which He can, with his whole love and his whole might, as it were with body and soul, as though He must embrace them more heartily and completely take them to Himself and pass wholly into them, as the final separation more certainly threatens; as though He were impelled, so far as He could, to leave behind for them all the best part of Himself, at the time when He most painfully realises that He must leave them. Thus would every good man wish to part from the circle of his beloved ones: but who could be more anxious, when separated to sight for ever, to yet remain constantly wholly present, than was He! When now, on the day before the Passover, that is on Thursday the 13th of the month Nisan, on the fifth day from the entry into Jerusalem, from all the signs of the times, and especially from the bearing of Iscariot, if yet undecided, yet to his sharp eye no longer hidden, He saw how near his earthly end was, and alone with the Twelve was just about towards evening to preside at the daily meal; He rose suddenly, before the preparations for the meal were finished (δείπνου γινομένου according to the correct reading), laid aside his over-garments, like a servant who has something to do in the house, girded Himself with an apron like a servant, who, according to a custom there, would wash his lord's feet before meal-time after the walking and labour of the day, and took a basin filled with water to wash the feet of the Twelve. No action could arise with Him more naturally through the hasty impulse of a momentary thought: but his presentiment that this would be the last meal with them combined with his boundless love long shewn to the Twelve, so that this love would now suddenly overflow, and He hardly knew what greatest proof of love to shew them. When then, as natural, He wished to begin with Peter as the one recognised by Himself as head of the

Twelve, Peter strove very earnestly against the thought of being served by Him whom he himself should serve, but gladly gave way on learning that only if he so suffer himself to be served by Him has He part in Him and is one of his; he then wishes to be washed by Him in his whole body, as he eagerly exclaims, and has to be equally set right in the other direction; that in the case generally of those who belong to Christ, no such violent handling and change (no complete bath) is any more necessary (as for example at John's baptism), but a gentler handling and amendment (as for example the washing the feet) must be sufficient. After He had thus served them all, He first declares to them Himself the higher meaning of this proof of love: He had touched them with his own hand, and with this touch rendered more than a small earthly service—He had wished with his hand, so to speak, to impress his spirit of love, with the water of the washing to rub it into them: and could any man of feeling among them ever forget that his hand had thus touched and consecrated him with more power than with kiss and laying on of hands? The spiritual meaning of the act reaches here beyond its outward and visible meaning, and all words are strictly here too weak to exhaust the whole infinite depth of the meaning. Hence He only tells them, how He had in this given them the example of the genuine love through which alone this his Church had been founded and must sustain itself after his visible departure. Not as if such self-sacrificing love (which must constantly proceed most from those very men who stand highest) is to take away the distinction between the various offices and callings; the true Lord remains what He is, in spite of his condescending and all-embracing love: and unhappily Christ knows very well that even among the Twelve whom He had thus touched, not all among them are alike in love to Him, nay, that the traitor is already lurking among them; but nevertheless the blessing of true love rests on all proofs of it, from those above to those below, as that of the master to the servant or of the teacher to the disciple, and conversely from those below to those above, as the love of the servant, or one who is in any position of receiving, to his master and benefactor.

Thus commenced this meal, the last which Christ, according to his true presentiment, could enjoy undisturbed in company with his own, as John with the most touching simplicity tells us in his representation of the Exalted One: and so we easily understand how in a like spirit it was continued, and if possible was finished, with yet higher elevation of the feelings of purest and most exalted love which here crowded in. He *must* have in this meal reached to them Himself bread and wine, still serving them like one who loved them, and following therein all the boundless thoughts and most sublime truths which here flowed together, and so to speak, in the eating, offering Himself to them to be absorbed into them and transmuted into their every feeling and their life. As He in view of his death breaks this bread to them and reaches this wine to them, as if He were giving with them his body also and his blood soon to be shed for them: so is it his will that they have Him continually *in* themselves though now vanishing from their sight, and keep Him in themselves as still living and present among them; *it is his will* and wish that it be so, and those who thus in faith enjoy this food given them by Him take in the substance rather than bodily food, Himself into them with his infinite love and power. Thus then is He even inwardly already a different being: since He has thus given Himself with all that He yet has of earthly to his own, He has already, as it were, renounced the whole visible world, and now, as one who belongs no more to Himself, goes the more easily and more majestically to meet the outward death.

There are moments in this fleeting earthly life, in which the highest experiences, discoveries and intuitions of all mankind are compressed together, and all which anyone in his whole previous striving and working has accomplished, would fain gather into one word and one token, in order thus to last for ever. Such was this moment at the Saviour's last meal in reference to that which for a year and a half had been the great end of his earthly labour, the Church of His own. All at this one moment done by Christ and his disciples goes infinitely beyond its immediate object; and all earthly matter is transfigured here into the purest spiritual. For the unfathomed lessons, which through the finished work of Christ and his purest strongest love sought for a home on earth, had long been delivered; they waited, as it were, only for this moment to be overpoweringly and visibly so far as possible transfigured, and thus found even in the most trivial and smallest occasion the right instrument for their most significant expression and never-to-be-forgotten truth; for the highest meaning can be summed up even in the smallest thing and, to the eye of sense, the least important. But in truth all this could not have gained its highest significancy until the Apostolic period. It is evident that the Church, to which He had thus given Himself at the last moment, the more constantly and the more earnestly they afterwards reflected on this moment, could deem nothing more comforting than the remembrance of it, and nothing holier than, so far as possible, to repeat that which had at that time taken form in creative originality. But of the events of Christ's proof of his love on this day, the meal alone could be repeated; for this the disciples had themselves enjoyed with Him, and they might always conceive to themselves the heavenly Saviour as with his whole spirit present with them; whilst the washing of the feet could in nowise be repeated, as being something in which the disciples had been purely receptive, and which the Lord's love was only, we may say, to impart with his own hands. The feast of the Supper could be repeated; and we shall see below, how in the Apostolic period much that was quite sensual could easily attach itself to it: but many Christians certainly accustomed themselves very early, in place of keeping the festival of the Lord's Supper yearly, the last day before the Passover, that is before the 14th of the month Nisan, to repeat it on the day itself and connect it with the Passover, on grounds which will likewise be better enquired into below. The entrance of this custom and, still more, the consideration of the death of Christ become predominant, had in fact a reaction on the usual repetition of the Gospel history. For after it had become quite usual to name Christ Himself the Christian Paschal Lamb slain as an offering, as his death had happened as nearly as possible at the time of the Passover, and the first Christians found therein a confirmation of many of their dearest truths: for this reason the account of the first celebration of this Supper readily took the shape of Christ Himself having really celebrated it with the Twelve as a Paschal Supper, and only after it given to his disciples bread and wine in the new higher meaning. This account, in accordance with which several reminiscences took characteristic forms in the separate narratives, lies now before us, in the form it was generally repeated in the three first Gospels; and a further result was that the fifteenth of this month, or the first great day of the feast, had to be regarded as the proper day of the crucifixion and death of Christ. But, as is always the case with small displacements, the original reminiscence is not entirely obliterated by this displacement, and may be actually again recognised pretty correctly in a broken form under the outer surface. If that Supper had been really an eating of the Passover, then Christ would have given to his own, as the most correspondent token of his body now going to death, the flesh especially, still more if this love feast had entirely coincided with the Passover, as it must seem to have done under St. Luke's representation: but it is only of bread and wine that we are always told. Further, on the night of the Passover, until the morning of the first great day of the feast of unleavened bread, according to known laws which the chief-priests of that time might least break, the arrest and the trial could not have followed. And as the day of the death, according to that account also, was a Friday, it agrees in so far with the more correct history (if we presuppose that there was generally a clear recollection that in that year Sunday was the third day from that of the crucifixion). But this narrative, in fact, sets before us no other reasons for regarding the night of the arrest and the following day of the death as the time of the great feast of unleavened bread; rather, through the reminiscence that the chief-priests had hastened the condemnation in order that it might ensue *before* the feast, clearly indicates the original reminiscence of the real time. But here again it is St. John who, in the perfectly plain account in his Gospel, restored the whole in its proper sequence to its original simplicity. But if he related only the washing of the feet omitted in the earlier narrative, and not the distribution of bread and wine, he does so, partly because the last was universally known, just as he holds it unnecessary to relate in his story so many universally known particulars, and partly because on an earlier occasion (Chap. VI.) he had already explained the higher meaning of such eating of Christ's bread and of Christ's flesh and blood, so that it was superfluous for him here to recur to it.

The contradiction however between the Gospels as to this date, in another aspect to be here referred to, is not of much importance. On more careful consideration, the whole account which leads to the belief that the evening of the betrayal and the love feast was the Passover evening, as we have further shewn in "die drei ersten Evangelien," may be traced back to St. Mark's original account alone. But we have preserved in St. Luke the beginning of a much simpler account taken from the oldest Gospel narrative. This states that Christ, when the day (that is the feast of unleavened bread) approached when the Passover must be killed, sent Peter and John into the city to make preparations for it. The language of this might suggest that the day *before* the Passover is meant; the preparations besides had to be made in good time. In this case the Supper, which was eaten in the inn thus engaged, would have been not indeed the Passover, but partaken of with minds full of the Passover; and might the more easily be looked on as taking its place, as the disciples doubtless on the following day, amid the greatest horror and extremest fear, found neither a place nor inclination to partake. In any case, the Passover was much connected with the history of these two days, which St. John in his Gospel does not dwell on, because in general everything merely Jewish was indifferent to him. So far may suffice for the more accurate date of this crisis. But in the development of the great history, the sole principal point is that Christ had thus done on his part all which He could, in order that the mortal blow foreseen by Him might not strike the Twelve unprepared, and that they, at least after the stunning blow, might get up again, and again find their way in those eternal truths to found which alone He had come. But the nearer the blow approached, the more fearful He shewed Himself in the intimations of it. According to the universal Gospel reminiscence, all the Twelve became silent so soon as Jesus alluded more directly to it, and even those generally strongest in the faith could not admit this view; as it will soon appear further that even Peter wavered for a moment. What was here to happen, and what Christ prophesied to them ever more clearly, was a blow to all the earliest and most confident hopes of the Messiah; as in fact the multitude (John xii. 34), from their previous intuitions, readily discerned: how could they be otherwise than most deeply moved and, as it were, thrown out of their balance, when their whole life's hope had most inseparably grown up with the Messianic! It is, in fact, one of the best proofs of the pure goodness and truth of Christ's whole cause, that, with the highest spiritual freedom and clearness to which He Himself had educated the Twelve, in this hour of the severest temptation, the decision of Iscariot alone went wrong; although He had called forth among them neither any false expectations of the goods and honours of this world, nor any perverted national hope. It is not however to be denied, that all this great uncertainty of affairs, whilst, through their already germinating higher belief and their greater innocence, the rest of the Twelve suffered less from it, was for Iscariot one of the causes which led him to his horrible act. As in general it is noticeable, that it is constantly not a single however powerful a cause, so much as a turmoil and conflict of the most various evil thoughts, which leads a man at last to the execution of an evil deed long ripening in his soul.

CHAPTER XXXVII.

The Arrest and its Consequences.

At that last Supper Iscariot, according to all reminiscences, had been present. He seemed not to notice when Christ, both before and during it, repeatedly alluded to treachery in the midst of the Twelve themselves. When he, even towards the end of the meal, after the unfathomed tokens of love which the Lord had shewn them all, was yet silent, Jesus, shocked at such callousness, felt that such a callous indecision could not last. He openly stated then, that one of them would betray Him: all the twelve—Iscariot out of confusion and surprise, the rest from sincerity—were most deeply moved, and most earnestly assured Him of the impossibility of it. But as Christ did not recall his asseveration, Peter wished, through John the bosom disciple, to get from Him more exact information, went up to him, and whispered his wish. He, as usual, sitting next to Christ, ventured equally secretly to enquire who was intended, and received for answer, he it was to whom He would now give an extra morsel (as if from particular attention and love). Doubtless the wretched

Iscariot had not clearly heard this, whispered between the two, (reported to us by St. John alone in his gospel); still less had the others heard it; and we may well suppose that it was hardly repeated at once by John to Peter. He might yet perhaps have been able to repent, when Christ's love, as it were, overflowed on him; but he felt now quite unworthy of so much love, and from the unusual singling him out, felt that Jesus must have completely seen through him; and on His now adding that he should do quickly what he was conscious of, he ran forth from the company, more strongly feeling what the Saviour might have meant by it, firmly resolved, as he was already seen through by Christ, to execute his plan at once. In truth, only a man with a guilty conscience could forbode auything wrong from this last saying of Christ; for as he, as steward of the community, had constantly all sorts of business to do for them, now especially when the Passover was at hand, Christ might have said this with no hidden meaning, and so the rest actually understood Him.

What time elapsed between this departure of Judas and his return for the capture we know not accurately, doubtless some hours: and as we know from St. John that it was already night when he went out, the arrest may probably not have followed before midnight. The older account, which looks on that Supper as the Passover, mentioned quite shortly what the Saviour said and did after the Supper, and the singing the Psalm which concluded the Paschal celebration during these last moments of his being alone with his own. They went this night also to the Mount of Olives to sleep there as usual: on the way Christ did not disguise from them his certain foreboding, that they would all be offended at his fate. When Peter would at least except himself, He who knew him better told him that he was the one, who that night before the cock crowed would deny him thrice; yet he, like the rest, would not think of the possibility of it. Arrived at the Garden of Gethsemane, on the western slope of the Mount of Olives, He left first the rest behind, and went further on with his three especial friends among the Twelve, in order to be at the last somewhat more alone, and in this last crisis to find in God the last serenity and strength; He retired then a little further even from these three, and only wished they would keep watch that night of the presentiment of death. As He thus felt the completion of the treachery only too certainly as very near at hand, the human fear of death was like once more to seize on Him: all his human feelings were still uninterruptedly strong and healthy; and if the sense of coming death may for brief intervals overcome every healthy heart, what pain and bitter suffering must He feel would with his death follow for his own! Was there no possibility that the Messianic cause should conquer in another way? The thought of this might, rather must, while his human feeling was yet undisturbed, once more penetrate his heart, while He braced Himself at this last moment by thinking on God alone: but it only made Him recover at once in God more absolute true devotion to the supreme Will. But whilst thus at the last hour He strengthened Himself by wrestling aloud in prayer, resisting every movement of human weakness and temptation, He had wished in vain that the three at least might be able to resist sleep; He finds them three times asleep after the strong excitements of the last days and hours, and had to give up even this human hope of finding at least his dearest friends watching with Him. Thus had He at last, quite alone and like one forsaken by all the world, to undergo the sense and pains of coming death—how much more then to bear alone the actual pain of death! even those nearest and truest to Him could not help Him, not even with their spirit: and if He wished, as a man at least, through their watchful spirit to strengthen his own, He had when the time came to give up even this last human hope. In this older simpler narrative some indisputably of the most important recollections of that moment of trembling decision have been faithfully preserved: it is short and incomplete, as Christ certainly, in these last hours of his freedom, might have said much more that was worthy of recollection; but yet it gives us in some broad touches the clear picture of the purport of such never-to-be-forgotten last hours. But as in general the history of Christ's last earthly history was early (as the Gospels themselves shew) followed up with particular interest, and in many ways multiplied and put into new forms, so is it the case with the recollection of these last hours before his arrest; and to suit the grandeur of these hours the representation of the events became ever also more sublime. We see this variously shewn in St. Luke's

Gospel. On one side, in fact, it was a favourite alteration to shift to these last hours many of the most important sayings of Christ, so many seemed to occur appropriately then: then it was frequent to lengthen the time between the Last Supper and the move towards the Mount of Olives, as this Supper must have furnished the richest matter for further solemn parting remarks. Thus St. Luke inserts here an important fragment from the Spruchsammlung, and two others from the "Book of the higher Gospel History" (Luke xxii. 21—38). On the other hand, the conception of Christ in his agony of soul excited not a little the attempt to paint it less unworthily of its whole sublimity: some grand touches of Christ in this light have been preserved by St. Luke from the same somewhat subsequent Gospel history (Luke xxii. 43 f.).

But St. John goes much further in this. As in his Gospel he always endeavours to entirely exhaust all important matter of more general bearing; so at this moment, in which Christ after the departure of the traitor is once more alone with those quite true to Him, he inserts the most eloquent as well as the most complete discussion of the whole relation between Him and his. It is the purest and tenderest relationship which can be declared in a Gospel, and is also the highest subject of all true religion: but nowhere are these truths in their whole compass transfigured with such depth and exhaustiveness, as in this crowning passage of *that* work, which of all the books of the Bible is most absolutely inspired. Doubtless, as we need not remark, in this very long discourse of Christ there prevails the same freedom of repetition and putting into form, which mark all such discourses in this Gospel; in fact, without this freedom it could never have come into being in this upward soaring of the thoughts and entire exhaustion of the subject: there is also no doubt that, as in other passages of this Gospel, St. John starts from certain passages of earlier Gospels as his key-note, and returns to them again, like, we may say, a performer of genius, who transfigures the few notes given to him through the freest and yet the truest and most fascinating variations. But here also, with the elevation of this extraordinary subject, the exposition rises in a manner elsewhere unknown in a discourse of any length. And the fundamental thought of this long discourse, which through several interruptions only increases in inward clearness and in warmth of expression, is only the same which in other parts of the Gospel serves as so strong an under tone, namely, that Christ's deepest humiliation now, after the traitor's departure, impending immediately and without escape, will be his highest glory. But whilst the Speaker, from this thought and from the great Christian fundamental law of true love, contemplates in all its aspects his relations to his own and to God, such as it had hitherto been and must soon perfect itself through the last great change, He first discusses on one hand what He will do *for* his own, and then, on the other hand, conversely what is their part towards Him.

His part, if we may so speak, is, even at and after his departure out of the visible world, not to forsake them, but to prepare with the Father a place for them for their eternal happiness, and from thence reappear to them, even while yet on earth, Himself or by the sending of the Holy Spirit: their part, on the other hand, is to keep towards Him, as to one who wishes not so much to be their Lord as their friend, amid all the temptations and trials from the world, that fidelity which seems so hard to hold fast, and yet is really so easy for everyone who completely understands His mind, and has taken it into himself in its heavenly clearness. As however all which Christ here, in such a parting hour, divines and desires for his own glorifying as well as that of his own, if they shew fidelity, can only through the Father be accomplished, the whole discourse changes of itself at length into a loud earnest prayer, which once more, in summing up in pregnant words everything most sublime, must necessarily linger chiefly at the supplication for his own, but at length embraces, even beyond the narrower circle of the Twelve, all the infinite multitude who should come like them, and in the way they had come arrive at the knowledge of the True. Thus the principal matter of the sayings of Christ on his way to and in the Garden, as given us by the older accounts, is here by St. John exhausted, looking at the whole scope of this last great concluding discourse and this sublime parting. St. John hence omits (after this discourse spoken at the conclusion of this Supper in the city itself) the whole further account of Christ's time in the Garden and the mortal agony, which here, according to the older Gospels, falls on Him; it would moreover, after the pure sublimity of this parting address, be hardly conceivable. We have here the most striking proof of how St. John, in the boundlessness of the purely heavenly matter spread before Him to overflowing, throws off all earthly matter. He had moreover had an opportunity of painting how at least the passing thought of another issue had power earlier to agitate Christ's soul.

Meanwhile, on the part of the enemy all arrangements had been made for arresting Him this night at the place where they expected to find Him according to the traitor's information. The chief priests had supplied the traitor partly with Roman soldiers from the company quartered in Jerusalem, partly with a division from the temple-guard, under command of the high-priest (John xviii. 3), the last led by a certain Malchus: the whole company were well armed, and well provided with torches and lanterns, in order not to miss the right man, who might, as they thought, hide Himself. As they were prepared to expect resistance, Iscariot was not above making use of a ruse : he was, on arriving at the Garden, to go in front of the company, and first seek Jesus alone, in order thus to single Him out before the eyes of the leader of the company. The traitor was so lost to shame as not only to look Him out, but even, as if all were between them as of old, to greet Him in the most friendly terms and kiss Him, and so give the token agreed on between him and the soldiers: with short solemn reply Christ rejected his hypocrisy, went rather by Himself to meet the officers, with the question, Whom did they seek? and freely made Himself known to them. Such courage was unexpected by the high-priest's bailiffs: it seemed suddenly as if a higher fear prevented them from taking *that* man, who from the midst of his friends had met them quite alone with the open brow of innocence; they sank, so to speak, to the ground. He may at this moment have addressed them in that solemn saying which the older account has preserved: they should at least know what they would do; they had come out as against a robber, with swords and staves, to take in the darkness of the time Him whom they might daily have taken much more easily while He taught in the temple. But He wished not to escape from them: He therefore desired them, as their superior officers had bidden them, to arrest Him, but to let his companions go free. The officers could for the present have no objection to this, as the idea evidently was, that through the destruction of this one they should be able to stifle the whole cause. When they would actually lay hands on Him, Peter felt himself suddenly too excited to remain quite composed: he drew his sword and smote Malchus on the right ear; but a word of reproof from the Lord quenched his unseasonable and unrighteous zeal. When the Saviour indeed now let Himself be taken quite quietly and be completely bound, horror and fear fell on the Twelve and the rest (who seem to have poured in with the officers) at so unexpected a result. They fled in all directions: and if on the one hand St. John truly remarks how Christ's nobleness had approved itself in, according to his desire and prophecy, no one during his earthly companying with them having suffered injury; on the other hand, as the older account tells us, only one young man, not further named, almost naked, just as he had been aroused from his sleep and had come up to protect Christ, followed Him at first faithfully, as if in order to make an alarm and summon all to aid, but, when they would arrest Him, likewise at last took to flight. The enemy's first stroke had now, through the traitor's help, succeeded almost contrary to expectation; other strokes might soon be expected to follow.

CHAPTER XXXVIII.

The Condemnation.

For in the enemy's camp all had evidently been carefully prepared in advance for a speedy condemnation, as they were in the greatest hurry to prevent any popular movement, and especially to have the execution early on the following morning, before the evening of the Passover and the feast of unleavened bread should interrupt the trial and unite the crowd. It had long been known that the people in Jerusalem, always so fickle, were never more inclined to disturbance, nor shewed the ruling powers such bold tokens of their discontent, as when they met in crowds on feast-days, under the protection, so to speak, of the law. The condemnation had to be a double one, as the Roman governor (Nach. s. 14—16) had, from his own view of the case, to give his assent to a sentence of death resolved on by the supreme court of the high-priest: Pilate's accidental presence in Jerusalem at that time made, however, this course of proceeding more easy. But further, the condemnation in the supreme court must be preceded by a hearing which settled the principal point in the charge, and was thus of the weightiest moment. That a case could not be brought at once before the highest court, is at once understood: but as the intention was to turn the charge in Jesus' case to that of a capital offence against the religious commonwealth, the first hearing had to be tried by the supreme judge. The reminiscence of such a double procedure had survived in the older account also, but dimly: here again it is St. John who distinguishes it all more accurately. For the older account makes the regular high-priest of the time, Caiaphas, preside at the first hearing, which is in itself improbable, because the acting high-priest was only the regulator of all the superior courts, and only in the Sanhedrim had the presidency: but St. John mentions that Jesus was first led to Annas, and tried by him, and then, when he had pronounced Him guilty, led next bound to Caiaphas, and so before the Sanhedrim, that that court might pronounce sentence of death, and send Him to the Roman governor. If we now assume what necessarily follows, that Annas, a member of the Sanhedrim, was at the same time the supreme judge, to which office he, as former high-priest and father-in-law of the present, may have been raised, it is all easily intelligible.

For the chief-priests plainly endeavoured to make the legal procedure quite regular; although about higher justice they only too little troubled themselves. If we enquire more particularly according to what law they meant to try and condemn Jesus, it is plain that, supposing Him innocent in civil matters, there was no written law which they could have used against Him.

The case of anyone giving himself out to be the Messiah, whether his view therein were more earthly or heavenly, had not been provided for in the old sacred law. Conscientious judges must then have entirely acquitted Jesus, supposing that under pretence of being the Messiah He had not been guilty of any civil offence, which no one charged Him with; and the breaches of the Sabbath, with which He had earlier been often charged, supposing even He had not been able to satisfactorily defend Himself on this ground, according to the then existing usage, did not amount to a capital charge. It was then on grounds quite apart from the sacred law and the true religion, apart indeed from all laws at that time in force, that the chief-priests were led to insist on the punishment of death, even though no actual legal pretext should be found against Him. It was the dull sense that here was rising a spiritual power, continually in development and advancing, which must overthrow their own existing power, together with their priest-rule. Fools, who, only to have quiet for the moment, overthrew the purest and most divine possible, and hence only brought on a speedier and more irretrievable ruin for their own cause! If they were once determined accordingly to know nothing more of Christ as He came closer to them, and opposed themselves to Him in ever blinder fury—as in increasing hardness of heart they had done hitherto— there was nothing left to them, supposing they found nothing to be legally brought against Him, except, among themselves and in presence of their followers, to express a vague horror at the presumption of this man, who exalts Himself above all existing sacred laws, and makes Himself equal to God; in presence of the Romans, on the other hand, to feign a strong fear of popular uproar which this King might arouse, and hence actually great devotion towards the Imperial Roman Empire: indeed, for an acute man who thought Himself exceptionally clever among these chief-priests, and wished above everything not to throw away the good will of Rome—and such a man was the high-priest at that time—the last reason was quite sufficient (Chap. XXXI). The result of this pretended trial was very easy to foresee: and doubtless Christ Himself foresaw it with all possible certainty. But it behoved Him, even in these last earthly transactions, to maintain His dignity.

The hearing before Annas was doubtless held late in the evening, in order to lay the cause as early as possible in the morning, regularly prepared, before the Sanhedrim. The high-priest first asked Jesus of his disciples and of his doctrine: the first question he had no conceivable right to put, so long as the defendant was not charged with being a popular leader; He answered accordingly, briefly, only to the second question, in the only way it became Him to answer, namely, that his doctrine had long been known. It is only too probable that the blow on the face, of which St. John speaks, was then given Him by an overzealous officer of the court, for supposed disrespectful speech before the court. But as the judge did not succeed in catching Him in his words, he brought forward the witnesses standing all prepared; who may (as one of the Gospels styles them) be styled, in fact, false witnesses, because they were put forward with bad intent to state something they had heard from Christ which might damage Him, and yet could say next to nothing against Him: it appeared too, on closer enquiry, that no two of them completely agreed together. The most damaging charge seemed to be the saying about the destruction of the temple, which had been retained from the earliest period of his public activity, and was now served up again: no two, however, who stated it were able to state it with such agreement that a legal condemnation could be passed on their testimony. When now Christ was simply silent to all this witness, the high-priest began to lose patience, reproached Him with his silence, and asked, adjuring Him (for no other means was left to him), if He really believed Himself Messiah the Son of God. But hardly had Jesus, as He could not help, solemnly assented to this, when the judge of the court thought He had thus condemned Himself. On what passage from the law he founded his judgment we are not informed—probably on a passage from Deuteronomy directed against false prophets; for the attendants of the court jeered at Him now as a false prophet, and prepared to send Him as an already convicted false prophet, strongly fettered, to the Sanhedrim for a final verdict.

During this somewhat protracted procedure two of his most intimate disciples, recovering from their first alarm, had collected about the house in which the inquiry was going on, following at a distance the band which had led away their beloved Lord. The older account mentions this only of Peter. This is, however, merely from its having to tell us how in these terrible hours he stood about the court-house, and in the cold night warmed himself, in company with the warders and attendants, at a great fire kindled in the court; and how to the question thrice asked by the men outside, whether he were not a follower of the accused, he answered not in the affirmative. Without doubt the much-tried man afterwards often himself told, how he at that time, out of mere human fear, had not freely enough acknowledged his part in the Lord, full of bitter repentance even at what, in so trying a time, seems so small an offence: thus only was it, doubtless, that this recollection found its way into the Gospel history. St. John, in his narrative, adds how it was possible for him to come into the well guarded court of that palace; that he was himself known in the palace, and on his application Peter was also admitted. It is thus also intelligible how Peter could be asked whether he *also* was one of Jesus' disciples; and, as the recognised head of the Twelve, he had in truth most cause for personal fear. The Sanhedrim itself, as more difficult to assemble, did not meet till the early morning; but its session was this time pushed through with greater haste, and the procedure might here be quite brief, if Christ, as was the fact, did not appeal. He was accordingly led very early before Pilate (who, according to Roman custom, was before sunrise present in the Prætorium for business), in order to get confirmed by him the sentence of death already approved by the higher court: but at the same time, in the statement to him it was plainly desired that he should have the Saviour crucified in the Roman manner, as a seditious character who was guilty of treason against the supremacy of Rome. For the execution of a false prophet, according to the ancient sacred law, would have been by stoning, under the initiative of the witnesses: but witnesses, as above stated, were here not to be found; and if they succeeded in putting Him to death in the Roman manner as guilty of high treason, the disgrace, they counted, must be much greater, and at the same time the public responsibility would pass from them to the Roman governor. The proceedings connected with Pilate are given in the earlier account pretty accurately, but far more accurately by St. John: and as Pilate in these proceedings acted quite openly, partly before his court-house, partly within it, yet always in the presence of several Romans, it is not surprising that for their importance they were retained in memory with sufficient fidelity.

Those arriving with the hurried bill of accusation could not go into the heathen Prætorium, because those intending to keep a feast might not enter the houses of heathen; for such was their traditional interpretation of the rule about keeping themselves clean for three days beforehand. Pilate then, leaving the accused bound in the house, came out to them before the door, but (as from the indictment he could quickly discover the trifling character of the charge) shewed at first no wish at all to interest himself in the case, and wished to leave it to them to inflict a smaller punishment: they however insisted on his ratifying the punishment of death, that is of crucifixion, which they had called for from the first. He went then back into the Prætorium, to ask Jesus whether He were really the King of the Jews: and doubtless He could have briefly denied the question so put, if the governor had put it to Him as coming merely from himself. But as He saw that in this very notion rested the charge brought against Him, He declared that He was indeed a king, but that his kingdom was unlike any other in this world—it was the kingdom of Truth itself, standing open to every one; and this, when called upon, He repeated as distinctly as possible. What Truth is—whose kingdom Jesus was advancing, appeared to Pilate of very small moment, as he expressed himself without disguise and almost in mockery: but if he were to treat the accused as one of the many fools, as the chief Romans with extreme coldness treated all the endless systems of philosophy and religion becoming known to them, he could not look on Him as deserving of punishment by death, and so thought to release Him.

It was certainly at this stage of the proceeding that Pilate resolved to send Jesus to Antipas—who was then likewise present at Jerusalem for the feast—as being his Galilæan prince; in the sure hope that this prince would not judge the accused so hardly as the chief-priests: he wished too thus to gratify the Tetrarch, and to remove some ill-feeling which had arisen between them. It is true that St. Luke alone records the interlude; but one does not see how it can be purely fictitious: Antipas besides (Nach. s. 14) was at that time living not far off. The vain Tetrarch, who as it happened had never seen Jesus, much as he had heard of his miracles, was well pleased to see Him, but found Him quite silent; just as the older narrative in the enquiry before Pilate dwells much on Jesus' sparing discourse with Pilate; and why should He say much? The Tetrarch then was contented with mocking Him in many ways, with the rough warriors who were present, and at last sending Him back to Pilate, with a mock royal robe of state. He could not better meet the feeling of this Roman than by the judgment it involved, that the man charged with seeking a kingdom was to be treated as a madman: it was remarked among the people, that from that day these two rulers became friends.

Meanwhile Pilate had repeatedly assured the complainants and the rest of the people, who at the instigation of the chief-priests assembled about the court-house, that he could discover no guilt, but also he thought in the worst case he could lay before them a choice, which, as he shrewdly calculated, would necessarily lead to the discharge of the accused. According to custom the governor released yearly at the Passover to the prayer of the people one prisoner: Pilate then would give them the choice, either to set free a certain other Jesus, usually however called Barabbas, a public disturber, murderer and robber, or the other accused; imagining they would surely not ask for the release of so dangerous a man. And as Jesus now returned from the Tetrarch, Pilate first tried the course indicated to him by the Tetrarch; had him scourged by the soldiers and otherwise ill-treated, put in derision a crown of thorns upon his head and a purple robe about his shoulders, and introduced Him to the people thus chastised and mocked as king, in hope they would be touched with compassion for Him. But the people, who now became uproarious, wished the crucifixion of Jesus and the release of Barabbas; thus was Pilate caught in his own cunning. He wished then at least not to give his own soldiers for the crucifixion, that it might not happen under Roman approval: he even, when it was called out to him that one who gave Himself out to be God's Son must be publicly executed, like a superstitious man, became afraid, had Jesus again brought into the court-house to ask Him about it, and so finally again gave Him a chance of release. How deeply rooted among the people was the notion of a superstitious fear on the part of the governor, appears from the tradition inwoven in one of the present Gospels, that Pilate's own wife, troubled the night before by a dream, sent a message to him during the procedure, to release the innocent man. When, however, on that superstitious question of the governor the Saviour remained mute, he became for a moment angry with Him, asking Him whether He knew that he could kill Him or release Him? but the Saviour now quietly answered, he would have no power over Him had it not been given by God to him, as the then supreme authority in the Holy Land: and so far as human guilt was to blame, not he, but that man had the greater guilt who had faithlessly given Him up to his supreme jurisdiction. The governor proposed indeed to the people once more the release; but they called out, would he really not punish a disturber of the imperial power? This subdued the man trembling at every accusation at Rome against Him: he made preparation for pronouncing sentence from the seat of judgment (s. 14), this probably, according to usage, containing only a short summary of the case. But it is easily intelligible how the simple popular tradition told that Pilate at length yielded to prevent an increase of popular excitement, but before pronouncing sentence washed his hands in public, in presence of the multitude and of the sun just rising, removing from himself all higher responsibility.

CHAPTER XXXIX.

THE CRUCIFIXION AND BURIAL.

THUS then, without further grace and without the least delay, a punishment of death was to be executed on the Saviour, the most terrible and disgraceful possible. In this peculiar sort of punishment, the criminal at the place of crucifixion was either, as he lay, nailed with his hands to the cross, and generally with his feet as well, and this was then set upright and fixed in the ground, or else he was in this way fixed to the cross already set up. The cross was usually not high, and had in the middle a small wooden projection on which the criminal had to sit, while the cross-beam above likewise projected before the upright: thus he had to stoop forwards, to prevent him with the weight of his whole body sinking too far, or losing equilibrium, whilst at the same time the increased duration of the torment, till death at length appeared, through this small rest granted to the body, became only more unendurable. As a punishment devised with such devilish art of torture, as all like punishments, it was looked on strictly as the punishment of slaves or others degraded to this lowest order of being:

the Carthaginians and Persians indeed punished with this those charged with high treason; but by the Romans this most horrible punishment was almost either confined to their enormous multitude of slaves, or in the provinces executed as well against those charged with high treason. To the spirit of the Old Testament religion, and to the old customs of Israel, it was quite strange; so much the more wicked that it was now called for by the chief-priests against a member of their own people, and that too an innocent one. Roman, that is the most civilized, heathenism must combine with the most degenerate and irreclaimable material of the old community of the True God, to carry out the most fearful crime which could ever be committed.

When Pilate mounted the chair of judgment to pronounce the final sentence, it was, according to St. John, about the sixth hour, that is, about the time of sunrise, or at any rate not much after that hour; according to the older account it was 9 A.M., as we reckon, when the Saviour was nailed to the cross: and in fact, from the moment of the sentence, in the making the final preparations, and then in the procession to the place of execution, two or three hours might well elapse before the crucifixion actually began.

A part of the preparation consisted, according to usage, in drawing up the statement of the crime to be settled by the supreme authority, which, written in large capitals, had to be fixed to the cross. Pilate commanded to put above the cross simply, "Jesus of Nazareth, the

King of the Jews," in the Hebrew, Latin, and Greek languages. The chief-priests, who, now reproached by an evil conscience, looked on it as almost an injury to the Jewish name that such a man should be publicly executed as their king, wished he would state in the superscription that He had only given Himself out for it, but never been recognised by them: but the governor did not give in to this too late stirring of the national pride, quite worthy of the whole proceeding in the matter, which seemed to him merely ridiculous. St. John alone relates this more particularly: it is a trait apparently trifling, but very significant for the whole behaviour of the persons active in the matter.

The place of the crucifixion, where doubtless at that time all such executions took place in Jerusalem, lay not far indeed from the city, but yet without its walls and surrounded by gardens: for the ancient horror of the people at contact with a corpse, a horror ratified by law, would never have suffered them to permit such a place, no more than the burial places, within the city. It was called Golgotha, or, as all the old Gospels translate it, "Place of a skull"; even St. Luke, who always avoids foreign terms, has merely adopted this name in a translation. The name 'skull' indicates a bare and barren hillock projecting from the ground; it was indeed the place best fitted for a place of execution: but the name, so far as we know, does not occur earlier, and probably in the modern Jerusalem replaced the name of a hill of similar purport in the ancient Jerusalem, probably the hill Gareb, (Jerem. xxxi. 39). It may have lain to the north-west of the city, but evidently at a greater distance than the place where, since Constantine's time, men believe they have discovered the Holy Sepulchre, and since then constantly shewn it. This place lies indeed in the probable direction, and an old reminiscence of its situation may long have been generally preserved. If now the court-house, at which Pilate was stopping, (Nach. s. 14) stood pretty well in the east of the city, the way from it to Golgotha was of some length; as we can further see from special recollections of the events of that quite unparalleled day of judgment and death. For Christ, like every other condemned to such a death, had to bear His cross from the court of judgment to the place of execution, surrounded by Roman soldiers and accompanied by two robbers to be crucified with Him: the burden, for the length of the way, was too heavy for Him to bear, and one Simon of Cyrene, just returning from his field and thus meeting the procession, was compelled to carry it for Him, which the older account thinks sufficiently important to inform us of. That a crowd followed the procession, and in particular many women, with loud wailing, we can well understand, as also that among them were many of His truest venerators, now seized with horror and deepest grief: but St. Luke is the first who gives us, from a later account, some words of solemn comfort, which Christ directed more especially to the wailing women. The Eleven, of whose doings on this day the history is silent, save for the exception soon to be mentioned, appear to have stood somewhat further off, to escape from the first raging of the storm: He was also Himself great enough to wish to bear his deepest misery alone, and not now to desire the presence of his closest friends. Thus they arrived at the place of execution: the rough soldiers, when just about to nail his hands and feet, and to set up his cross between those of the two robbers, offered Him, as usage demanded, a stupifying drink; but He wished to bear all his pain in full possession of his faculties, and even found strength for Himself in the prayer to his Father to forgive those who knew not what they did: these soldiers were indeed only the unwitting instruments for carrying out commands whose right they understood not, but in truth by their own guilt indifferent enough not to ask seriously about the right. There were of them—all this we know more particularly from St. John—four, who together formed the watch at the cross: they parted among them as usual the garments of the crucified, cutting his over-garment into four pieces, but throwing lots for his under-garment which was woven from one piece. Now at length, when with his whole cause He seemed humanly speaking lost, the scorn and mockery of the world could pour forth unrestrained, and the malice of the chief-priests broke out aloud. Imagination fails to picture this scorn of men, to which the joy of the feast close by formed an accompaniment; and the older account relates further, quite simply, how the Roman soldiers, whose imagination would be strongly agitated by the crime imputed to Him of wishing to be the king of the Jews, poured forth all their derision on Him simply as king: the same account tells us how the idle and frivolous lookers-on at the cross in passing by, the chief-priests keeping somewhat further off, and even the two robbers crucified with Him, all according to their several frames of mind, gave free utterance to their insulting speech. But the Christian feeling preferred soon to turn from the thought on these horrors, struck by the all-subduing majesty of Christ's prayer, in prospect of such sufferings praying the divine mercy for his torturers: and it seems to have been the impossibility of thinking that all, even of those who had not known Christ more closely, could have been able to join in this derision, which led to the tradition of the reviling of the two crucified with Him being so beautifully changed to the opposite, as we now have it in St. Luke; according to whom, one at least of them, brought now through the punishment itself to repentance, and seeing on the other hand the guiltless suffering of the Just, reproved the other for his blasphemy, and asked not in vain for the intercession of the Crucified. And if St. Luke cannot let the thought of the last earthly moments of the Holy One of God be disturbed by the account of the various blasphemies of men—which indeed have no need to be dwelt on—still less can St. John, all the less that in other parts of his Gospel he has sufficiently intimated their historical occurrence. The more fondly does St. John recollect a trait of purest love and tenderest thoughtfulness, which Christ on the cross revealed. Whilst the disciples and other near friends of Christ during the fury of this storm kept themselves further from its scene, the faithful women, who indeed as women had less to fear at this moment, stood round the cross somewhat further off: four now of these women, the mother of Jesus herself and her sister Salome (Chap. VII.) with two other Marys and with John from the Twelve, stood somewhat closer. Then in few words He pointed John to his mother as her son, and her to him as his mother, thus cementing a new relationship peculiarly touching for both, and especially for the beloved disciple, in place of the relationship between Himself and his mother now completely dissolved. His brothers in the flesh had not yet become believers: thus then his brother adopted by Him at his departure out of this life took his mother to his own house: and if in his Gospel he determined not to pass over this, and much else which certainly has in the first place only a private importance, he evidently did this not from vain-glory, but at the close of his life it was a sweet reward for Him to bring it all back in livelier recollection: for his readers it is an undesigned proof that he alone can have written all this.

But the same older account, which, in accordance with its predominant plain simplicity, had not been silent about that deepest derision of the world, has also the depth to comprehend that from this very deepest humiliation arises the highest transfiguration, and that the infinitely painful turning-point of this whole divinely human story begins where by the world it is least dreamt of. If the infinite meaning here concealed may be expressed in words, we have the simplest and at the same time most beautiful account, how, after that Christ during the first three hours on the cross had endured the greatest conceivable depths of misery, just at noon a darkness of three hours, lasting till his death, came over the earth, as though from that mysterious place of punishment for all human guilt there rose already the prelude of future just punishment in the mourning of the whole world for the coming death of the Holy One through man's immeasurable guilt. But the Holy One Himself also (this account goes on), in this terrible darkness and nearness of the final death-struggle, cast forth, as if wrung from Him, in the words of the deepest penitential psalm, that human despair, which hitherto, even under the extremest pains, He had always overmastered; as though, by that cry of the dying man going through the whole world, He called on God Himself to carry on the work which He on earth must now give up: thus certainly did the purely human feeling remain in Him even to the last moment. And we can well understand that his friends standing around, thrilled through by that mighty call of the Holy One, misled by a misunderstanding of one of his words, thought He called for Elias to help; and that one of them hastened to refresh Him with a drink of vinegar, as though Elias might actually come to save Him. But the last human hope, wherever or however it looked for help, must give way, and with one last mighty cry He breathed forth his spirit; whilst—as if for a heavenly token that with this life that of all the existing national religion was already virtually at an end—the veil before the Holy of Holies in the temple was rent from top to bottom, and even the heathen captain standing by had to acknowledge that here God's Son suffered and died. In this account all is grandly exhaustive and in close mutual connection: and he who will, may further enquire whether the purely heavenly occurrences, the darkness of those three hours and the rending of the veil of the temple, may have an ordinary historical meaning, and from what events of experience they may have been interwoven in the account. But as such unfathomable moments of history as this, to him who will exhaust their deeper meaning, are beyond every attempt to describe them in their greatness and miraculousness, in their connection with all the spiritual and bodily universe, and on this very account continually excite to new attempts; we see accordingly, from the present St. Matthew's Gospel, how further attempts were made to paint the moment of this one death grandly as became the subject. Not only on that noon was the earth darkened, but three hours afterwards, in that dreadful moment of death, it was so shaken that the rocks were cleft and the graves were opened: and as though this moment were prolonged over all time and the completion of all things, and the last judgment would appear, many of the saints who slept actually arose from out of their graves and shewed themselves in the holy city. Thus truly was this moment of death regarded as the great boundary line of all time, and as the period of the deepest shaking of the whole existing course of the world. But, as even the sublimest pictures of the importance of this moment never come up to it, it is not less worthy of St. John, that he describes in a few grand words the close of the history of this earthly life. And as for all the most prominent features of the close of this history, which was unexpected and to many proved a stumbling-block, he seeks the more carefully for Old Testament types; so he tells us Christ, when He saw that all was accomplished, as though even his last thought without design corresponded to the Messianic prophecies, complained of thirst—as in fact the crucified do suffer much from thirst: when they had put to his mouth a sponge full of vinegar put on a hyssop-stalk, and He had received the vinegar, with the cry 'It is finished' He let his head fall forward and gave up the ghost. Thus is St. John's narrative also a very simple one, but in truth in quite another style from that oldest account.

This endeavour to find a fulfilment of Old Testament types, especially in the close of this history which thus makes its way into the arena of Universal history, is apparent in St. John once more in the course of the history. According to a legal order in Deuteronomy, criminals hung should not remain unburied after evening fall: there was no legal right to extend this humane law to those crucified in the Roman manner, but because on that Friday not only an ordinary Sabbath, but in this year the great day of the Passover likewise was impending, on which it was still more essential that great quiet and peace should extend over the country, Pilate was asked for permission to be allowed to kill on the cross the crucified before evening. They hence broke as usual the legs of the crucified: but when it came to

Jesus' turn, and He was observed to be already dead, one of the soldiers merely thrust his spear into his side to convince himself of death having actually occurred. But that *He*—who was slain about the time of the slaughter of the Paschal offering, and had fallen as the infinitely nobler Paschal or Atonement offering—thus sacrificed as an offering, was also like the Paschal offering in this unexpected and extraordinary coincidence, in not having his bones broken; *that* seemed to St. John so remarkable, that he cannot sufficiently assure us how he saw and observed this with his own eyes. But this remark would only be looked on as so extremely important in the Apostolic period, as will further appear below. That the Saviour was really quite dead on taking down from the cross, we have not the remotest reason for doubting. For though the crucified live on over the first even to the third or fourth day, and extremely wonderful spasmodic alterations, nay, even transfigurations, may appear in their whole countenance, called forth by the acutest of all pains, in men of youthful vigour; yet, to say nothing of the carefulness of the authorities then, under these circumstances so strict, and passing over the express testimony of St. John, Christ had been greatly exhausted by the days preceding, and especially by the night before (as had appeared in his attempt to carry the cross, nay, on the evening before in Gethsemane), so that the earlier coming on of death in his case could surprise no one. Only, from the short duration of his crucifixion, and as according to all accounts He had a strong voice quite unbroken and loud, we must certainly assume that at last a sudden inward convulsion, through breaking of the heart, occasioned death; and this the flowing forth of blood and water indicates. As the chief-priests, who, insensible as they were towards the higher truth, retained with such anxiety the lower legal truth, had before all to respect the peculiar nature of this day, they had doubtless early in the day asked the governor in good time for leave to finish early the crucifixion; and this breaking the bones on the cross happened probably pretty soon after three o'clock in the afternoon, or not long after Jesus' death. Meanwhile the Crucified remained hanging until the two others, whose deaths had been thus accelerated, were also quite dead. About this time one of the secret honourers of Jesus, Joseph of Arimathæa, came to Pilate with the request to be allowed to remove the Saviour's body and bury it: the governor, after he had assured himself that He was dead, gave the permission, and the Saviour's friend placed the body, wrapped according to custom with linen towels, in the new rock-hewn grave situated in a garden close by. They could not look for a more distant place suited for the laying-out of the body, on account of the eve of the Sabbath being close at hand: they were satisfied then to place it temporarily in this the nearest place that was suitable. According to St. John, who always follows up the part taken by Nicodemus, he specially contributed by bringing rich incense and aloes: and although, according to the older account, the women also, who staid not far from the cross and observed where He had been laid, recollected likewise the last office of love, they came with their profound paralyzing grief too late, as immediately at sunset the Sabbath began.

CHAPTER XL.

The Eternal Exaltation.

Thus, so far as man's will and power were able, had *He* been slain as a criminal, who, neither as man, nor as, what none other could be, the Messiah of Israel, was guilty of the smallest offence: *He*, who alone appeared as the rightful true Messiah and Israel's sublime and blessed hope, the Messiah for so many centuries expected,—*He* had been now rejected and treated with the lowest contumely by those who since the last fifteen hundred years were the heads of God's people in its existing form, as well as by the great multitude of this people themselves: *He*, whose purpose was to found the imperishable salvation of Israel and, through this, of all nations, and who shewed in the only right way how all human salvation can blossom and ripen, had been, by the highest courts both of Israel and of heathenism, branded as the most dangerous deceiver of men; *He*, who, against all the errors, the sins, and abominations, which from the beginning of the human race had been for so many thousand years growing ever greater and more unbearable, had used no weapon, save the highest wisdom, purest divine love, and the most inexhaustible meekness, had fallen through the combination of the sin of Israel's hardness of heart with heathenism's frivolity. In that nation, which beyond all others ought to be God-beloved, pure and holy, but yet for fifteen hundred years had suffered so many errors and sins to spring up within itself, the whole weight of all these errors and sins grown old and rigid, gathered into one mass, collected against Him: for He fell not in consequence of a single, as it were accidental question, as the Baptist had fallen, nor, as it were by accident, in a sudden rising of the people; but simply in the one great question of the whole development of Israel, that is of the Church of the true religion, and in the culmination of the struggle for its highest truth and whole existence upon earth. But even the hardness of heart of all the error and all the sin in Israel, as it now took form in the chief priesthood, could not by itself destroy Him, and had to take as its ally the Roman, that is the most terrible and strongest rule of all heathendom. Thus the weight of all the sins of the whole ancient world turned against Him standing alone, the single, weak, defenceless man, who strove for no human power and majesty. Here are condensed the most extreme and sharpest contrasts in all previous history—for heathen history had already inseparably entwined itself with that of Israel. And with the single founder of a Church of the completed true religion, this Church seemed, when hardly founded, to be again completely crushed.

The way however in which, from the very moment

in which it seemed crushed, together with the King of the completed Kingdom of God—and little striking in appearance was this King—the way in which its unconquerable power was most miraculously shewn, and how out of the grave of its Founder, killed only through the culmination of all human sin, there rises infinitely more mighty quickening and eternal glory; to describe and illustrate this in a connected history belongs to the following period. Christ's death and burial are in history phenomena soon over, yet are they the true concluding moments of all ancient history. The end of this was not previous to that of Christ's earthly existence, but doubtless they close together as if this grave only closed, in order that the whole period also of ancient humanity should close with it. We may not deprive Christ's death and burial of this its true importance; nor may we confuse the new following life of Christ with the old, now violently interrupted, as though it were the very same: in so doing the deep suffering of this death is lost to us, and its infinite importance for us diminished. Hence, if the Gospels annex briefly some events lying beyond this grave, they do this only because they had then known though only for too short a time this new glorified life of Christ, which first reflects on his earthly life the most brilliant light, being as it were its necessarily following higher side: whilst St. Luke's example, in his second history, shews that all which happened after the death and burial is better connected with the history of the Apostolic period. We must therefore say, that all which the Saviour, in fulfilment of the ancient holy expectation and hope, as likewise from the true nature of the cause itself, had to suffer, was already completely achieved in all his previous actions, and not least in this suffering and death; that, consequently, what of Him reaches beyond this grave is the fruit of the earthly completion of his work, and hence passes over into a quite new province. Even the highest divine power, when it veils itself in mortal body and appears in definite time, finds in this body and this time its limits: and never did Jesus as the Son and Word of God take the place of God and the Father, nor presume to make Himself equal to Him. Thus then the ancient Messianic hope certainly, in its grasp of the whole conceivable future in all its circumstances and in its whole extent, contained more than Christ, in this frail body and in this fleeting time, could accomplish. But we must not look for the certain truth of a prophecy and hope, touching the whole of God's kingdom, as to be fulfilled at once: nor is its true fulfilment once in the course of ages and for ever. And thus He had now appeared, who alone at this period and amid this people could be the true Messiah of the kingdom of God to be formed: and not only had He fulfilled what these prophesies in their deepest meaning demanded from Him, but, working and establishing, suffering and dying, amid all the difficulties of the period, He had absolutely done far more than any ancient prophet had been able so accurately to foresee and prophesy. That call had struck on his ear, which, going through the whole ancient history of all nations, had been most firmly and clearly perceived in Israel; through all that people's earlier history that call had sounded with irresistible force—the call that One must first come forth, who, unmoved and unsubdued by the errors and sins which in the whole history of youthful humanity had taken ever stronger root, must completely do the will of God: and, behold, his whole life and working was the answer to this call. The call came to Him, not simply as bidding Him act and take thought for Himself, but in the way it must come to Him in Israel, in harmony with that nation's unparalleled ancient history, as to Him who, unseduced by all the sins of the world, could *so* follow in everything simply the will of God, that He should be the leader of all towards the like perfection, through the founding of the Church of the perfected true religion: and, behold, He fulfilled also this double call so insurpassably, that it is vain to ask whether He is greater as an individual, or as leader and head of a Church founded by Him.

When He followed the call, the whole weight of all the errors and sins, which since time began had been growing ever heavier and more hopeless, not only of mankind in general, but of the ancient people of the true religion in particular, threw itself entirely on Him, to hinder his work or to crush Himself: all the perversities and sins in the ancient Church, unremoved since the earliest times, grown ever more fixed and darkened, raged against Him from far and near, and at length He came into conflict, in addition, with the frivolity and stupidity of the most violent heathenism; then it was that the most painful requital conceivable fell on the most innocent even to extremity; the deepest hatred of the world turned against Him, who had shewn towards it nothing but the purest truth and the kindest benevolence, as though this hero and this innocence had been great and strong enough to endure what none other endured: yet not one moment did He waver, and was in enduring and bearing, in suffering and dying, equally great as in working and combating. He drew friends towards Him, brought disciples into his more intimate circle; but He had at last to bear and suffer all, even to extremity, quite alone and forsaken by all, only to be pronounced happy in this, that as his labouring and working, so also his deepest suffering, reached their goal not very remotely in time. For all with Him reached a climax in such a manner, that his temporal temptation through suffering, though most extreme, yet also was very brief and sufficient. But if He suffered to extremity, forsaken by all, yet not by the true God, through whose power He alone wrought all and suffered all, to win thereby in the last outward destruction the highest victory. For all those spiritual powers, which in Israel (as the people of the true religion striving with mighty effort towards its perfection) had severally been active and dominant, once more massed together to form one whole, so as at once to throw off all the defects which infected them singly, and whose ever stronger prominence and ever more dangerous combination put a stop at length to all true progress in the development, and prevented the great completion which ought in proper sequence to follow. In Him in these late days was renewed once more the prophetic power as the first fundamental power of the Church of the true religion, and that with an immediately divine certainty, such as had never existed since Moses, in proclaiming new truths and creating a new empire, but free from the violence which clave originally to the prophetic activity: every truth shone only by its own lustre, and was recommended by its own goodness, so that even the last trace of the ancient prophetical dress disappeared, and in the most human language there streamed forth only the most divine certainty and the calmest truth. In Him the long-extinguished existence of a true King of Israel revived, founding and sustaining a kingdom, with kingly word deciding the hardest question, and with supreme power ruling in all, but establishing and working only through the purest piety as the highest instrument, and founding only the unchangeable dominion of the perfected true religion, which must go forth out of Israel, but, immediately making its way beyond, must embrace all men and nations; no longer bound up in Israel, and indissolubly connected with its human weaknesses. In Him also the ancient priestly power gives new might, reconciling man with God, and leading Him purified back to Him, but no more bound up with a purely prophetic law, nor with a law holy merely from antiquity, and consecrated through its antiquity or anything external, but following only the highest truth, and with the truth's advance continually receiving new life. (Compare Matt. xiii. 52.) All however those highest spiritual powers, once dispersed through Israel, united in Him to form one never before existent strong Whole, because the power and impulse of the perfected true religion, in which they were all included, was at length manifested in Him, as according to the divine will it ought to have been shewn forth from the beginning of all creation, but yet was unable to manifest itself, excepting now, and only in this nation, and only in the first place in this one.

Thus then He brought the very element, which alone was wanting for the completion of the ancient true religion in the Church, which this Church was long desiring; namely, the cheerfulness, power, and activity of the purest divine love, to be subdued by nothing, penetrating all knowledge as well as all action, fulfilling all existing good laws, but alive equally to every new divine duty and all new knowledge; giving to the world the most sensible proof, in ruling, working, helping, and leading, but also in all obedience, all self-restraint, and all self-sacrifice. Thus was He the Son of God in a way none other had been; in mortal body and in fleeting time the purest reflection and the most glorious picture of the Eternal Himself. He was the Word of God; through his human word as well as through his whole manifestation and working, speaking from God, and illustrating to the world God's most secret thought, nay, as it were the spirit of his working, with such absolute power and such immortal brilliance, as none hitherto, and as none can surpass: and so He was the only true Messiah, the eternal King of the kingdom of God among men, perfected for the first time in his person; the One towards whom, as Leader and Lord, everyone after Him must constantly look and strive, whom the Spirit leads, whether in thought, in labour, or in suffering, to strive purely and wholly up to God. Is the perfect possible in the humanly imperfect; the imperishable and eternal possible in the perishable and transitory? The answer to this He demonstrates as it has never been before or since: and He will for ever manifest and prove it to all those who do not flee from his light. Before Him, among all the nations of the earth, no one even rightly conceived the task that was to be accomplished. Socrates in a long life hardly succeeded even in rightly discerning it at a distance; whilst his pupils immediately lost themselves again in mere questions of science, and hardly among the Stoics did a remote recollection of the task survive. Buddha strove towards it through the creation of the same divided nature in man and in nations, which in Christendom satisfies only the Pope and friends of Popery, and ended by putting Himself in God's place and thus driving every true god from his circle; the inferior gods, and as such less disturbed, were allowed to continue their being. Kung-tso conceived the project of founding and sustaining the best kingdom merely through good instruction, good morals, and, at most, by a striving after the perfect apart from a living true God. How far does He stand removed even from these greatest men outside of Israel! and if nevertheless the kingdom of the two last endures so wonderfully, what must we expect from the firmness and duration of his kingdom? There is probably no nation which might not see at length what they have most zealously longed for during many centuries, and sought for with the deepest earnestness and the most patient striving, achieved at last most completely in one of its members. All its noblest powers and most exalted efforts seem united in this *one*, and hence mount in Him higher and higher with his very success, most unexpectedly and marvellously: and in every noble and aspiring people a culminating effort at the close of a long history thus gathers most naturally into the condensed kernel-like strength of a single man. Thus all that was most fair and exalted in what the Greeks strove after (a divided effort swaying them from the first) met in the two so unlike contemporaries, Aristotle and Alexander; and the best to which the Romans could rise, in one man, Julius Cæsar. Among the Arabians again, Mahomet became such a hero. In Israel also all at length that was most noble and immortal in it, which for hundreds and thousands of years had been striven for and hoped for, was summed up in the working of Jesus of Nazareth: only in this nation could He come, and He came here as the long-desired and expected, for whom the way had long been prepared, though no one before Him was able actually to find it. But as the highest effort of this people, from the time of the founding the Church of the true God was infinitely more exalted and divinely imperative than all which to other nations seemed the highest end of life, and this final goal of all the noblest work of this people, in the course of ages amid all their changing destinies, nay, even amid their deepest troubles and most lasting gloom, was only the more clearly recognised and the more zealously pursued anew; so now in Him a hero had appeared in the earth, far less imposing, more short-lived and weaker than those named above, and yet infinitely more exalted, more mighty, and more immortal than any of them. The Highest had now come which could come as the fruit and reward of all the combats and victories of the incalculable host of men of God in Israel, to which more or less distinctly the hope and desire of all noblest antiquity had been directed, and which for the whole future was to have an incomparably higher importance; but had come infinitely nobler, and hence also infinitely more through Messiah's own working and suffering than through that of all the men of God before Him.

NOTES.

Chap. I.

The first two chapters were translated by the Editor from an earlier edition through inadvertence. The following corrections are accordingly given here from the last edition. The statement as to Josephus' regret for the putting to death of Jesus has been amended and referred to the rightful subject, namely, James his brother. The amended sentence runs as follows:—

"They lamented the death inflicted on James the brother of Jesus, and wished it had been left undone. Their dissatisfaction might indeed also have been influenced by the old opposition between the Pharisees and Sadducees, as Josephus was a Pharisee: but although Annas, at whose instigation, with that of his son-in-law Caiaphas, Christ was crucified, was, with all his family, an adherent of the Sadducees, yet the case of Christ's execution rightly seemed to him quite different from that of the Baptist, because He had been crucified by Pilate on the indictment of those in higher authority (namely, of the whole Sanhedrim), and so had not, like James (s. Unten), been executed without the observance of the established laws."

Antiquity of the Sources of the Gospel History.

It is pure prejudice, which in later times has led many learned men to try to establish that the whole Gospel literature was not commenced till very late: all more exact enquirers shew rather that it began very early, and was in process of formation in the most various forms before the destruction of Jerusalem, though doubtless it was continued long after that date.

Chap. II.

If we were able to discover the date of the appearance of the star, it would seem that we should be able to arrive at the date of Christ's birth. Now the star is generally taken to be the remarkable propinquity of Jupiter and Saturn in the year 747 U.C. Taking this however as the date of the appearance in the heavens, it is disputed whether we are to suppose the birth of Christ to have followed shortly after: in this case, the date of the birth would agree very well with the date of the census which, as Ewald supposes, was carried out by Herod not long after 746 U.C. He observes in a note to this chapter, that the time given by the Magi since the appearance of the star, of two years, leads to the inference that the child was nearly two years old when visited by the Magi; for it was believed that the star which foretels a birth only rises a few months before the actual birth. If to this interval from the star's first appearance we add the time spent by the child in Egypt, we are led to place the birth not much later than 747 U.C.

It may be said however that though the appearance of the star would be popularly supposed to occur shortly before the birth, it does not follow that it did.

The chief difficulty, if we allow this long interval between the birth and the appearance of the Magi, is, that we have then to suppose two visits of the parents of Jesus to Bethlehem: we have certainly however no reason for asserting that there were not two such visits.

On the question of the census, the author in the text takes S. Luke's meaning to have been, that the census was some time previous to the later one which took place under Quirinus.

The $\pi\rho\omega\tau\eta$, he observes, before $\dot{\eta}\gamma\epsilon\mu o\nu\epsilon\acute{u}o\nu\tau os$ $K\upsilon\rho\eta\nu\acute{\iota}ou$ is only the stronger comparative (a similar idiom being frequent in Sanskrit), and the meaning is this census fell *much earlier* than the government of Quirinus. Compare $\pi\rho\hat{\omega}\tau\acute{o}s$ $\mu o\upsilon$ (John i. 15, 30, xv. 18). The author rejects the view of A. W. Zumpt, namely, that Quirinus may actually have been governor of Syria, and in that capacity ordered this census; as we know in fact that he was about this time engaged in subduing the Homonadenses in Cilicia, and it seems not improbable that Cilicia may have been at that time included in the province of Syria: Ewald however says that St. Luke's words will not bear the meaning which it is thus sought to give them.

Chap. III.

On the grand conception of a theocracy, originating with the Jews, Ewald observes in the passage referred to (p. 20):—

"In the idea of the theocracy was introduced the sharpest contrast to all human kingdoms whose end and aim goes not beyond themselves, which come into existence and pass away only through human power and arbitrary will: here for the first time is a kingdom which itself knows its issue and its purpose to be apart from itself, which has neither arisen nor can grow through human will, a kingdom which, because its will is the divine, contains in itself a germ of eternal duration; as accordingly, in spite of all following changes, it survives for ever in its eternal truth, and only rises up again in Christianity with new youth and self-complete. But if the individual man find it difficult to devote his life for ever to the service of the Invisible alone, which he needs to keep every moment consciously before him, for which no outward support and hope is of the smallest use; how much harder must it be for a whole people, without any human kingdom and the outward order and firmness which it introduces, to find its unity and strength only in the invisible mysterious King, nay, designedly to destroy every other support of its kingdom!"

On the rise of the Messianic hope, Ewald observes (vol. iii. Schlussergebniss der gansen Königlichen Zeit):—

"The first period of the history of Israel had bequeathed the lesson; how ruinous was the intentional avoiding of a human kingdom. Accordingly, the establishment and the continuance of this kingdom became the soul of the second period. Yet the true religion was insufficient to prevent the kingdom from degenerating into a tyranny, because it itself suffered from this evil. Thus the perfected king could not come, whom yet religion now required. But the truth of the religion, so far as it had been won and secured, could not perish through any outward losses and overthrows: and if the great power of this second period, the kingdom, shewed itself too weak to bring forth the perfected King of this kingdom, and if at last it passed away with the overthrow of the kingdom and the dispersion of the people, the perfected King, with the perfection of the true religion and its kingdom, must be continually hoped for and striven for. Isaiah might indeed hope that with the speedy coming of the Messiah all would at once amend; but after that a century had again passed, and the hope remained unfulfilled, and the good Josiah himself in his work and in his death had but increased the confusion and sufferings of the time; then must the clear prophetic glance discern that it was not only the coming of a Messiah which was wanted, that the ground of the pressing evils of the people and kingdom lay much deeper : the deficiencies of the ancient religion had in general become apparent, and for the first time the need of a radically renewed religion must have been experienced. In the early days of the people, the individual felt himself supported by the Whole; Jehovah was only as the God of Israel his God. When now this Whole, after it had gradually through David and Solomon been carried to the highest glory it was capable of, and with the external might of the ancient religion there vanished that confidence which had hitherto been the strongest support of the individual; this very religion must either in its deepest essence perish, or it must habituate the individual to look away from that earlier majesty, and trust purely to the religion's deeper powers, and hold fast in it such new truths which earlier had not become sufficiently prominent in it. But whilst the more concealed enduring power of this religion, questioned and tried by thousands in their thousand needs, now first suffered its treasures to be rightly sought for and called forth, nay, suffered truths akin to it to leap forth exulting, truths which hitherto had not been clearly enough brought into light; it sank with its most peculiar power and certainty ever deeper into the mind and heart of individuals, and taught them, in spite of the vanishing of the national kingdom, nay, midst heathen conquerors and heathen-minded rulers of Israel, to hold fast more simply to their eternal truths. All historical traces shew this changed religious tone when more accurately examined: but we can follow it out most clearly in that book of the Old Testament, which is the clearest revelation of the secret emotions of the heart—the Psalter."

Chap. IV.

By the "Great Unnamed One" Ewald denotes the author of Isaiah (xl—lxiii): it was he, according to the Evangelists, whose spirit-stirring appeals moved the Baptist to his great enterprise. He looks on him as one of the captivity, but thinks him to have incorporated in his work some earlier prophecies.

Chap. VII.

Ewald brings forward the following arguments for the priestly parentage of the Virgin. St. John was apparently her nephew, as being the son of Salome the sister of our Lord's mother: now we have the following intimations of St. John being of priestly family. First, he was known to the high-priest, (John xviii. 15, 16). Secondly, the reminiscence given by Polycrates at the end of the second century (Euseb. iii. 31), that he was a priest and bore the πέταλον, the high-priest's mitre; for, from passages like Deut. xxxiii. 8—10, it might be concluded that the Levites were entitled to this at least as an honorary decoration. Though this language doubtless sounds partly metaphorical, it yet does not appear to have been used of anyone who was not of the tribe of Levi. Epiphanius in the fourth century uses the same expression in speaking of James the Lord's brother, after stating that he was a priest:

Οὗτος ὁ Ἰάκωβος καὶ πέταλον ἐπὶ τῆς κεφαλῆς ἐφόρεσε.
Adv. Hær. III. ii. 14.

This author states that the Heretics of his day used to ask how the Lord's mother could marry into the tribe of Judah while Elizabeth married into the family of the high-priests: his view is that the tribes of Levi and of Judah had the special privilege of intermarriage, as in fact we know that Aaron married Elizabeth of the tribe of Judah.

The Two Genealogies of our Lord.

The author, it will be seen, cuts the knot here, instead of trying to untie it. It will evidently be the safest to rest, as he does, the descent from David on the general belief of our Lord's contemporaries, rather than on the witness of these genealogies.

If only we allow with Ewald the historic truth of our Lord's descent from David, it is evidently a matter of small importance what mistakes may have crept into the genealogies; except in the view of proving the entire immunity from error of the inspired writers.

I would here express my entire dissent from the view of Ewald, that the histories of the infancy in St. Matthew and St. Luke are contradictory. They certainly shew, as Ewald observes, entire independence, and therefore we have double reason for assuming the truth of that wherein they agree, as of our Lord's descent from David, and the birth of the infant at Bethlehem at a time when the parents were from home: this is however quite consistent with St. Luke's view that the parents were visiting Bethlehem, having come up from their home in Nazareth: the episode of the flight into Egypt is simply omitted by St. Luke; he tells us nothing inconsistent with it.

It is satisfactory to find Ewald protesting against the view that the flight into Egypt was a fiction intended to serve as a fulfilment of the prophecy (Hosea xi. 1): so far-fetched an application of the prophecy can only, he observes, have been suggested by an undoubted fact.

Chap. IX.

The Earlier and the Later Scene of John's Baptism.

The earlier place was at Bethany (John i. 28), the reading Bethabara in the Textus Receptus being taken from certain late MSS. on a conjecture of Origen, who, not finding any Bethany on the banks of the Jordan, suggested Bethabara (mentioned in Judges vii. 24). It is remarkable that Bethany is read in many MSS. for Bethsaida (Mark viii. 22), as is observed in the remarks on Lazarus' history: the place intended lay pretty far to the north.

As to the later place of baptism, Ænon, near to Salem, the author differs from Robinson, who, following the Onomasticon, places it at Ainun ("Later Biblical Researches"). He inclines to the

Shalkhim (not Shilkhim) and Ayin, put together as contiguous places (Josh. xv. 32) in the south-east of Judah.

Ænon in any case lay away from the Jordan, as we are told that John found "much water" there.

Which brother's wife did Herod Antipas take from her husband? St. Mark asserts that it was the wife of Philip. Josephus (Ant. xviii. 5) asserts that it was Herod, brother of this Philip both on the father and the mother's side. That this Herod was a private man makes it more likely that Josephus is here correct: Philip too, we know, married his niece Salome. It is generally assumed, in order to make St. Mark's account agree with Josephus, that this Philip had Herod for his second name. It does not however seem probable that there should be two brothers named respectively Herod and Philip Herod, still it is certainly not impossible.

Chap. XI.

Ewald, it will be observed, adopts the view first suggested by Townson, that St. John reckons his hours, not from 6 o'clock in the morning, but from midnight and noon, as we do. Townson endeavours to shew that this mode of reckoning time was in common use in Ephesus, where St. John wrote his Gospel. He alleges in proof that Polycarp is said to have been martyred at the eighth hour: as the spectacles in the amphitheatre are allowed generally to have taken place early, it is, he observes, more likely that this was at 8 o'clock (as it would be if his view be correct) than at 2 o'clock. Pionius, who was martyred in the same city eighty-four years later, is said to have been martyred at the tenth hour, or 10 A.M. in Townson's view, 4 P.M. in the ordinary view.

The statement of St. John xix. 14, as to the time of Pilate's sentence on our Lord, can neither be reconciled with the other Evangelists' statement, nor with St. John's own statement (xviii. 28), unless we admit this view.

Chap. XIII.

On the Purport of our Lord's Reply (John ii. 19).

With Ewald's interpretation of this agree generally the deepest German expositors, Olshausen, Neander, &c: those however who, with

Neander, look on the reply as having been correctly reported, find their great difficulty in the mention of the three days. Ewald would doubtless take these words to be an unconscious alteration of our Lord's words, naturally occasioned by what St. John looked on as their fulfilment. It does not seem that St. John's remark forbids us to look for a fulfilment of our Lord's words beyond the fulfilment mentioned by him here. It seems to be the especial glory of the Biblical prophecies, that they are ever receiving new fulfilments. What was at one time looked on as a great or perhaps the only fulfilment, is found afterwards quite put into the shade by an after fulfilment. It was only to be expected that St. John should not see, as we may now, in the growth of Christ's spiritual temple the most complete fulfilment of the prophecy; that the undoubted fulfilment of it in Christ's own person should have completely satisfied him. There is another instance in which St. John imputes a motive to our Lord, which, as will be seen, Ewald questions—the motive of the question to Philip, "Whence shall we buy bread that these may eat?" I am certainly inclined to prefer looking on these words as a simple question for information. It is entirely in keeping with the lesson taught us by our Lord's temptation, that he should look for natural means for supplying men's needs before using supernatural. Viewing the question in this light, we get a much more graphic and touching picture of the human heart of our Lord melting towards His fainting hearers. In thus imputing to the Evangelist a misconception of our Lord's intention, Ewald might appeal to the example of Chrysostom, in his comment on the cursing of the fig-tree (Hom. in Matt. xvii).

Ewald's view that our Lord had primarily Himself in view as "the man" who had no need of human testimony, I have met nowhere else. It seems very improbable that He should thus have spoken of Himself.

"Ye worship ye know not what." Ewald observes on this:—

"This can only describe a religion which is actually ignorant of what is the exact purpose and final issue of the truth which lies or may lie in it; whilst the Jews, amongst whom alone the Messianic hopes flourished with their original vigour and certainty, possessed, at least in these, a clear and certain religion for all time to come: and only such a religion which embraces also the whole future development of its own living subject, and contains an eternal living hope, can be a true religion. Very analogous is St. Paul's saying to the Athenians (Acts xvii. 23)."

"Other men laboured, and ye are entered into their labours." Ewald notices this as an instance of our Lord's delicate modesty that He will avoid the use of the pronoun I. He finds another instance in John iii. 11, "We speak that we do know." On the general sense of the words he observes, Christ is Himself a reaper (v. 36), but still more His disciples (viii. 37), and Christ only as Christ glorified is the reaper; so that in this is a fulfilment of the proverb, No one can at once sow and reap, and the sower is always other than the reaper.

Chap. XIV.

The Healing of the Centurion's Son (St. John iv. 46—54).

This is taken by Ewald to be the same occurrence as is recorded by the first three Evangelists; the boy is by St. John called the Centurion's υἱός, by St. Matthew his παῖς, by St. Luke his δοῦλος. Ewald observes that St. Matthew's term might denote a son, while it might at the same time have been taken by St. Luke to signify a servant, and been in consequence by him changed into δοῦλος.

Chap. XV.

The Temptation of our Lord.

The view of our Lord's temptation as an inward, not as an outward one, is held by Neander, Olshausen, and most of the modern German commentators. By way of further elucidating Ewald's views, a passage is here given from "Die drei ersten Evangelien." "In St. Mark's words the Spirit drives Him into the wilderness: that mighty Spirit itself which had now come upon Him, and leaves Him no rest till He has accomplished all to which He was called, drives Him at once not into public life, but, on the contrary, first into the profound solitude of the wilderness, where fitting quiet reflection is possible, and where the true composure of spirit for the execution of the work can be won. The wilderness is the land of every horror and of every want, of wild beasts and of hunger and thirst; and its terrors and its wants become greater when one is quite alone in it, as the Saviour was there, and retires, as He did, into its most remote waste places; it is therefore the land of evil spirits, as the New Testament also often tells us; where consequently Satan is ever near enough at hand. But yet quite other temptations than these outer terrors and wants lay in the solitude itself, and in meditation on the carrying out of a resolution: every meditation of the sort brings before the mind's eye the wrong means and ways also, which likewise are very near to the spirit, and Satan is ever waiting with his temptations on the mere thought of what is wrong (Matt. xvi. 23). Nay, especially so long as the right and safe way has not yet been found of meeting a great Divine undertaking and work, so long waits (we may truly say) Satan continually at hand with his temptations and snares."

He explains as follows the lessons taught in the accounts of St. Matthew and St. Luke. There are three special dangers which meet the spirit in all public working, three weaknesses and passions which every man must overcome, if he will work with the Holy Spirit for a providential end; three true and lofty virtues, with whose help he must fight in order to win the final victory; and these three have a deep inward connection, but do not come before the spirit successively until the development in time of a great public activity. When such activity begins and its impediments also appear, the man would, to meet these impediments, retain all his eagerness for and dependence on external necessities, and apply every means in order to satisfy his craving, and to remove in the best way rising difficulties; whilst, on the contrary, independence of all external resources, forbearance from and renunciation of every false means of removing a rising difficulty, is the first requirement and the first lofty virtue for manifesting rightly and successfully a great activity: but when the spirit, thus severely self-contained and independent of external means, has already accomplished many a lofty project, and is at its most successful working, then it readily becomes fool-hardy, and in rash confidence tries even the most desperate actions: whilst, on the very contrary, with the growing success, moderation and collectedness need to grow all the more. And when at length through that success he has won the highest power possible to him, there lies in it for him the last and worst temptation, that namely of using the very power won, as a means for satisfying his own ambition and other lusts; whilst, on the contrary, the most single eye to the service of God must direct power at its greatest elevation, in order that the eternal divine purpose itself may be thus accomplished without disturbance."—*Ewald.*

As applying the general lesson to Christ's particular case, we may say with Neander, the first temptation was the temptation to work miracles for his own comfort or advantage, the second to work miracles in order to prove Himself the Christ, the third to establish His Messianic kingdom by human means and devices of human expediency.

Chap. XVI.

The author considers the narrative in St. Luke, of Christ's call to his first three Apostles, to be coloured by the recollection of the later experience of the Apostles. He considers the reminiscence described by John (xxi. 6—22) to be the foundation of St. Luke's narrative here. The connection which, according to our Lord's teaching, ought always to be found between temporal blessings and spiritual, was no doubt present to St. Luke's mind.

Are Matthew and Levi different names of the same man? The narratives in St. Matthew of the calling of Matthew the publican, and in St. Mark and St. Luke of the calling of Levi the publican, seem certainly to refer to the same event. There would be no difficulty in supposing that Matthew was the name adopted by Levi after his calling, were it not that in this case we should have expected the Evangelists, who had already spoken of him under the name of Levi, would, when speaking of him under a different name, inform us of the identity of Matthew with Levi. Still this hypothesis seems preferable to that of Ewald—that the name of Matthew was inserted by its last editor in place of the less known Levi, who knew that their former position in life and their calling had been similar.

Chap. XVII.

The narrative of Christ's day's work, given, according to our author, as a specimen of the nature and activity of Christ's daily work, is given in the first three Gospels in essentially similar form, as well as the healing of the leper. But in St. Matthew this last event is recorded as an event not followed by any particular consequences. St. Mark and St. Luke both tell us, as the consequence, that the Saviour avoided going into towns. Ewald supposes this narrative was placed by St. Matthew in its present place to avoid the inference from the other Gospels that it happened in a town.

The healing of the centurion's son (or servant), if it be taken as identical with the healing the nobleman's son (John iv. 46—54), brings the two narratives at this point into contact.

Chap. XIX.

That the Saviour was excommunicated about this time is not stated in the Gospels, but, with the growing enmity of the spiritual rulers in Jerusalem, we can hardly conceive it to have been otherwise: we know that this punishment was at a somewhat later time inflicted on any who believed in Him. That the punishment did not extend to general exclusion from the synagogues is certain, since we find Christ later constantly teaching in the synagogues. See especially John xviii. 20.

Chap. XXII.

Ewald, as might be expected, has no doubt of the identity of the similar discourses given by St. Matthew and St. Luke, known as the "Sermon on the Mount." He, it will be observed, looks on St. Luke's intimation, that a part of the discourse was delivered "on the plain" and in the audience of the multitude, as a true reminiscence. In fact St. Matthew tells us at the conclusion of this sermon as reported by him, that *the people* were astonished at his doctrine; whilst yet the words with which He introduces it, and much of the discourse itself, seem to shew that it was addressed exclusively to disciples. The only conclusion seems to me that it was never delivered by our Lord *as a whole* in the form given us in St. Matthew. St. Luke confirms this view by inserting fragments from it in his Gospel at other periods in our Lord's life, in that portion of his Gospel especially between Chap. ix. 51 and the end of Chap. xvi. Ewald believes that a report of the Ordination address originally existed in St. Mark's Gospel between III. 19 a and 19 b. He believes that St. Luke took it from him and abbreviated it. In "Die drei ersten Evangelien" our author gives an admirable running commentary on the "Sermon on the Mount."

Chap. XXVI.

The Children's Play (Matt. xi. 16, 17).

Ewald observes: "This play here alluded to was, as far as we can see, a guessing game, in which the one party, which sat and represented the judge and king, had to give up their seats when they had twice failed to guess the meaning of what the other party by action and movement represented; *e.g.* if they had understood neither the sound of the flute nor that of the weeping, and had failed to give the corresponding action."

Who are the children of Wisdom here who justify her?

Our author takes them to denote the self-imagining wise men of our Lord's generation; who, by their rejection of God's message in whatever guise it might come to them, obviated the possible objection, that the message was not received because God had not sent it in the wisest and most taking way.

The remark thus understood seems to fit more naturally into the narrative than if we take "Wisdom's children" to denote the truly wise, and understand her justification in a subjective, instead of, as in the other view, in an objective signification.

Chap. XXVII.

It will be observed that in this Chapter the author places the return of the Twelve shortly after the mission of the Baptist to

Christ. St. Matthew, it is true, does not mention their return, but
neither does he mention their going out, as do the other Evangelists.
If St. Matthew then omitted the one, it is likely he omitted the
other, which yet found place in the original narrative.

St. Luke records the return of the Seventy immediately before
this outburst of joy from our Lord. Ewald believes St. Luke to
have taken the address to the Seventy from the same narrative of
the Spruchsammlung from which St. Matthew quotes more at length
in his report of the address to the Twelve. Without agreeing with
this, we may suppose that the time appointed to the Seventy for
their return may have been the same as that appointed to the
Twelve. Our author finds a confirmation of his view of the depression of our Lord being succeeded by exultation, in God's general
dealings in meting out disappointments and hopes to his servants.
"Thus contrasts in life follow close on each other; a troublous event
is shortly succeeded by one which dissipates all trouble."

Chap. XXIX.

What Place is denoted by Dalmanutha?

St. Matthew gives in place of this name the doubtless more
familiar name of Magadon, which is supposed to be the same which
by the Masorites has been written Megiddo. In fact, in the
Apocalypse xvi. 16, this name Megiddo is written Magedon. It lay
in the plain of Esdraelon which was situated to the south-west of
the lake of Tiberias. Ewald suggests that Dalmanutha may have
been a Galilæan form of the name Tsalmon, in which, according to
the Mishna, many Jews dwelt. As we are told that there were
fruitful vineyards here, we are naturally led to place it in South
Galilee.

The way in which the author takes the words of Mark ix. 29, is
very far-fetched, referring the term τοῦτο τὸ γένος to the Pharisees
instead of to the dæmons. The sense given, by those who take this
view, to ἐξελθεῖν, "to go to work," seems quite unwarranted.

Chap. XXX.

Will He go to the Dispersed among the Gentiles and teach the Gentiles?

The author refers to the earlier part of the volume, p. 57 in the original work (Second Edition), for some account of the intercourse and acquaintance of Jewish teachers with Roman. He observes that in the reign of Augustus (Suetonius August. c. 76 and 93) a general desire had seized on all Romans, including the Emperor, to be initiated into the Oriental religion and mysteries; many women were engaged in the study. The grounds indeed which moved them thereto were often impure, and much empty curiosity or even worse was mixed up therewith. Accordingly a Jew of bad reputation, on account of offences against the laws forced to fly from Palestine, came and settled in the metropolis of the world, and advertised himself as an expounder of the laws of Moses. He was convicted however in Rome of being an impostor, and of swindling Fulvia the wife of Saturninus, a man of high influence. This event happened about the same time as the frauds of the priests of Isis, and concurred with them in leading to the banishment, in the nineteenth year of Tiberius, of all Jews from Italy.

Chap. XXXIV.

The giving up of the Ass's Foal by its Owner to the Messiah.

Our author compares the presents made to Saul just after he had been anointed king by Samuel. The presents thus freely offered to him were foretold him by Samuel as auguries of a prosperous reign and the willing devotion of his subjects. It is on this account, he observes, that the Evangelist lays such stress on the free offering of the animal to Messiah for His royal entry into His capital.

Chap. XXXVI.

What was the Fate of Judas?

There seems some difficulty in reconciling the account of Judas' end given in the Gospels with that in Acts (Chap. i.). The difference in the accounts as to the manner of his death is not of much importance, and probably, if we had fuller particulars, the two accounts might be found compatible. The most important difference is that the Evangelists seem to speak of the traitor's death as following directly on Christ's condemnation. But τότε is often used in a vague sense, and seems often used to imply rather a connection in the thought of the writer, than an immediate connection in time. It seems clear however that Acts i. v. 18 does not give us St. Peter's words, but is added by way of explanation—probably it was originally a gloss.

THE END.

CAMBRIDGE:—PRINTED BY JONATHAN PALMER.

A SELECTED LIST

OF

STANDARD PUBLICATIONS & REMAINDERS

Offered for Sale at remarkably low prices by

JOHN GRANT, BOOKSELLER,

25 & 34 George IV. Bridge,

EDINBURGH.

Moir's (D. M.) Works.

Poetical Works, with Portrait and Memoir, edited by Thomas Aird, 2 vols, fcap 8vo, cloth (pub 14s), 5s. Blackwood & Sons.

"These are volumes to be placed on the favourite shelf, in the familiar nook that holds the books we love, which we take up with pleasure and lay down with regret."—*Edinburgh Courant.*
"'Delta' has produced many pieces which will possess a permanent place in the poetry of Scotland."—Professor WILSON.

Lectures on the Poetical Literature of the Past Half-Century, fcap 8vo, cloth (pub 5s), 2s. Blackwood & Sons.

"A delightful volume; exquisite in its taste, and generous in its criticisms."—HUGH MILLER.

Domestic Verses, fcap 8vo, cloth (pub 5s), 9d. Blackwood & Sons.

"This little work will be felt as a rich boon and treat to the feeling heart."—*Scotsman.*

Sent Carriage Free to any part of the United Kingdom on receipt of Postal Order for the amount.

JOHN GRANT, 25 & 34 George IV. Bridge, Edinburgh.

Beattie (James)—Poetical Works of, with Life, portrait and illustrations, crown 8vo, cloth extra, gilt edges (pub 2s 6d), 9d.
A neatly got up edition; very suitable as a gift.

The New Library Edition of
The Works of Robert Burns, large paper copy, edited by W. Scott Douglas, with Explanatory Notes, Various Readings, and Glossary, illustrated with portraits, vignettes, and frontispieces, with India proof plates, by Sam Bough, R.S.A., and W. E. Lockhart, R.S.A., all newly engraved on steel, woodcuts, facsimiles, maps, and music, 6 vols, royal 8vo, cloth extra (pub £8 8s), £2 15s, W. Paterson, 1880.

Lyndsay (Sir David, of the Mount)—A Facsimile of the ancient Heraldic Manuscript emblazoned by the celebrated Sir David Lyndsay of the Mount, Lyon King at Arms in the reign of James the Fifth, edited by the late David Laing, LL.D., from the Original MS. in the possession of the Faculty of Advocates, folio, cloth, gilt top, uncut edges (pub £10 10s), £3 10s.
Impression limited to 250 copies.

Also Uniform.
Scottish Arms, being a Collection of Armorial Bearings, A.D. 1370-1678, Reproduced in Facsimile from Contemporary Manuscripts, with Heraldic and Genealogical Notes, by R. R. Stodart, of the Lyon Office, 2 vols, folio, cloth extra, gilt tops (pub £12 12s), £4 10s.
Impression limited to 300 copies.

Several of the manuscripts from which these Arms are taken have hitherto been unknown to heraldic antiquaries in this country. The Arms of upwards of 600 families are given, all of which are described in upwards of 400 pages of letterpress by Mr Stodart.

The book is uniform with Lyndsay's Heraldic Manuscript, and care was taken not to reproduce any Arms which are in that volume, unless there are variations, or from older manuscripts.

Wilson (Professor)—The Comedy of the Noctes Ambrosianæ, by John Skelton, Advocate, with portraits of Wilson and Hogg, crown 8vo, cloth (pub 7s 6d), 3s, Blackwood & Sons.

"Mr Skelton has erected what is perhaps the most durable monument to Wilson's fame that we possess. In it we find the immortal trio at their best throughout. From beginning to end their meetings are inspired and sanctified by Bacchus and Apollo."—*Academy.*

Younger (John, shoemaker, St Boswells, Author of " River Angling for Salmon and Trout," " Corn Law Rhymes, &c.)—Autobiography, with portrait, crown 8vo (457 pages), cloth (pub 7s 6d), 2s 6d.

"'The shoemaker of St Boswells,' as he was designated in all parts of Scotland, was an excellent prose writer, a respectable poet, a marvellously gifted man in conversation. His life will be read with great interest; the simple heart-stirring narrative of the life-struggle of a highly-gifted, humble, and honest mechanic,—a life of care, but also a life of virtue."—*London Review.*

Sent Carriage Free to any part of the United Kingdom on receipt of Postal Order for the amount.

JOHN GRANT, 25 & 34 George IV. Bridge, Edinburgh.

Historians of Scotland, complete set in 10 vols for £3 3s.
This Grand National Series of the Early Chronicles of Scotland, edited by the most eminent Scottish Antiquarian Scholars of the present day, is now completed, and as sets are becoming few in number, early application is necessary in order to secure them at the reduced price.

The Series comprises:—

Scoticronicon of John de Fordun, from the Contemporary MS. (if not the author's autograph) at the end of the Fourteenth Century, preserved in the Library of Wolfenbüttel, in the Duchy of Brunswick, collated with other known MSS. of the original chronicle, edited by W. F. Skene, LL.D., Historiographer Royal, 2 vols (pub 30s), not sold separately.

The Metrical Chronicle of Andrew Wyntoun, Prior of St Serf's Inch at Lochleven, who died about 1426, the work now printed entire for the first time, from the Royal MS. in the British Museum, collated with other MSS., edited by the late D. Laing, LL.D., 3 vols (pub 50s), vols 1 and 2 not sold separately. Vol 3 sold separately (pub 21s), 10s 6d.

Lives of Saint Ninian and St Kentigern, compiled in the 12th century, and edited from the best MSS. by the late A. P. Forbes, D.C.L., Bishop of Brechin (pub 15s), not sold separately.

Life of Saint Columba, founder of Hy, written by Adamnan, ninth Abbot of that Monastery, edited by Wm. Reeves, D.D., M.R.I.A., translated by the late A. P. Forbes, D.C.L., Bishop of Brechin, with Notes arranged by W. F. Skene, LL.D. (pub 15s), not sold separately.

The Book of Pluscarden, being unpublished Continuation of Fordun's Chronicle by M. Buchanan, Treasurer to the Dauphiness of France, edited and translated by Skene, 2 vols (pub 30s). Vol 2 separately (pub 12s 6d), 8s 6d.

A Critical Essay on the Ancient Inhabitants of Scotland, by Thomas Innes of the Sorbonne, with Memoir of the Author by George Grubb, LL.D., and Appendix of Original Documents by Wm. F. Skene, LL.D., illustrated with charts, out of print (pub 21s), 10s 6d.

In connection with the Society of Antiquaries of Scotland, a uniform series of the Historians of Scotland, accompanied by English translations, and illustrated by notes, critical and explanatory, was commenced some years since and has recently been finished.

So much has recently been done for the history of Scotland, that the necessity for a more critical edition of the earlier historians has become very apparent. The history of Scotland, prior to the 15th century, must always be based to a great extent upon the work of Fordun; but his original text has been made the basis of continuations, and has been largely altered and interpolated by his continuators, whose statements are usually quoted as if they belonged to the original work of Fordun. An edition discriminating between the original text of Fordun and the additions and alterations of his continuators, and at the same time tracing out the sources of Fordun's narrative, would obviously be of great importance to the right understanding of Scottish history.

The complete set forms ten handsome volumes, demy 8vo, illustrated with facsimiles.

Sent Carriage Free to any part of the United Kingdom on receipt of Postal Order for the amount.

JOHN GRANT, 25 & 34 George IV. Bridge, Edinburgh.

Leighton's (Alexander) Mysterious Legends of Edinburgh, illustrated, crown 8vo, cloth (pub 5s), 2s 6d.
CONTENTS:—Lord Kames' Puzzle, Mrs Corbet's Amputated Toe, The Brownie of the West Bow, The Ancient Bureau, A Legend of Halkerstone's Wynd, Deacon Macgillvray's Disappearance, Lord Braxfield's Case of the Red Night-cap, The Strange Story of Sarah Gowanlock, and John Cameron's Life Policy.

Steven's (Dr William) History of the High School of Edinburgh, from the beginning of the Sixteenth Century, based upon Researches of the Town Council Records and other Authentic Documents, illustrated with view, also facsimile of a School Exercise by Sir Walter Scott when a pupil in 1783, crown 8vo, cloth, a handsome volume (pub 7s 6d), 2s.
Appended is a list of the distinguished pupils who have been educated in this Institution, which has been patronised by Royalty from the days of James VI.

Exquisitely beautiful Works by Sir J. Noel Paton at a remarkably low price.

Paton's (Noel) Compositions from Shakespeare's Tempest, a Series of Fifteen Large Outline Engravings illustrating the Great Drama of our National Poet, with descriptive letterpress, oblong folio, cloth (pub 21s), 3s. Chapman & Hall, 1845.

Uniform with the above.

Paton's (Noel) Compositions from Shelley's Prometheus Unbound, a Series of Twelve Large Outline Engravings, oblong folio, cloth (pub 21s), 3s. Chapman & Hall, 1846.

Pollok's (Robert) The Course of Time, a Poem, beautifully printed edition, with portrait and numerous illustrations, 12mo, cloth, 6d. Blackwood & Sons.
"'The Course of Time' is a very extraordinary poem, vast in its conception, vast in its plan, vast in its materials, and vast, if very far from perfect, in its achievement."—D. M. MOIR.

The Authorised Library Edition.

Trial of the Directors of the City of Glasgow Bank, before the Petition for Bail, reported by Charles Tennant Couper, Advocate, the Speeches and Opinions, revised by the Council and Judges, and the Charge by the Lord Justice Clerk, illustrated with lithographic facsimiles of the famous false Balance-sheets, one large volume, royal 8vo, cloth (pub 15s), 3s 6d. Edinburgh.

History of the Queen's Edinburgh Rifle Volunteer Brigade, with an Account of the City of Edinburgh and Midlothian Rifle Association, the Scottish Twenty Club, &c., by Wm. Stephen, crown 8vo, cloth (pub 5s), 2s 6d. Blackwood & Sons.
"This opportune volume has far more interest for readers generally than might have been expected, while to members of the Edinburgh Volunteer Brigade it cannot fail to be very interesting indeed."—*St James's Gazette.*

Edinburgh University—Account of the Tercentenary Festival of the University, including the Speeches and Addresses on the Occasion, edited by R. Sydney Marsden, crown 8vo, cloth (pub 3s), 1s 6d. Blackwood & Sons.

Sent Carriage Free to any part of the United Kingdom on receipt of Postal Order for the amount.

JOHN GRANT, 25 & 34 George IV. Bridge, Edinburgh.

Grampian Club Publications, of valuable MSS. and Works of Original Research in Scottish History, Privately printed for the Members:—

The Diocesan Registers of Glasgow—Liber Protocollorum M. Cuthberti Simonis, notarii et scribæ capituli Glasguensis, A.D. 1499-1513; also, *Rental Book of the Diocese of Glasgow*, A.D. 1509-1570, edited by Joseph Bain and the Rev. Dr Charles Rogers, with facsimiles, 2 vols, 8vo, cl, 1875 (pub £2 2s), 10s 6d.

Rental Book of the Cistercian Abbey of Coupar-Angus, with the Breviary of the Register, edited by the Rev. Dr Charles Rogers, with facsimiles of MSS., 2 vols, 8vo, cloth, 1879-80 (pub £2 12s 6d), 10s 6d.

——— The same, vol II., comprising the *Register of Tacks of the Abbey of Cupar, Rental of St Marie's Monastery*, and Appendix, 8vo, cloth (pub £1 1s), 3s 6d.

Estimate of the Scottish Nobility during the Minority of James VI., edited, with an Introduction, from the original MS. in the Public Record Office, by Dr Charles Rogers, 8vo, cloth (pub 10s 6d), 2s.

The reprint of a manuscript discovered in the Public Record Office. The details are extremely curious.

Genealogical Memoirs of the Families of Colt and Coutts, by Dr Charles Rogers, 8vo, cloth (pub 10s 6d), 2s 6d.

An old Scottish family, including the eminent bankers of that name, the Baroness Burdett-Coutts, &c.

Rogers' (Dr Charles) Memorials of the Earl of Stirling and of the House of Alexander, portraits, 2 vols, 8vo, cloth (pub £3 3s), 10s 6d, Edinburgh, 1877.

This work embraces not only a history of Sir William Alexander, first Earl of Stirling, but also a genealogical account of the family of Alexander in all its branches; many interesting historical details connected with Scottish State affairs in the seventeenth century; also with the colonisation of America.

Sent Carriage Free to any part of the United Kingdom on receipt of Postal Order for the amount.

JOHN GRANT, 25 & 34 George IV. Bridge, Edinburgh.

Scott's (Dr Hew) Fasti Ecclesiæ Scoticanæ, Historical and Biographical Notices of all the Ministers of the Church of Scotland from the Reformation, A.D. 1560, to the Present Time, 6 large vols, demy 4to, cloth, uncut (pub £9), £4 15s, Edinburgh, W. Paterson.

David Laing, the eminent antiquarian, considered this work a valuable and necessary addition to the Bannatyne, Maitland, or Abbotsford Club Publications. The work is divided into Synods, and where priced the volumes can be had separately.

Vol 1.—Embraces Synods of Lothian and Tweeddale. Not sold separately.
Vol 2.—Synods of Merse and Teviotdale, Dumfries and Galloway (pub 30s), 15s.
Vol 3.—Synods of Glasgow and Ayr (pub 30s), 15s.
Vol 4.—Synods of Fife, Perth, and Stirling (pub 30s), 15s.
Vol 5.—Synods of Argyll, Glenelg, Moray, Ross, Sutherland, Caithness, Orkney, and Shetland, not sold separately.
Vol 6.—Synods of Aberdeen, and Angus and Mearns (pub 30s), 15s.

Historical Sketches of the Highland Clans of Scotland, containing a concise account of the origin, &c., of the Scottish Clans, with twenty-two illustrative coloured plates of the Tartan worn by each, post 8vo, cloth, 2s 6d.

"The object of this treatise is to give a concise account of the origin, seat, and characteristics of the Scottish Clans, together with a representation of the distinguishing tartan worn by each."—*Preface.*

Historical Geography of the Clans of Scotland, by T. B. Johnston, F.R.G.S., F.R.S.E., and F.S.A.S., Geographer to the Queen, and Colonel James A. Robertson, F.S.A.S., demy 4to, cloth, with a map of Scotland divided into Clans (large folding map, coloured) (pub 7s 6d), Keith Johnston, 3s. 6d.

"The map bears evidence of careful preparation, and the editor acknowledges the assistance of Dr William Skene, who is known for eminent services to Highland archæology."—*Athenæum.*

Keltie's (John S.) History of the Scottish Highlands, Highland Clans, and Highland Regiments, with an account of the Gaelic Language, Literature, Music, &c., illustrated with portraits, views, maps, &c., engraved on steel, clan tartans, numerous woodcuts, including armorial bearings, 2 vols, imperial 8vo, half morocco (pub £3 10s), £1 17s 6d.

Sent Carriage Free to any part of the United Kingdom on receipt of Postal Order for the amount.

JOHN GRANT, 25 & 34 George IV. Bridge, Edinburgh.

***Burt's** (Capt.) Letters from the North of Scotland (1754)*, with an Introduction by R. Jamieson, F.S.A. ; and the History of Donald the Hammerer, from an authentic account of the Family of Invernahyle, a MS. communication by Sir Walter Scott, with facsimiles of all the original engravings, 2 vols, 8vo, cloth (pub 21s), 8s 6d. W. Paterson.

"Captain Burt was one of the first Englishmen who caught a glimpse of the spots which now allure tourists from every part of the civilised world, at a time when London had as little to do with the Grampians as with the Andes. The author was evidently a man of a quick, an observant, and a cultivated mind."—LORD MACAULAY.
"An extremely interesting and curious work."—LOWNDES.

***Chambers's** (William, of Glenormiston) History of Peeblesshire*, its Local Antiquities, Geology, Natural History, &c., with one hundred engravings, vignettes, and coloured map from Ordnance Survey, royal 8vo, cloth (pub £1 11s 6d), 9s. W. Paterson.

"To the early history and antiquities of this district, and to old names and old families connected with the place, Mr Chambers lends a charm which is not often met with in such subjects. He discerns the usefulness of social as well as political history, and is pleasantly aware that the story of manners and morals and customs is as well worth telling as the story of man," &c.—*Athenæum*.

***Douglas'** (Gavin, Bishop of Dunkeld, 1475-1522) Poetical Works*, edited, with Memoir, Notes, and full Glossary, by John Small, M.A., F.S.A. Scot., illustrated with specimens of manuscript, title-page, and woodcuts of the early editions in facsimile, 4 vols, beautifully printed on thick paper, post 8vo, cloth (pub £3 3s), £1 2s 6d. W. Paterson.

"The latter part of the fifteenth and beginning of the sixteenth century, a period almost barren in the annals of English poetry, was marked by a remarkable series of distinguished poets in Scotland. During this period flourished Dunbar, Henryson, Mercier, Harry the Minstrel, Gavin Douglas, Bellenden, Kennedy, and Lyndesay. Of these, although the palm of excellence must beyond all doubt be awarded to Dunbar,—next to Burns probably the greatest poet of his country,—the voice of contemporaries, as well as of the age that immediately followed, pronounced in favour of him who,
' In barbarous age,
Gave rude Scotland Virgil's page,'—
Gavin Douglas. We may confidently predict that this will long remain the standard edition of Gavin Douglas ; and we shall be glad to see the works of other of the old Scottish poets edited with equal sympathy and success."—*Athenæum*.

***Lyndsay's** (Sir David, of the Mount, 1490-1568) Poetical Works*, best edition, edited, with Life, Notes, and Glossary, by David Laing, 3 vols, crown 8vo, cloth (pub 63s), 18s 6d. W. Paterson.

"When it is said that the revision, including Preface, Memoir, and Notes, has been executed by Dr David Laing, it is said that all has been done that is possible by thorough scholarship, good judgment, and conscientiousness."—*Scotsman*.

Sent Carriage Free to any part of the United Kingdom on receipt of Postal Order for the amount.

JOHN GRANT, 25 & 34 George IV. Bridge, Edinburgh.

Crieff: Its Traditions and Characters, with Anecdotes of Strathearn, Reminiscences of Obsolete Customs, Traditions, and Superstitions, Humorous Anecdotes of Schoolmasters, Ministers, and other Public Men, crown 8vo, 1s.

"A book which will have considerable value in the eyes of all collectors of Scottish literature. A gathering up of stories about well-known inhabitants, memorable local occurrences, and descriptions of manners and customs."—*Scotsman.*

Dunfermline—Henderson's Annals of Dunfermline and Vicinity, from the earliest Authentic Period to the Present Time, A.D. 1069-1878, interspersed with Explanatory Notes, Memorabilia, and numerous illustrative engravings, large vol, 4to, half morocco, gilt top (pub 21s), 6s 6d.

The genial Author of "*Noctes Ambrosianæ.*"

Christopher North—A Memoir of Professor John Wilson, compiled from Family Papers and other sources, by his daughter, Mrs Gordon, new edition, with portrait and illustrations, crown 8vo, cloth (pub 6s), 2s. 6d.

" A writer of the most ardent and enthusiastic genius."—HENRY HALLAM.

"The whole literature of England does not contain a more brilliant series of articles than those with which Wilson has enriched the pages of *Blackwood's Magazine.*"—Sir ARCHIBALD ALISON.

The Cloud of Witnesses for the Royal Prerogatives of Jesus Christ; or, The Last Speeches and Testimonies of those who have Suffered for the Truth in Scotland since the year 1680, best edition, by the Rev. J. H. Thompson, numerous illustrations, handsome volume, 8vo, cloth gilt (pub 7s 6d), 4s 6d.

"The interest in this remarkable book can never die, and to many we doubt not this new and handsome edition will be welcome."—*Aberdeen Herald.*

"Altogether it is like a resurrection, and the vision of Old Mortality, as it passes over the scenes of his humble but solemn and sternly significant labours, seems transfigured in the bright and embellished pages of the modern reprint."—*Daily Review.*

M'Kerlie's (P. H., F.S.A. Scot.) History of the Lands and their Owners in Galloway, illustrated by woodcuts of Notable Places and Objects, with a Historical Sketch of the District, 5 handsome vols, crown 8vo, roxburghe style (pub £3 15s), 26s 6d. W. Paterson.

Wilson's (Dr Daniel) Memorials of Edinburgh in the Olden Time, with numerous fine engravings and woodcuts, 2 vols, 4to, cloth (pub £2 2s), 16s 6d.

Hamilton's (Lady, the Mistress of Lord Nelson) Attitudes, illustrating in 25 full-page plates the great Heroes and Heroines of Antiquity in their proper Costume, forming a useful study for drawing from correct and chaste models of Grecian and Roman Sculpture, 4to, cloth (pub £1 1s), 3s 6d.

Sent Carriage Free to any part of the United Kingdom on receipt of Postal Order for the amount.

JOHN GRANT, 25 & 34 George IV. Bridge, Edinburgh.

Hay's (D. R.) Science of Beauty, as Developed in Nature and Applied in Art, 23 full-page illustrations, royal 8vo, cloth (pub 10s 6d), 2s 6d.

Art and Letters, an Illustrated Magazine of Fine Art and Fiction, edited by J. Comyns Carr, complete year 1882-83, handsome volume, folio, neatly bound in bevelled cloth, gilt top, edges uncut, and Parts 1 and 2 of the succeeding year, when the publication ceased, illustrated with many hundred engravings in the highest style of art, including many of the choicest illustrations of "L'Art," published by arrangement with the French proprietors (pub £1 1s), 8s 6d.

The artistic excellence of this truly handsome volume commends itself to all lovers of what is beautiful in nature and art. The illustrations, which are numerous and varied, embrace—Specimens of Sculpture Old and New, Facsimile Drawings of the Old Masters, Examples of Art Furniture, with objects exhibited in the great European Collections, Animals in Art illustrated by Examples in Painting and Sculpture, Art on the Stage, Products of the Keramic Art Ancient and Modern, the various forms of Art Industry, &c. &c., accompanied by interesting articles by men thoroughly acquainted with the various subjects introduced.

Stewart's (Dugald) Collected Works, best edition, edited by Sir William Hamilton, with numerous Notes and Emendations, 11 handsome vols, 8vo, cloth (pub £6 12s), the few remaining sets for £2 10s. T. & T. Clark.

Sold Separately,

Elements of the Philosophy of the Human Mind, 3 vols, 8vo, cloth (pub £1 16s), 12s.

Philosophy of the Active Powers, 2 vols, 8vo, cloth (pub £1 4s), 10s.

Principles of Political Economy, 2 vols, 8vo, cloth (pub £1 4s), 10s.

Biographical Memoirs of Adam Smith, Principal Robertson, and Thomas Reid, 8vo, cloth (pub 12s), 4s 6d.

Supplementary Volume, with General Index, 8vo, cloth (pub 12s), 5s.

"As the names of Thomas Reid, of Dugald Stewart, and of Sir William Hamilton will be associated hereafter in the history of Philosophy in Scotland, as closely as those of Xenophanes, Parmenides, and Zeno in the School of Elea, it is a singular fortune that Sir William Hamilton should be the collector and editor of the works of his predecessors. . . . The chair which he filled for many years, not otherwise undistinguished, he rendered illustrious."—*Athenæum.*

Sent Carriage Free to any part of the United Kingdom on receipt of Postal Order for the amount.

JOHN GRANT, 25 & 34 George IV. Bridge, Edinburgh.

Campbell (Colin, Lord Clyde)—Life of, illustrated by Extracts from his Diary and Correspondence, by Lieut.-Gen. Shadwell, C.B., with portrait, maps, and Plans, 2 vols, 8vo, cloth (pub 36s), 10s 6d, Blackwood & Sons.

"In all the annals of 'Self-Help,' there is not to be found a life more truly worthy of study than that of the gallant old soldier. The simple, self-denying, friend-helping, brave, patriotic soldier stands proclaimed in every line of General Shadwell's admirable memoir."—*Blackwood's Magazine.*

Crime—Pike's (Luke Owen) History of Crime in England, illustrating the Changes of the Laws in the Progress of Civilisation from the Roman Invasion to the Present Time, Index, 2 very thick vols, 8vo, cloth (pub 36s) 10s, Smith, Elder, & Co.

Creasy (Sir Edward S.)—History of England, from the Earliest Times to the End of the Middle Ages, 2 vols (520 pp each), 8vo, cloth (pub 25s), 6s, Smith, Elder, & Co.

Garibaldi—The Red Shirt, Episodes of the Italian War, by Alberto Mario, crown 8vo, cloth (pub 6s), 1s, Smith, Elder, & Co.

"These episodes read like chapters in the 'History of the Seven Champions;' they give vivid pictures of the incidents of that wonderful achievement, the triumphal progress from Sicily to Naples; and the incidental details of the difficulties, dangers, and small reverses which occurred during the progress, remove the event from the region of enchantment to the world of reality and human heroism."—*Athenæum.*

History of the War of Frederick I. against the Communes of Lombardy, by Giovanni B. Testa, translated from the Italian, and dedicated by the Author to the Right Hon. W. E. Gladstone, (466 pages), 8vo, cloth (pub 15s) 2s, Smith, Elder, & Co.

Martineau (Harriet)—The History of British Rule in India, foolscap 8vo (356 pages), cloth (pub 2s 6d), 1s, Smith, Elder, & Co.

A concise sketch, which will give the ordinary reader a general notion of what our Indian empire is, how we came by it, and what has gone forward in it since it first became connected with England. The book will be found to state the broad facts of Anglo-Indian history in a clear and enlightening manner; and it cannot fail to give valuable information to those readers who have neither time nor inclination to study the larger works on the subject.

Mathews (Charles James, the Actor)—Life of, chiefly Autobiographical, with Selections from his Correspondence and Speeches, edited by Charles Dickens, portraits, 2 vols, 8vo, cloth (pub 25s), 5s, Macmillan, 1879.

"The book is a charming one from first to last, and Mr Dickens deserves a full measure of credit for the care and discrimination he has exercised in the business of editing."—*Globe.*

"Mr Dickens's interesting work, which should be read by all students of the stage."—*Saturday Review.*

Reumont (Alfred von)—Lorenzo de Medici, the Magnificent, translated from the German, by Robert Harrison, 2 vols, 8vo, cloth (pub 30s), 6s 6d, Smith, Elder, & Co.

Sent Carriage Free to any part of the United Kingdom on receipt of Postal Order for the amount.

JOHN GRANT, 25 & 34 George IV. Bridge, Edinburgh.

Oliphant (Laurence)—The Land of Gilead, with Excursions in the Lebanon, illustrations and maps, 8vo, cloth (pub 21s), 8s 6d, Blackwood & Sons.

"A most fascinating book."—*Observer.*
"A singularly agreeable narrative of a journey through regions more replete, perhaps, with varied and striking associations than any other in the world. The writing throughout is highly picturesque and effective."—*Athenæum.*
"A most fascinating volume of travel. . . . His remarks on manners, customs, and superstitions are singularly interesting."—*St James's Gazette.*
"The reader will find in this book a vast amount of most curious and valuable information on the strange races and religions scattered about the country."—*Saturday Review.*
"An admirable work, both as a reeord of travel and as a contribution to physical science."—*Vanity Fair.*

Patterson (R. H.)—The New Golden Age, and Influence of the Precious Metals upon the War, 2 vols, 8vo, cloth (pub 31s 6d), 6s, Blackwood & Sons.

CONTENTS.
VOL I.—THE PERIOD OF DISCOVERY AND ROMANCE OF THE NEW GOLDEN AGE, 1848-56.—The First Tidings—Scientific Fears, and General Enthusiasm—The Great Emigration—General Effects of the Gold Discoveries upon Commerce—Position of Great Britain, and First Effects on it of the Gold Discoveries—The Golden Age in California and Australia—Life at the Mines. A RETROSPECT.—History and Influence of the Precious Metals down to the Birth of Modern Europe—The Silver Age in America—Effects of the Silver Age upon Europe—Production of the Precious Metals during the Silver Age (1492-1810)—Effects of the Silver Age upon the Value of Money (1492-1800).
VOL II.—PERIOD OF RENEWED SCARCITY.—Renewed Scarcity of the Precious Metals, A.D. 1800-30—The Period of Scarcity. Part II.—Effects upon Great Britain—The Scarcity lessens—Beginnings of a New Gold Supply—General Distress before the Gold Discoveries. "CHEAP" AND "DEAR" MONEY—On the Effects of Changes in the Quantity and Value of Money. THE NEW GOLDEN AGE.—First Getting of the New Gold—First Diffusion of the New Gold—Industrial Enterprise in Europe—Vast Expansion of Trade with the East (A.D. 1855-75)—Total Amount of the New Gold and Silver—Its Influence upon the World at large—Close of the Golden Age, 1876-80—Total Production of Gold and Silver. PERIOD 1492-1848.—Production of Gold and Silver subsequent to 1848—Changes in the Value of Money subsequent to A.D. 1492. PERIOD A.D. 1848 and subsequently. PERIOD A.D. 1782-1865.—Illusive Character of the Board of Trade Returns since 1853—Growth of our National Wealth.

Richardson and Watts' Complete Practical Treatise on Acids, Alkalies, and Salts, their Manufacture and Application, by Thomas Richardson, Ph.D., F.R.S., &c., and Henry Watts, F.R.S., F.C.S., &c., illustrated with numerous wood engravings, 3 thick 8vo vols, cloth (pub £4 10s), 8s 6d, London.

Tunis, Past and Present, with a Narrative of the French Conquest of the Regency, by A. M. Broadley, Correspondent of the *Times* during the War in Tunis, with numerous illustrations and maps, 2 vols, post 8vo, cloth (pub 25s), 6s, Blackwood & Sons.

"Mr Broadley has had peculiar facilities in collecting materials for his volumes. Possessing a thorough knowledge of Arabic, he has for years acted as confidential adviser to the Bey. . . . The information which he is able to place before the reader is novel and amusing. . . . A standard work on Tunis has been long required. This deficiency has been admirably supplied by the author."—*Morning Post.*

Sent Carriage Free to any part of the United Kingdom on receipt of Postal Order for the amount.

JOHN GRANT, 25 & 34 George IV. Bridge, Edinburgh.

Cervantes—History of the Ingenious Gentleman, Don Quixote of La Mancha, translated from the Spanish by P. A. Motteux, illustrated with a portrait and 36 etchings, by M. A. Laluze, illustrator of the library edition of Moliere's Works, 4 vols, large 8vo, cloth (sells £3 12s), £1 15s. W. Paterson.

Dyer (Thomas H., LL.D.)—Imitative Art, its Principles and Progress, with Preliminary Remarks on Beauty, Sublimity, and Taste, 8vo, cloth (pub 14s), 2s. Bell & Sons, 1882.

Junior Etching Club—Passages from Modern English Poets, Illustrated by the Junior Etching Club, 47 beautiful etchings by J. E. Millais, J. Whistler, J. Tenniel, Viscount Bury, J. Lawless, F. Smallfield, A. J. Lewis, C. Rossiter, and other artists, 4to, cloth extra, gilt edges (pub 15s), 4s.

Smith (J. Moyr)—Ancient Greek Female Costume, illustrated by 112 fine outline engravings and numerous smaller illustrations, with Explanatory Letterpress, and Descriptive Passages from the Works of Homer, Hesiod, Herodotus, Æschylus, Euripides, and other Greek Authors, printed in brown, crown 8vo, cloth elegant, red edges (pub 7s 6d), 3s. Sampson Low.

Strutt's Sylva Britanniæ et Scotiæ ; or, Portraits of Forest Trees Distinguished for their Antiquity, Magnitude, or Beauty, drawn from Nature, with 50 highly finished etchings, imp. folio, half morocco extra, gilt top, a handsome volume (pub £9 9s), £2 2s.

Walpole's (Horace) Anecdotes of Painting in England, with some Account of the Principal Artists, enlarged by Rev. James Dallaway ; and Vertue's Catalogue of Engravers who have been born or resided in England, last and best edition, revised with additional notes by Ralph N. Wornum, illustrated with eighty portraits of the principal artists, and woodcut portraits of the minor artists, 3 handsome vols, 8vo, cloth (pub 27s), 14s 6d. Bickers.

—————— The same, 3 vols, half morocco, gilt top, by one of the best Edinburgh binders (pub 45s), £1 8s.

Warren's (Samuel) Works—Original and early editions as follows :—

Miscellanies, Critical, Imaginative, and Juridical, contributed to *Blackwood's Magazine*, original edition, 2 vols, post 8vo, cloth (pub 24s), 5s. Blackwood, 1855.

Now and Then ; Through a Glass Darkly, early edition, crown 8vo, cloth (pub 6s), 1s 6d. Blackwood, 1853.

Ten Thousand a Year,, early edition, with Notes, 3 vols, 12mo, boards, back paper title (pub 18s), 4s 6d. Blackwood, 1853.

Sent Carriage Free to any part of the United Kingdom on receipt of Postal Order for the amount.

JOHN GRANT, 25 & 34 George IV. Bridge, Edinburgh.

Wood (*Major Herbert, R.E.*)—*The Shores of Lake Aral*, with large folding maps (352 pages), 8vo, cloth (pub 14s), 2s 6d, Smith, Elder, & Co.

Arnold's (*Cecil*) Great Sayings of Shakespeare, a Comprehensive Index to Shakespearian Thought, being a Collection of Allusions, Reflections, Images, Familiar and Descriptive Passages, and Sentiments from the Poems and Plays of Shakespeare, Alphabetically Arranged and Classified under Appropriate Headings, one handsome volume of 422 pages, thick 8vo, cloth (pub 7s 6d), 3s. Bickers.

Arranged in a manner similar to Southgate's "Many Thoughts of Many Minds." This index differs from all other books in being much more comprehensive, while care has been taken to follow the most accurate text, and to cope, in the best manner possible, with the difficulties of correct classification.

Bacon (*Francis, Lord*)—*Works*, both English and Latin, with an Introductory Essay, Biographical and Critical, and copious Indices, steel portrait, 2 vols, royal 8vo, cloth (originally pub £2 2s,) 12s, 1879.

"All his works are, for expression as well as thought, the glory of our nation, and of all later ages."—SHEFFIELD, Duke of Buckinghamshire.

"Lord Bacon was more and more known, and his books more and more delighted in; so that those men who had more than ordinary knowledge in human affairs, esteemed him one of the most capable spirits of that age."

Burnet (*Bishop*)—*History of the Reformation of the Church of England*, with numerous Illustrative Notes and copious Index, 2 vols, royal 8vo, cloth (pub 20s), 10s, Reeves & Turner, 1880.

"Burnet, in his immortal History of the Reformation, has fixed the Protestant religion in this country as long as any religion remains among us. Burnet is, without doubt, the English Eusebius."—Dr APTHORPE.

Burnet's History of his Own Time, from the Restoration of Charles II. to the Treaty of the Peace of Utrecht, with Historical and Biographical Notes, and a copious Index, complete in 1 thick volume, imperial 8vo, portrait, cloth (pub £1 5s), 5s 6d.

"I am reading Burnet's Own Times. Did you ever read that garrulous pleasant history? full of scandal, which all true history is; no palliatives, but all the stark wickedness that actually gave the *momentum* to national actors; none of that cursed *Humeian* indifference, so cold, and unnatural, and inhuman," &c.—CHARLES LAMB.

Dante—*The Divina Commedia*, translated into English Verse by James Ford, A.M., medallion frontispiece, 430 pages, crown 8vo, cloth, bevelled boards (pub 12s), 2s 6d. Smith, Elder, & Co.

"Mr Ford has succeeded better than might have been expected; his rhymes are good, and his translation deserves praise for its accuracy and fidelity. We cannot refrain from acknowledging the many good qualities of Mr Ford's translation, and his labour of love will not have been in vain, if he is able to induce those who enjoy true poetry to study once more the masterpiece of that literature from whence the great founders of English poetry drew so much of their sweetness and power."—*Athenæum*.

Sent Carriage Free to any part of the United Kingdom on receipt of Postal Order for the amount.

JOHN GRANT, 25 & 34 George IV. Bridge, Edinburgh.

Dobson (W. T.)—*The Classic Poets*, their Lives and their Times, with the Epics Epitomised, 452 pages, crown 8vo, cloth (pub 9s), 2s 6d. Smith, Elder, & Co.

CONTENTS.—Homer's Iliad, The Lay of the Nibelungen, Cid Campeador, Dante's Divina Commedia, Ariosto's Orlando Furioso, Camoens' Lusiad, Tasso's Jerusalem Delivered, Spenser's Fairy Queen, Milton's Paradise Lost, Milton's Paradise Regained.

English Literature: A Study of the Prologue and Epilogue in English Literature, from Shakespeare to Dryden, by G. S. B., crown 8vo, cloth (pub 5s), 1s 6d. Kegan Paul, 1884.

Will no doubt prove useful to writers undertaking more ambitious researches into the wider domains of dramatic or social history.

Johnson (Doctor)—*His Friends and his Critics*, by George Birkbeck Hill, D.C.L., crown 8vo, cloth (pub 8s), 2s. Smith, Elder, & Co.

"The public now reaps the advantage of Dr Hill's researches in a most readable volume. Seldom has a pleasanter commentary been written on a literary masterpiece. . . . Throughout the author of this pleasant volume has spared no pains to enable the present generation to realise more completely the sphere in which Johnson talked and taught."—*Saturday Review.*

Jones' (Rev. Harry) East and West London, being Notes of Common Life and Pastoral Work in St James's, Westminster, and in St George's-in-the-East, crown 8vo, cloth (pub 6s), 2s. Smith, Elder, & Co.

"Mr Jones gives a graphic description of the trades and industries of East London, of the docks and their multifarious populations, of the bonded stores, of Jamrach and his wild animal repository, of Ratcliffe Highway with its homes and its snares for sailors, until the reader finds himself at home with all sorts and conditions of strange life and folk. . . . A better antidote to recent gloomy forebodings of our national decadence can hardly be found."—*Athenæum.*

Kaye (John William, F.R.S., author of "History of the War in Afghanistan")—*The Essays of an Optimist*, crown 8vo, 8vo, cloth extra (pub 6s), 1s 6d. Smith, Elder, & Co.

"The Essays are seven in number,—Holidays, Work, Success, Toleration, Rest, Growing Old, and the Wrong Side of the Stuff,—themes on which the author discourses with bright and healthy vigour, good sense, and good taste."—*Standard.*

"We most sincerely trust that this book may find its way into many an English household. It cannot fail to instil lessons of manliness."—*Westminster Review.*

Selkirk (J. B.)—*Ethics and Æsthetics of Modern Poetry*, crown 8vo, cloth gilt (pub 7s), 2s. Smith, Elder, & Co.

Sketches from Shady Places, being Sketches from the Criminal and Lower Classes, by Thor Fredur, crown 8vo, cloth (pub 6s), 1s. Smith, Elder, & Co.

"Descriptions of the criminal and semi-criminal (if such a word may be coined) classes, which are full of power, sometimes of a disagreeable kind."—*Athenæum.*

Sent Carriage Free to any part of the United Kingdom on receipt of Postal Order for the amount.

JOHN GRANT, 25 & 34 George IV. Bridge, Edinburgh.

By the Authoress of " The Land o' the Leal."

Nairne's (Baroness) Life and Songs, with a
Memoir, and Poems of Caroline Oliphant the Younger, edited by Dr Charles Rogers, *portrait and other illustrations*, crown 8vo, cloth (pub 5s)   Griffin   0 2 6

" This publication is a good service to the memory of an excellent and gifted lady, and to all lovers of Scottish Song."—*Scotsman.*

Ossian's Poems, translated by Macpherson,
24mo, best red cloth, gilt (pub 2s 6d)   0 1 6
A dainty pocket edition.

Perthshire—Woods, Forests, and Estates of
Perthshire, with Sketches of the Principal Families of the County, by Thomas Hunter, Editor of the *Perthshire Constitutional and Journal*, *illustrated with 30 wood engravings*, crown 8vo (564 pp.), cloth (pub 12s 6d)   Perth   0 6 0

" Altogether a choice and most valuable addition to the County Histories of Scotland."—*Glasgow Daily Mail.*

Duncan (John, Scotch Weaver and Botanist)
—Life of, with Sketches of his Friends and Notices of the Times, by Wm. Jolly, F.R.S.E., H.M. Inspector of Schools, *etched portrait*, crown 8vo, cloth (pub 9s)   Kegan Paul   0 4 0

" We must refer the reader to the book itself for the many quaint traits of character, and the minute personal descriptions, which, taken together, seem to give a life-like presentation of this humble philosopher. . . . The many incidental notices which the work contains of the weaver caste, the workman's *esprit de corps*, and his wanderings about the country, either in the performance of his work or, when that was slack, taking a hand at the harvest, form an interesting chapter of social history. The completeness of the work is considerably enhanced by detailed descriptions of the district he lived in, and of his numerous friends and acquaintance."—*Athenæum.*

Scots (Ancient)—An Examination of the An-
cient History of Ireland and Iceland, in so far as it concerns the Origin of the Scots; Ireland not the Hibernia of the Ancients; Interpolations in Bede's Ecclesiastical History and other Ancient Annals affecting the Early History of Scotland and Ireland—the three Essays in one volume, crown 8vo, cloth (pub 4s)   Edinburgh, 1883   0 1 0

The first of the above treatises is mainly taken up with an investigation of the early History of Ireland and Iceland, in order to ascertain which has the better claim to be considered the original country of the Scots. In the second and third an attempt is made to show that Iceland was the ancient Hibernia, and the country from which the Scots came to Scotland; and further, contain a review of the evidence furnished by the more genuine of the early British Annals against the idea that Ireland was the ancient Scotia.

Magic and Astrology—Grant (James)—The
Mysteries of all Nations: Rise and Progress of Superstition, Laws against and Trials of Witches, Ancient and Modern Delusions, together with Strange Customs, Fables, and Tales relating to Mythology, Miracles, Poets, and Superstition, Demonology, Magic and Astrology, Trials by Ordeal, Superstition in the Nineteenth Century, &c., 1 thick vol, 8vo, cloth (pub 12s 6d)   1880   0 2 6

An interesting work on the subject of Superstition, valuable alike to archæologists and general readers. It is chiefly the result of antiquarian research and actual observation during a period of nearly forty years.

A Story of the Shetland Isles.

Saxby (*Jessie M., author of " Daala-Mist," &c.*)—*Rock-Bound,* a Story of the Shetland Isles, second edition, revised, crown 8vo, cloth (pub 2s), 6d. Edinburgh, 1877.

"The life I have tried to depict is the life I remember twenty years ago, when the islands were far behind the rest of Britain in all that goes to make up modern civilisation."—*Extract from Preface.*

Burn (*R. Scott*)—*The Practical Directory for the Improvement of Landed Property,* Rural and Suburban, and the Economic Cultivation of its Farms (the most valuable work on the subject), plates and woodcuts, 2 vols, 4to, cloth (pub £3 3s), 15s, Paterson.

Burnet's Treatise on Painting, *illustrated by 130 Etchings* from celebrated pictures of the Italian, Venetian, Flemish, Dutch, and English Schools, also woodcuts, thick 4to, half morocco, gilt top (pub £4 10s), £2 2s.

The Costumes of all Nations, Ancient and Modern, exhibiting the Dresses and Habits of all Classes, Male and Female, from the Earliest Historical Records to the Nineteenth Century, by Albert Kretschmer and Dr Rohrbach, 104 coloured plates displaying nearly 2000 full-length figures, complete in one handsome volume, 4to, half morocco (pub £4 4s), 45s, Sotheran.

Dryden's Dramatic Works, Library Edition, with Notes and Life by Sir Walter Scott, Bart., edited by George Saintsbury, portrait and plates, 8 vols, 8vo, cloth (pub £4 4s), £1 10s, Paterson.

Lessing's (*Dr J.*) *Ancient Oriental Carpet Patterns, after* Pictures and Originals of the 15th and 16th Centuries, 35 plates (size 20 × 14 in.), beautifully coloured after the originals, 1 vol, royal folio, in portfolio (pub £3 3s), 21s, Sotheran.

The most beautiful Work on the " Stately Homes of England."

Nash's Mansions of England in the Olden Time, *104* Lithographic Views faithfully reproduced from the originals, with new and complete history of each Mansion, by Anderson, 4 vols in 2, imperial 4to, cloth extra, gilt edges (pub £6 6s), £2 10s, Sotheran.

Richardson's (*Samuel*) *Works, Library Edition, with* Biographical Criticism by Leslie Stephen, portrait, 12 vols, 8vo, cloth extra, impression strictly limited to 750 copies (pub £6 6s), £2 5s, London.

Sent Carriage Free to any part of the United Kingdom on receipt of Postal Order for the amount.

JOHN GRANT, 25 & 34 George IV. Bridge, Edinburgh.

www.ingramcontent.com/pod-product-compliance
Lightning Source LLC
Chambersburg PA
CBHW032015220426
43664CB00006B/255